The Second Economy

The Race for Trust, Treasure and Time in the Cybersecurity War

Steve Grobman

Allison Cerra

Foreword by Christopher Young, Cybersecurity Executive

Apress®

The Second Economy: The Race for Trust, Treasure and Time in the Cybersecurity War

Steve Grobman
Santa Clara, California, USA

Allison Cerra
Plano, Texas, USA

ISBN-13 (pbk): 978-1-4842-2228-7
DOI 10.1007/978-1-4842-2229-4

ISBN-13 (electronic): 978-1-4842-2229-4

Library of Congress Control Number: 2016955488

Managing Director: Welmoed Spahr
Lead Editor: Natalie Pao
Technical Reviewer: Patty Hatter
Editorial Board: Steve Anglin, Pramila Balan, Laura Berendson, Aaron Black, Louise Corrigan, Jonathan Gennick, Robert Hutchinson, Celestin Suresh John, Nikhil Karkal, James Markham, Susan McDermott, Matthew Moodie, Natalie Pao, Gwenan Spearing
Coordinating Editor: Jessica Vakili
Copy Editor: Lori Jacobs
Compositor: SPi Global
Indexer: SPi Global
Artist: SPi Global

Distributed to the book trade worldwide by Springer Science+Business Media New York, 233 Spring Street, 6th Floor, New York, NY 10013. Phone 1-800-SPRINGER, fax (201) 348-4505, e-mail orders-ny@springer-sbm.com, or visit www.springeronline.com. Apress Media, LLC is a California LLC and the sole member (owner) is Springer Science + Business Media Finance Inc (SSBM Finance Inc). SSBM Finance Inc is a **Delaware** corporation.

For information on translations, please e-mail rights@apress.com, or visit www.apress.com.

Apress and friends of ED books may be purchased in bulk for academic, corporate, or promotional use. eBook versions and licenses are also available for most titles. For more information, reference our Special Bulk Sales–eBook Licensing web page at www.apress.com/bulk-sales.

Any source code or other supplementary materials referenced by the author in this text are available to readers at www.apress.com. For detailed information about how to locate your book's source code, go to www.apress.com/source-code/. Readers can also access source code at SpringerLink in the Supplementary Material section for each chapter.

Printed on acid-free paper

Contents at a Glance

Contents

About the Authors

Steve Grobman A self-proclaimed cybersecurity pragmatist, Steve Grobman (@stevegrobman) has spent over two decades in senior technical leadership positions related to the field of cybersecurity. He has the distinction of serving on both sides of the white hat fight: both in defending his company against adversaries and in building innovative cybersecurity defense technology to protect consumers and organizations around the world. An avid student and teacher of the trade, Grobman earned his bachelor's degree in computer science from North Carolina State University, has published multiple technical papers and books, and holds 24 US and international patents in the fields of security, software, and computer architecture, with another roughly 20 patents pending. He regularly provides perspectives on the adversary, the evolving threatscape, and the measures organizations and consumers alike can take in protecting themselves to industry insiders, media, analysts, and customers the world over—all delivered in laymen's terms that distill extraordinarily complex problems into actionable prescriptions.

Allison Cerra (@acerra1) found her life's calling at 18 years of age, when she fortuitously stumbled into a lifelong career of marketing complex technologies. A frustrated anthropologist at heart, Cerra enjoys understanding how the technologies around us are fundamentally altering the way we live, work, learn, and play. Whether in dissecting how broadband upends traditional economies, how technology influences and reflects company culture, or how virtual and physical worlds converge to create a new human psyche, Cerra has explored the intersection of technology and behavior in several books. In 2015, motivated by a desire to stand on the good side of a fight too important to lose, Cerra joined the ranks of cybersecurity professionals, where she currently marries her calling for marketing with a cause of educating unwitting participants in a virtual battle that is underestimated, if not ignored, by far too many.

About the Technical Reviewer

Patty Hatter (@pattyhatter) is guided by a fundamental philosophy centered on building connections across the information technology (IT) ecosystem. The multiplier effect of her collaborative approach means better outcomes by every measure. She has led all parts of the business, from sales and service to operations and IT. As a result, she intimately understands her customers. For more than two decades, she's developed an authentic leadership style marked by clear communication and tackling challenges head-on. She often appears at industry events to share her uniquely qualified perspective as a chief information officer (CIO) and cybersecurity leader. Hatter's advocacy of STEM education, mentoring of women, and full inclusion in technology amplifies the impact of her leadership on these critical industry issues. She also donates her free time to support children's education and the arts, and currently is on the board for the Silicon Valley Education Foundation (SVEF).

Acknowledgements

The authors wish to gratefully acknowledge the contributions of the following individuals who helped make this project a reality:

- Patty Hatter, for your critical insights and invaluable perspectives as a technical reviewer of the content.

- Vincent Weafer, for your expertise in framing the nuances of the current threat intelligence landscape.

- Tom Quillin, Raja Patel and John Loucaides, for your constructive review of the material and helpful advice.

- William Chance Hoover, for your research assistance.

- Mark Murray, for your mastery in deconstructing complex principles into elegant simplicity.

Thanks also to all our white-hat comrades the world over, for faithfully defending your organizations and consumers against virtual adversaries few even realize exist. It is a privilege to stand in the fight with you.

Foreword

The second economy is at risk. It need hardly be said that the magnitude and prevalence of cybersecurity threats in our lives is increasing. In 2006, McAfee Labs counted an average of 25 threats a day; by 2016, the number was more than 400,000, or more than 300 threats per minute. New malware alone is up 60 percent, there has been a 30 percent increase in targeted attacks, and a billion personal records are stolen every year. As it has been for more than 30 years, cybersecurity is the very definition of dynamic.

In 1997 three business partners and I embarked on a startup journey in cybersecurity. You might say we were among the last white hats to enlist in the cybersecurity cause before the new century began. Online security then was largely a back-office function, and often it was physically situated in the basement, or fitted into some other less than desirable piece of real estate, as if an afterthought. It's not that the computing experience wasn't already under threat by then, or that online safety wasn't important to each of us living digital lives. Nuisance attacks via numerous worms and viruses in the 1980s generated a great deal of media coverage and drove broad public awareness. Accordingly, much of the focus in the late 1990s was on deploying antivirus software and monitoring e-mail for corrupt attachments. We were still a few years away from targeted efforts that began with attacks on credit cards in the early 2000s.

My partners and I had a business vision that was easy to rally behind 20 years ago: protect trust. Others might guess we would have defined our work as something like this: keep outsiders from getting inside by monitoring for suspicious activity across systems. While that's technically true—it's what our software did—our higher aim was to ensure trusted, and trustworthy, computing. After all, safe information powers the world. The data that defines us, the patents and designs that differentiate our brands, the records of our institutions, and government—indeed, the knowledge of all humankind—is the very stuff of which the Internet is made.

Still, two decades ago, my partners and I didn't foresee how cybersecurity would evolve. How quickly trust would come under relentless attack. How eventually cybersecurity would move from the basement to the boardroom. And I certainly didn't know then that cybersecurity now would be my life's work. The second economy is built on trust, and protecting it is my personal focus. That hasn't changed since my startup days, even as many things about the cybersecurity landscape have.

The caricature of the social misfit hacker working alone popularized in popular culture is outdated. Attacking computer infrastructure is now mainstream and global. Coordinated efforts of nation-states, criminal organizations, and networks of politically motivated hacktivists have brought targeted attacks to the front pages. From thefts of retail customer data to publication of national security data to billion-dollar international financial industry attacks, the breadth and scope of cybersecurity attacks have increased exponentially. The size of the target has also increased. Where once individual retailers or banks would be targeted, now entire supply chains, financial networks, and stock markets are targeted.

What was once a threat to one computer at a time now has the potential to affect the integrity of international financial systems or a country's GDP (gross domestic product).

Furthermore, as automation pervades more and more of our world, the targets for cyberattacks increase as well. Many systems once isolated and mechanically driven are now networked and automated or controlled remotely via the Internet, often wirelessly, greatly expanding the target surface and nature of cyberattacks. The race to be the first to market with new automation technologies has also meant that some devices in the growing "Internet of Things" are proving to be vulnerable to hacking with only moderate effort. Location tracking is also routinely accessed by phone apps, providing yet another security risk to consumers if hacked. And this is all before drones and autonomous transportation have become commonplace.

Before I made cybersecurity my career, all this was more limited in scope. Computer access was less pervasive, and systems were limited in their ability to connect to other networks and devices. The issue of cybersecurity was the province of a small number of specialists within the information technology (IT) community, working within the operations team within individual organizations. Today, even in the Oval Office, cybersecurity is front and center, and I'm certainly proud and gratified to have been appointed by President Obama to the NSTAC (National Security Telecommunications Advisory Council). Securing our communications infrastructure is central to everything we value in the 21st century, and protecting data and systems across all aspects of government, and throughout every sector, is only increasing in importance with each passing day.

But while events in the news have by and large gotten everyone's attention, those in the executive suite often have no tools, history, context, or experience to understand the magnitude and nature of new threats. Recently, chief information officers (CIOs) of several large corporations admitted that they had only paid attention to cybersecurity for a few years. How can critical organizational decisions be made in an informed way in such an environment?

This book helps explain in clear layman's terms the fundamental landscape of the second economy, its foundations, basic concepts in security, and the threats to it, so that you can better understand the issues at hand. If you are a cybersecurity professional, the book will magnify your world through a different lens, particularly by challenging conventional wisdom that is rooted in cybersecurity's early beginnings. If you are an executive, you will gain an appreciation for the complexity of the issues at hand and be provided with practical takeaways to ensure your cybersecurity agenda is not compromised by internal politics or flawed incentive systems. And, if you are an employee, you will grasp the magnitude of the virtual battle that is fought each day, many times with your unwitting participation. But what exactly is meant by the *second economy*, anyway?

Not that long ago, references to a second economy would have referred exclusively to the underground economy of unregulated and illegal commerce (as, for example, the black market in the former Soviet Union). Though this secondary underground economy differed in many ways from the first economy, it was bound by the same physical limits and operated at the pace of humans transacting business directly in the physical world.

In today's society, the second economy refers to the vast and interconnected set of digital systems that move alongside or serve as underpinnings for our first economy. Billions of IP (Internet Protocol)-enabled sensors are like oxygen in the always on, always connected world. Through the proliferation of smart devices in this new second economy, transactions occur instantaneously and globally, often with no direct human involvement.

But the unregulated and illegal activities of the physical world have successfully migrated to this second virtual economy as well. Whatever nefarious schemes go down in the physical world can happen in the virtual world as well. How do we combat threats that know no physical barriers and attacks that occur either instantaneously with apparent damage or surreptitiously but gradually, causing great cumulative harm? While the first economy relies on physical barriers and safety mechanisms for security, the second economy relies on trust: consumer trust in a company's security structure for ecommerce, for instance.

But, the second economy is also about treasure—be it the enemy's pursuit for profit, principle, or province and the defender's relentless fight to protect what is most sacred. This book covers the economic principles undergirding incentive structures for black hats and white hats. It does so by juxtaposing the clarity of incentive schemes for adversaries against the unclear, and sometimes misdirected, reward structures of their targets. In this highly asymmetric battle, it's critical that those of us on the good side of the fight understand our enemy and how we may be unintentionally playing into its hands with rewards that do not drive optimal cybersecurity outcomes.

Finally, the second economy is about time. When a breach does occur, time becomes the ultimate weapon. Adversaries use it to their advantage to surreptitiously pilfer their loot, if not surprise their victim with a very visible attack designed to grab news. Victims are in a virtual race against both their enemy and the clock—detecting and remediating threats as quickly as possible becomes the goal in a race where every second matters. Time is critical. And, the "supply" of time available in one's war reserves—or how quickly an organization is able to shift from its heels to its toes when an attack occurs—depends on an organization's tools, policies, and political structures in place before any such notion of a threat is even recognized.

Unfortunately, not every organization has evolved to meet the demands placed on it by today's industrialized hackers. Often, separate divisions within a corporation or organization still have separate security policies, allowing one lax team to open up the others to attack. Inertia and reluctance to comply with corporate standards compound the problem of keeping security measures up to date.

Although this situation is changing to one where cybersecurity standards are being more consistently enforced within organizations, the complexity of electronic connectivity with business partners, cloud computing, automated supply chains, and connected devices have provided more opportunities for attacks along with additional convolution. Cybersecurity vendors have naturally responded with more tools to help manage this increasingly complex landscape.

The cybersecurity industry is experiencing tremendous growth in response to well-publicized threats: in just four years, more than 1,200 new firms found VC (venture capital) backing of some $7 billion. Corporate expenditures for cybersecurity today are around $100 billion and growing. In addition to this expansion, the movement to pool threat information for mutual aid in such industry initiatives as the CTA (Cyber Threat Alliance) has provided enormous amounts of threat and attack data to analyze. Making cybersecurity a financial priority and working together to combat cyberattacks are both steps in the right direction.

However, within organizations, the need to justify expenditures and show a return on investment in the conventional way leads to, in many cases, simply purchasing (and perhaps actually deploying) the latest tools on the market, and reacting to each new threat by logging ever more alerts and collecting more and more data. To some extent, this tool sprawl is throwing money at a problem. What you get in return is not always more protection. Sometimes all you get is more complexity, higher costs, and massive volumes of data. As we have learned from intelligence initiatives in the past decade or so, sometimes just having the data won't protect you unless you can make sense of it. With all this attention and financial investment, there is a dire shortage of trained cybersecurity experts to rank all these alerts and analyze all this data in an intelligent way. And while data analytics and artificial intelligence are promising technologies, the need for better-trained and better-staffed cybersecurity teams remains a critical choke point in moving forward (i.e., we don't have enough white hats—we're on track to be short two million qualified personnel by the end of the decade). And we don't just need more bodies. Conventional paradigms must be challenged: the more the teams are expanded to include those not narrowly focused on IT security, the sooner fresh approaches and new perspectives can be gained to help with identifying and combating current attacks as well as anticipating potential targets that need to be protected.

Cybersecurity is about outcomes—it's that simple. Which is why a thorough change in the organization, from the boardroom to security operations, needs to occur in order to successfully address current threats and prepare for future ones. Are you asking the right questions? Skilled teams need to be developed to identify and assess the most likely serious threats based on an understanding of the business, the infrastructure, the data, and recent targeted attacks. For the foreseeable future, the most highly trained teams are a scarce and valuable resource, and they must be used wisely. This implies that metrics need to be rehashed and reevaluated to make sure that likely risks are given higher priority for more in-depth assessment by such teams, while lower-level alerts are dealt with using vetted cybersecurity software and best security practices. I often put it this way: deploy automation to deal with the 99 percent of threats that are noise, and put your best talent on the hunt for the 1 percent of attacks that would steal headlines.

A framework for dealing with risk needs to be established and then constantly revisited to check for inertia, institutional bias, incorrect or outdated assumptions, and the like. Understanding how to use a more cooperative and adaptive defense strategy requires a renewed interest and focus on cybersecurity at the highest levels of the organization. This book does a great job of presenting memorable and engaging illustrative examples from history and current events that provide key insights and perspectives gleaned from the collective experiences of the security industry in a context that helps it all make sense.

It takes courage and dedication to move from a siloed, reactive, back-office approach to cybersecurity to one that is adaptive, aggressive, and proactive in its orientation. In order to develop the framework to meet these demands and push these efforts forward, leaders must have a basic understanding of cybersecurity and what has and has not been effective in terms of corporate strategy to meet the cybersecurity threats head on. They need to know what is at risk, what is perceived as potentially vulnerable or a rich target, what motivates the black hats to develop their attack campaigns, and how the white hats can anticipate these attacks, defend against them, and move from defense to offense. This book provides a foundational understanding of the challenge in a thought-provoking way. It can be an invaluable jumping-off point for the evolution in thinking that needs to occur to adapt and survive in the world of the second economy. A world where trust, treasure, and time are the spoils.

—Christopher Young
Senior Vice President and General Manager
Intel Security

Prologue

"Because that's where the money is."

—*Quote attributed to notorious felon William Francis "Willie" Sutton when asked by reporter Mitch Ohnstad why he robbed banks*

Merriam-Webster defines an urban legend as "a story about an unusual event or occurrence that many people believe is true but that is not true." Willie Sutton's 40-year criminal record, in which he scored nearly $2 million and escaped from prison three times, is the stuff of which urban legends are made. Indeed, with an estimated 100 bank heists to his credit, Sutton rightfully earned his place in history as one of the most prolific bank robbers of the 20th century.

Yet, despite his prodigious career as criminal mastermind, the one defining mark of Sutton's legacy would become so inextricably linked to him that it could only be dubbed "Sutton's Law"—that is, his oft-quoted response to the question of why he robbed banks, to which Sutton allegedly quipped, "Because that's where the money is." Beyond demonstrating the brilliant simplicity (and wit) of one of the most famed bank robbers of a generation, Sutton's Law would live on in other more respectable trades. In the medical community, it served as a metaphor encouraging doctors to focus on the most likely diagnosis, rather than waste resources investigating every potential possibility. In management accounting, it gained traction in activity-based costing, where the highest-cost items are scrutinized to uncover commensurate savings.

Despite all the notoriety of Sutton's Law, the truth, according to Sutton himself, is that he never made the comment:

> The irony of using a bank robber's maxim as an instrument for teaching medicine is compounded, I will now confess, by the fact that I never said it. The credit belongs to some enterprising reporter who apparently felt a need to fill out his copy. I can't even remember where I first read it. It just seemed to appear one day, and then it was everywhere.[i]

And so it goes: urban legend born from one journalist's active imagination attributed to a one-man-crime-spree whose record hardly needed embellishment continues to this day. And, as Sutton's Law has gone down as one of the most fascinating (if not completely fictitious) retorts in modern history, it pales in comparison to the widespread popular opinion of early bank robbers and their reign of terror over what American historians would label the country's "frontier period." The mere mention of the "Wild Wild West" conjures images ripped from the silver screen of gun-wielding, mask-donning bank robbers, intent on cashing in before darting out on their trusty steeds. Here's the problem with this image: Like the Sutton quote, it is born of fiction.

To clarify, there certainly were bank robberies during this period, but the number hardly warrants the moniker, yet alone icon, associated with a "Wild West." In their book, *Banking in the American West from the Gold Rush to Deregulation*, authors Larry Schweikart and Lynne Doti examine primary and secondary sources from all the states of the "frontier west" during the period 1859-1900. Based on their extensive research, including additional interviews from well-intentioned sources bent on clarifying the record following the book's release, Schweikart and Doti report roughly a half dozen bank robberies over a 40-year period and across 15 states. Putting the number into context, there were more bank robberies in Dayton, Ohio, in one year at the turn of this century than there were in the entire Old West in a decade and perhaps in the whole frontier period.[ii]

While the results were not entirely surprising to Schweikart and Doti, the average layperson may be puzzled by the lack of robberies among what would have represented a lucrative target for inspired thieves. After all, whether Sutton said it or not, banks really were where the money was. In deconstructing the success of these early frontier bankers, the authors point to a relatively simple blueprint that established a financial bedrock for society.

- *Bankers were often first something else.* Despite several early bankers having ties to eastern financial firms, many did not inhabit a town and immediately set up a bank. Instead, they typically opened a general merchandise store. The reason was simple, if not profound. These early businessmen recognized that a bank's foundation was predicated on the psychological currency of trust. Introducing a general store allowed these leaders to build trust with those in the community before attempting to monetize it via a banking relationship.

- *Bankers looked the part.* Before the days of federal regulation or financial insurance, a banker's appearance was paramount in convincing customers of his authenticity and credibility. A banker's dress denoted success and wealth; more important, it conveyed assurance of a person behind the bank, one capable of supporting his business during times of trouble. With trust still the principal currency in play, a banker who effectively played the part connoted competence.

- *Banks were secure.* Often placed in the center of town and constructed by some of the leading architects in the country, the bank building itself was one that deterred would-be criminals. Flanked on both sides by other merchants, a bank's most vulnerable entry was through the rear of the building. Still, blasting through this rear entry proved no simple task, as many bankers double-reinforced this wall. Even if the most industrious of criminals found their way in, they would find themselves confounded with a seemingly impenetrable iron safe. The physical representation of the institution was the final marker upon which to build trust, one where customers had confidence in the construction of the bank itself.

Of course, there were exceptions to the rule and notorious bank robbers, including Butch Cassidy and his clan, were successful in major scores. While fiction is quick to glamorize the shoot-out matches likely present in these escapades, it fails to convey the excruciating planning behind such heists. As a case in point, Cassidy was known to be an expert with horses and would strategically station his stallions at deliberate checkpoints between his score and hideout, allowing his team to switch "vehicles" mid-course at precisely the moments the animals were most likely to fatigue.[iii]

But the capers of Cassidy and other notorious felons were rare cases. Based on Schweikart and Doti's own account, the Wild West bank robbery was virtually nonexistent. While the money certainly was at the bank, so too were considerable obstacles and risks to the criminally inclined. Instead, stagecoaches and trains became the risk-averse targets of choice, rendering most banks during the frontier era safe havens upon which a burgeoning economy would ultimately flourish—one where physical currency traded on the basis of an underlying trust relationship.

Only when the playing field was leveled between experienced and amateur robbers did the bank heist become a more common occurrence. Specifically, the introductions of the automobile and highway system allowed crooks the advantage once enjoyed exclusively by innovators like Cassidy – the ability to evade pursuit. Once banks became softer targets, thieves responded in kind.

Fast forwarding to modern times, the economics of bank robbery still prove elusive but for the most adept masterminds. According to a study by a team of economists at the University of Sussex, who crunched data on more than 350 robberies between 2005 and 2008, the average haul for a British robber was a rather insignificant £20,330 ($31,610). In the United States, the take was even lower—just $10,025, on average, according to the FBI.[iv] Just as mythical as the prolific Wild West bank heist is the notion that current bank robbers abscond with huge sums of money for their risk and trouble. Contrary to the images so common on a Hollywood set, less than 10 percent of US bank robbers even make it inside the vault, leaving their spoils subject to what can be collected at a bank teller's window.[v]

And so, the annals of bank robberies have been relegated but to the most notorious of criminals, including Sutton, Cassidy, and their ilk, leaving most thieves in the category of petty nuisance to the financial bastions they infiltrate. That is, until 2015, when security firm Kaspersky Labs uncovered what would be heralded as the largest bank heist in history. In an attack on more than 100 banks in 30 countries, criminals made off with close to an estimated $1 billion, of which only one-third was even traceable.[vi] There was no need to determine how to crack a seemingly impenetrable vault or orchestrate a strategic escape plan across jurisdictional lines. This attack was perpetrated by savvy hackers across Russia, China, and Europe.

First, the trap was set, as cybercriminals targeted bank employees with e-mails appearing to come from trusted colleagues (known as a phishing scheme in industry parlance). Once unwitting employees clicked on the e-mail attachments, malicious programs did their part to trace employee behavioral patterns. After capturing photo and video surveillance of employees' computers, the hackers used their victims' credentials to siphon money in what would otherwise appear as authorized bank or ATM (automated teller machine) transactions. One such tactic involved inflating individual bank account balances, such as showing $10,000 in an account where only $1,000 was actually deposited, allowing the criminals to abscond with the $9,000 in counterfeit withdrawals. And, perhaps the scariest fact in the case: unlike the quick in-and-out approach of "traditional" bank robberies, these perpetrators took their time, literally spending as much as two years camping out incognito within the virtual perimeter of their targets—collecting data, learning behavioral patterns, and inconspicuously taking up to $1 billion in treasure over several quarters.[vii]

Though newsworthy given the size of take, the $1 billion, nameless, faceless, virtual hack is one of so many stories that make daily headlines. In the financial industry alone, consider some of the more notable hacks in recent years.

- At 1:07 p.m. Eastern Standard Time on April 23, 2013, the official Twitter account belonging to the Associated Press released this tweet to its nearly two million followers: "Breaking: Two Explosions in the White House and Barack Obama is injured."[viii] Over a three-minute period that followed, the Dow nosedived nearly 150 points, temporarily obliterating $136 billion in equity market value before stabilizing. The recovery came when the tweet was exposed as fake. A group of Syrian hackers claimed credit for the breach and, though a financial institution was not the direct target, the group was able to wreak havoc on Wall Street for three minutes.[ix] Imagine the consequences if the hackers were successful in seizing the official Twitter accounts of multiple news organizations simultaneously with consistent counterfeit messages.

- British banking customers fell prey to another phishing scam in October 2015, losing up to £20 million to Eastern European hackers. The real target of the attack were global financial institutions as hackers lured consumers to click on otherwise legitimate e-mails which activated the insidious Dridex virus, succumbing the victims' computers—and online banking details—to the hackers' control.[x]

- In November 2015, four hackers were indicted for infiltrating a JPMorgan Chase server containing the contact records of more than 80 million customers. The case didn't involve a complex phishing scheme or zero-day attack exploiting an unknown software vulnerability. Instead, criminals simply stole the username and password of an employee.

  Normally, such a simplistic attempt would be thwarted, as most servers require two-factor authentication. Multifactor authentication is common security practice, requiring at least two forms of verification before allowing a user access to a system. As an example, consider a withdrawal from a cash machine, which requires both the authorized bank card and associated PIN (personal identification number) for the account, to be executed. In the JPMorgan Chase hack, a typical server would have required at least one more piece of verification beyond a user name and password for access. However, in JPMorgan Chase's vast network of servers, including those gained via mergers and acquisitions, the one that lacked this additional layer of security offered adversaries entry to more than 90 other servers on the bank's network.[xi]

Though no account data was stolen, the criminals still enjoyed a healthy payday—netting more than $100 million in a bogus stock-pumping scheme and online gambling operation.[xii] In the scam, the hackers used the stolen contact data to con victims into buying stocks and manipulate their prices. When asked whether buying stocks was popular in America, one of the perpetrators allegedly responded, "It's like drinking freaking vodka in Russia."[xiii]

Make no mistake: the nature of these attacks do not merely compromise a few companies' bottom lines. They call into question the stability and integrity of the financial system itself—a system that, at its foundation, is built on the psychological currency of trust. Early bankers knew that their very success depended on first gaining customer trust, hence the reason so many were first general merchants and carefully looked the part of credible financier capable of covering any potential losses. Historically, bank robbers proved more nuisance than threat, targeting banks meeting certain physical criteria and limiting their spoils largely to what they could quickly take when seconds matter.

However, with a virtual and highly interconnected monetary network now in play, cybercriminals increasingly have the entire financial system in their sights. The stakes of this game couldn't be higher as law enforcement officials are becoming all too aware. When federal prosecutor Preet Bharara brought charges against an Eastern European hacking ring in 2013, he presciently added, "Cybercriminals are determined to prey not only on individual bank accounts, but on the financial system itself."[xiv] These adversaries have a vast attack surface to target: a 2013 report from Iosco and the World Federation of Exchanges reported that 89 percent of the world's financial exchanges listed hacking as a "systemic risk."[xv]

And, the financial system is just one target. Hackers are not prone to discrimination, pursuing everyone from consumers to companies and everything from data centers to utility grids. Like the urban legends that pervasively represent a Wild West as a distant notion from reality, many still imagine a hacker as the pimple-faced teen in his parents' basement with nothing better to do with his time and talent. While hobbyist hackers still exist, the reality is that insidious cybercrime is increasingly at the hands of organized crime syndicates and nation-states, whose profits produce a staggering economic burden. According to the Center for Strategic and International Studies, a Washington think tank, the estimated global costs of cybercrime and economic espionage are nearly $450 billion, placing cybercrime in similar company with drug trafficking in terms of economic harm. Put another way, if cybercrime were a country, its GDP (gross domestic product) would rank in the top 30 of nations, exceeding the economies of Singapore, Hong Kong, and Austria, to name just a few.

And, similar to bona fide businesses, in the world of cybercrime, time equals money. Consider the dwell time—or the time between when a breach occurs and is finally detected—in which hackers enjoyed unauthorized access to their victims' most sensitive files and systems in some of the above-mentioned hacks:

- for JPMorgan Chase, cybercriminals were in the perimeter several months before being detected,[xvi]

- for at least some of the banks targeted in the $1B heist, up to two years went by with no knowledge of a breach,[xvii] and

- although the Associated Press Twitter hack lasted just a few short minutes before discovery, the temporary damage of more than $100 billion in market value was palpable nonetheless.

Cybercrime turns the tables on unsuspecting victims. Unlike physical threats that are readily seen and understood, virtual adversaries often enjoy a cloak of invisibility upon infiltration. The time of this clandestine advantage becomes a major weapon in the fight to contain damage or losses. Unfortunately, time is increasingly not on the side of the victim. A 2015 Ponemon Institute Survey reported the average dwell time at 98 days for financial services firms. For retail companies, the results were worse: breaches were not discovered for 197 days following attack.[xviii] Even more sobering, 58 and 71 percent of financial services and retail organizations, respectively, were not optimistic about improving their responsiveness to these virtual attacks within the coming year.[xix] Making matters worse, the volume of strikes would be sufficient on their own to cause concern, even if they could be immediately detected—more than 80 percent of financial service companies experience more than 12 attacks per week. Retail companies fared a bit better, but with nearly half of these companies reporting the same volumes at more than twice the dwell time of their financial counterparts, their results are equally disconcerting.[xx]

The physical world knows no such threat. Imagine a thief being in your house or place of business rummaging through your most sensitive belongings and remaining there undetected for months, seasons, or even years. Couple this with popular phishing schemes used to lure unsuspecting employees (Verizon reports 23 percent of recipients open phishing e-mails[xxi]) and you now also have a case where you, as the victim, offer the thug the key to your very own dwelling.

As adversaries have grown in number and sophistication, so too have their incentives. Just as the reporter who fabricated what would become known as Sutton's Law was seeking an answer to what would motivate such an individual, victims are left to ponder what would compel nameless, faceless hackers to strike. Assuming all are motivated by profit, as Sutton, seriously simplifies much more complex psychological undercurrents. Hacktivists enlist recruits to their virtual army to fight for principle. Nation-states identify targets to expand their province. And, yes, there are still hackers who view the hobby as a means to prank their victims. Whether for profit, principle, province, or prank, each attack serves to erode the trust of customers in a company's ability to withstand future breaches and protect their interests.

While threat actors may differ in incentive models, they universally share a currency of time. Time becomes the critical strategic weapon in the cyberwar. Whether using time against a victim, as in the recent spate of ransomware attacks, or dwelling inconspicuously for as long as possible to pilfer sensitive records, the way time is used in the battle depends on the hacker's incentive model. The two are often inextricably linked.

This book explores all of the above: the underlying incentives that are foundational to various cybercriminals and their victims, the time imperative when a cyberattack occurs, and the trust that is eroded between supplier and customer with each hack. *The Second Economy* pertains to all three: treasure, time, and trust. Like urban legends that seduce their believers into succumbing to an alternate reality, preconceived security notions—even those held by the most well-intentioned professionals employed to defend their organizations—are dangerous delusions that demand a second look to overcome an increasingly powerful enemy.

To thoroughly examine the problem, the book is divided in its approach. The first half explores the incentive models in play for cybercriminals acting for profit, principle, or province and the underlying trust economy that is ultimately corroded with each company breach. This part of the book is more observational in its orientation, as understanding how threat actors are changing their methods to abscond with treasure and trust is fundamental to formulating the solution. The second half offers a practical prescription for critical stakeholders of private and public organizations—including chief information officers (CIOs), chief executive officers (CEOs), and boards of directors—to remediate the threat and compete effectively in *The Second Economy*. This part of the book is more opinionated in its tone, as we respectfully challenge conventional security paradigms, based, in part, on a McAfee primary research study surveying more than 1,000 security professionals globally to understand attitudes, beliefs, and actions underlying their organization's security posture—many of which, we submit, must change for successful outcomes.

In writing a book like this, it is tempting to devolve to fear-mongering or hyperbole when discussing such a sensational topic. While we will resist such tendencies, we would be remiss in not placing a spotlight on how and where threat actors increasingly surround us. In fact, it is human nature to underestimate or misjudge risk entirely—a weapon the adversary exploits in his arsenal. As such, our intention is not to fuel exaggerated scare tactics but to inspire a sense of urgency among key decision makers to respond to their enemies in kind.

Organizations have historically lacked this bias for action, with cybersecurity dwelling in the shadows of traditional information technology (IT) organizations. Some have argued that IT, prone to commoditization, is a function best relegated to being a fast follower of innovation. However, the opposite is true for cybersecurity, as threat actors invest their own research and development preparing the next assault and seeking the most vulnerable victim—a follower, be it fast or not—to attack. It has only been fairly recently, with notable public hacks on significant targets like Sony, Target, and The Home Depot, that cybersecurity has elevated itself from a back-office function in IT to a conversation worthy of boardroom debate, as organizations scramble to prevent themselves from being the next headline or punch line.

The Second Economy provides a different lens through which to examine cybersecurity issues that ultimately affect each one of us, particularly as we increasingly inhabit a world comprised of the cloud, mobility, the "Internet of Things," and a seemingly infinite number of goods and services that are exchanged online. In the end, we hope to answer the reader's fundamental questions with regard to an ongoing and escalating battle of which we are all now part: as either prey, predator, or unwitting participant in this virtual marketplace. Among them are the following:

- How has the threat landscape changed over time and what is likely next?

- Where are preconceived security notions limiting successful outcomes for victims in the fight?

- What measures can organizations take to protect themselves?

We will also carefully embark on answering another critical question: Why? Why do cybercriminals do what they do? Specifically, for the financially motivated adversary, cause-oriented hacktivist or power-induced nation state, we will rely on the principles of another underlying economy in play—that of cybercrime itself. By deconstructing the incentives and addressable market available to different types of assailants, juxtaposed against the risk for various assaults, we will attempt to understand how motives are influenced by opportunity. While we will answer this question as it pertains to the mentality of those in pursuit of profit, principle, or province, the same cannot be offered for the mind-set of other cybercriminals who do not follow one of these walks of life and for whose motives we will likely never understand. And, while it is human nature to attempt to find an explanation for such destruction, sometimes the answer itself leaves one wanting more. It isn't surprising that a reporter asked the infamous Willie Sutton why he robbed banks, and when one considers his real answer, perhaps the falsified response becomes a bit more understandable. According to Sutton:

> If anybody had asked me [why I robbed banks], I'd have probably said it [because that's where the money is]. That's what almost anybody would say ... it couldn't be more obvious.

> Or could it?

> Why did I rob banks? Because I enjoyed it. I loved it. I was more alive when I was inside a bank, robbing it, than at any other time in my life. I enjoyed everything about it so much that one or two weeks later I'd be out looking for the next job. But to me the money was the chips, that's all.[xxii]

We may never fully understand what motivates these predators, though we can certainly examine the economic nature of crime itself as a precursor to knowledge. And, we can definitely make progress in altering our own beliefs and behaviors to be more successful in the battle. It starts with understanding what form of treasure is in play for various threat actors, why trust is often taken for granted, and how time is the most valuable weapon in the arsenal. It ends when we each recognize our part in *The Second Economy*.

Notes

i. W. Sutton and E. Linn, *Where the Money Was: The Memoirs of a Bank Robber* (New York: Viking Press, 1976), p. 160.

ii. Larry Schweikart, "The Non-Existent Frontier Bank Robbery," Foundation for Economic Education, January 1, 2001, http://fee.org/articles/the-non-existent-frontier-bank-robbery/, accessed March 28, 2016.

iii. Ibid.

iv. "The economics of bank robbery: More swagger than swag," *The Economist*, June 16, 2012, www.economist.com/node/21556980, accessed March 29, 2016,.

v. Ibid.

vi. Chris Smith, "The largest bank robbery ever: up to $900M possibly stolen, and no need for a getaway car," *BGR*, February 16, 2015, http://bgr.com/2015/02/16/300-million-bank-theft-hackers/, accessed March 29, 2016,.

vii. Ibid.

viii. Max Fisher, "Syrian hackers claim AP hack that tipped stock market by $136 billion. Is it terrorism?," *The Washington Post*, April 23, 2013, www.washingtonpost.com/news/worldviews/wp/2013/04/23/syrian-hackers-claim-ap-hack-that-tipped-stock-market-by-136-billion-is-it-terrorism/, accessed April 1, 2016.

ix. Ibid.

x. Nick Gutteridge, "Is YOUR computer affected? Hackers use virus to steal £20 MILLION from UK bank accounts," *Express*, October 13, 2015, www.express.co.uk/news/uk/611873/hackers-steal-money-UK-bank-accounts-malware-virus-national-crime-agency, accessed March 31, 2016,.

xi. Peter Bright, "JPMorgan Chase hack due to missing 2-factor authentication on one server," *ArsTechnica*, December 23, 2014, http://arstechnica.com/security/2014/12/jpmorgan-chase-hack-because-of-missing-2-factor-auth-on-one-server/, accessed April 1, 2016.

xii. Kim Zetter, "Four Indicted in Massive JP Morgan Chase Hack," *Wired*, November 10, 2015, www.wired.com/2015/11/four-indicted-in-massive-jp-morgan-chase-hack/, website accessed on March 31, 2016.

xiii.   Reuters and NBC News, "'Hacking as a Business Model': Three Indicted in JPMorgan Hack," November 10, 2015, www.nbcnews.com/tech/tech-news/jp-morgan-hack-three-indicted-cyberattacks-major-companies-n460671, website accessed on March 31, 2016.

xiv.   Owen Davis, "Hackers Steal $1 Billion In Biggest Bank Heist In History: Could They Take Down The Whole System Next Time?," *International Business Times*, February 16, 2015, www.ibtimes.com/hackers-steal-1-billion-biggest-bank-heist-history-could-they-take-down-whole-system-1818010, accessed April 1, 2016.

xv.   Ibid.

xvi.   Bright, 2note 11 *supra*.

xvii.   Smith, note 6 *supra*.

xviii.   Arbor Networks, "New Ponemon Institute Survey Reveals Time to Identify Advanced Threats is 98 Days for Financial Services Firms, 197 Days for Retail," Yahoo! Finance, May 19, 2015, http://finance.yahoo.com/news/ponemon-institute-survey-reveals-time-130000481.html, accessed April 1, 2016.

xix.   Ibid.

xx.   Ibid.

xxi.   Verizon 2015 Data Breach Investigations Report, file:///C:/Users/acerra/Downloads/rp_data-breach-investigation-report-2015_en_xg.pdf.

xxii.   Sutton and Linn, note 1 *supra*.

■ ■ ■

PART I

A Second Bite at the Problem

It isn't that they can't see the solution.
It is that they can't see the problem.

—Gilbert K. Chesterton
English writer, poet and philosopher

CHAPTER 1

■ ■ ■

The Second Side of the Story

If privacy is outlawed, only outlaws will have privacy.

—Philip Zimmerman, Creator of Pretty Good Privacy[1]

History has a way of repeating itself, even in the unlikeliest of cases. In 1917, a seemingly nondescript proceeding in the state of Oklahoma would find its way into the annals of legal precedent. In *Wilcox v. State*, the plaintiff appealed his criminal conviction for assault with a dangerous weapon, specifically a claw hammer. A claw hammer was (and still is) an ordinary household tool, one used to insert and remove nails in construction projects.

In his appeal, Wilcox referred to two earlier cases. In one, *Bourbonnais v. State*, the plaintiff had his two-year sentence reduced after the appellate court found it excessive given the evidence, or lack thereof. In the case, Bourbonnais appealed his conviction of assaulting a man with a piece of iron. In reviewing witness testimony, the appellate court found no proof where one could reasonably infer the object to be a deadly weapon.[2] In the other, *Moody v. State*, two plaintiffs successfully appealed their convictions after being found guilty of using a wooden plank to strike someone. The appellate court found that the wooden plank could not be, by itself, considered a dangerous weapon without further context:

> The charging part of the indictment was…too indefinite in that it did not describe the plank and designate in what manner it was used; it being their contention that a plank is not per se a deadly weapon; that, not being per se a deadly weapon, the county attorney was required to plead facts sufficient to show the character of the plank and the manner in which it was used, and that the facts so pleaded must show that the instrument used was of the character set out in the statute and used in such manner as to be reasonably calculated to produce serious bodily injury.[3]

With both legal precedents as support, Wilcox successfully had his conviction reversed when the court ruled, "a claw hammer is not per se a dangerous weapon, and especially it is not a dangerous weapon when considered without reference to its use, and a weapon cannot be said as a matter of law to be dangerous without reference to the manner of its use."[4] With the ruling, the claw hammer entered legal precedent as another tool that, without proper context of the user's intention, could not be deemed dangerous.

Claw hammers, iron pipes, and wooden planks may be subject to context in order to classify them as dangerous weapons or otherwise innocuous tools; automatic weapons utilized in mass shootings, on the other hand, require no such understanding. Nearly a century after the *Wilcox* case, a husband and wife team opened fire at their place of employment, the Inland Regional Center in San Bernardino, California, killing 14 and wounding 22 in what was, at the time, the deadliest terrorist attack on US soil since 9/11.[5] As is common with such tragedies, the event ignited vigorous debate over the impact of guns to society. Gun advocates point to the history of claw hammers, iron pipes and wooden planks for legal precedent, suggesting that guns per se do not kill—people do. Opponents claim stricter legal constraints to gun ownership would obviate mass shootings and save countless lives.

While the gun debate is hardly new, the San Bernardino case would also rekindle a more recent dialogue fundamental to technology security—one where context means everything. As is fairly common, the Inland Regional Center had issued a work-related iPhone to one of the perpetrators. The iPhone in question was encrypted, requiring a password to unlock the device. The employer and rightful owner of the device granted permission to the FBI to investigate its contents; however, the only one in possession of the phone's password was the now deceased assailant. The FBI took matters to Apple, asking the technology company to create a new version of its operating system and security firmware, one that disabled security features, to enable the FBI to use an automated passcode guessing attack to decrypt the device contents. When Apple refused, arguing that such a "backdoor" would ultimately endanger the security of tens of millions of American iPhone customers by also affording hackers a potential doorway through which to enter its installed base of devices, the FBI responded with an unprecedented lawsuit.

The Cryptowars

To fully understand the implications of the Apple suit requires a brief history lesson—one much more recent than the cases of Wilcox, Bourbonnais, and Moody. This time, we only need to travel as far back as 1993 when the Clinton administration introduced the "Clipper Chip." With the budding promise of Internet and wireless technologies, the US Government, long the bastion in using and cracking secret codes to transmit or intercept sensitive information, found itself outmatched by a torrid pace of technology change. New technologies introduced the need for stronger encryption to secure advanced communications, including e-mail and wireless transmissions. These advancements would benefit from the work of prodigious mathematicians of the 1970s—be it a seminal 1976 paper from researchers Whitfield Diffie and Martin Hellman that showed how ordinary businesses and individuals could securely communicate over modern communications networks using cryptography or the 1977 system developed by Massachusetts Institute of Technology mathematicians Ronald Rivest, Adi Shamir, and Leonard Adelman, which put Diffie and Hellman's encryption theory into practice.[6] With encryption securing more communications, the US Government began losing its grip as the singular authority in intercepting and deciphering these secured communications.

Enter the Clipper Chip—the American government's answer to balance the needs of national security with individual privacy. It called for a state-of-the-art microchip (the Clipper Chip) to be installed into consumer hardware telephones, fax machines and modems. The Chip would serve two purposes: it would provide the public with strong cryptographic capabilities to secure conversations but would also afford the US

Government access to these communications when legally warranted. Using a "key escrow" approach, a copy of each chip's unique encryption key would be stored with the federal government (with two separate agencies, requiring dual cooperation to break the encryption). With a key to unlock any Clipper Chip, the federal government was offered a pathway into the otherwise secured communications. And, while the Clipper Chip was not a mandatory standard, the government planned to seed the market with a massive volume of devices, intending to spawn its adoption.[7]

To appease public concern of a potential "Big Brother" government eavesdropping on sensitive conversations, a key selling point of the Clipper Chip involved its far superior encryption capabilities when compared to other alternatives at the time. Based on an encryption algorithm used by the National Security Agency (NSA) called Skipjack, the Clipper Chip offered what the US Government claimed was the best of both worlds: stronger encryption for the user with a doorway for government officials to tap Skipjack-encrypted communication. Parading out a panel of academic and industry experts espousing the advantages of the Clipper Chip and its associated Skipjack cryptographic standard, the US Government played offense in attempting to assuage public dissension against the Chip.[8]

Alas, public opposition grew. As echoed by cryptography's fathers, including Diffie, Hellman, and Rivest, the chorus of concerns over the government's proposal centered around three key trepidations. First, the very notion of offering the government potentially unrestricted access to its citizens' most intimate conversations gave pause to even the most trusting. Second, the reliance on a third party to break encryption negated the earlier work of Diffie and his ilk, which required no third-party intercept to decipher messages. And, combining the first and second concerns leads with the third: the federal government would be the only keyholder capable of breaking the code. With a growing list of very vocal public dissenters, it may come as no surprise that 80 percent of Americans opposed the Clipper Chip in a 1994 CNN/Time poll, with two-thirds saying that protecting privacy was more important than preserving the ability of police to conduct wiretaps.[9]

The US Government remained undeterred in the face of mounting opposition from the unlikeliest of bedfellows, including industry experts, conservative commentators, and one of the first hacktivist groups, labeled the Cypherpunks, a self-proclaimed "confederation of computer hackers, hardware engineers and high-tech rabble-rousers."[10] The final death knell to the Chip came when, in 1994, Matt Blaze, a computer scientist at AT&T Bell Laboratories, published a paper exposing a technical weakness in the technology that would allow one to circumvent the law-enforcement surveillance capabilities altogether.[11] With the government's exclusive access quashed, the Clipper Chip was no more, although the argument juxtaposing personal privacy against national security had only just begun —and would reach fever pitch in the 2016 Apple case.

In a standoff decades in the making, Apple challenged the US Government's right to force the company to introduce new software that would weaken the security defenses of its own products. Tim Cook, Apple's chief executive officer (CEO), pled the company's case in the court of public opinion with an open letter to customers, through which the ghosts of Diffie, Hellman, and their cohort were resurrected in the message:

> For years, cryptologists and national security experts have
> been warning against weakening encryption. Doing so would
> hurt only the well-meaning and law-abiding citizens who
> rely on companies like Apple to protect their data. Criminals
> and bad actors will still encrypt, using tools that are readily
> available to them.[12]

In this brief excerpt, the issue of context with regard to encryption becomes abundantly clear. Like the claw hammer before it, encryption can be used for either good or bad. And, weakening the defenses for the innocent only offers adversaries an easier target and backdoor through which to attack. Interestingly, the Apple case finished almost as quickly as it started, with the US Government unceremoniously and unexpectedly dropping its charges against Apple after claiming it had successfully worked with a third party to unlock the phone in question. The government is under no obligation to divulge how the encryption was broken and, as of this writing, has made no offer to Apple to do so, which would potentially serve to shore up security weaknesses in future product releases. Despite the abrupt closure to the case and what many would consider a victory for Apple, the company quickly pointed out that a more substantive public debate was in order to fully unpack some of the issues that had only been scratched in surface, asserting, "This case raised issues which deserve a national conversation about our civil liberties, and our collective security and privacy. Apple remains committed to participating in that discussion."[13]

Follow the Silk Road

If the cryptowars of the 1990s found a second life in 2016, device passwords would be only one battle. Using a unique cryptographic language, cryptocurrencies present their own duality where context matters. A cryptocurrency is digital money not issued, backed, by or tied to any particular government or nation.[14] Like encryption, cryptocurrencies rely on complex mathematical algorithms to secure and track all transactions and regulate the supply of virtual money to mitigate against inflation. To use cryptocurrencies, one need only access the Internet.

While many may struggle with exactly how cryptocurrencies like Bitcoin work, those in the know find themselves on opposite ends of a polarizing debate. Advocates point to the freedom such digital money affords those who otherwise lack access to an official bank account. This argument holds sway in developing regions such as Sub-Saharan Africa, where some countries have more adults using a mobile money account than one at a financial institution.[15] Cryptocurrency proponents also cite benefits associated with lower inflation risk (since the supply of currency is limited by mathematical rules), lower transaction fees versus other alternatives (like credit cards), and security of personal data (given the user's credit card is not involved in transactions).[16]

Opponents call into question the financial integrity of cryptocurrencies, pointing to the bankruptcy of Mt. Gox, the world's largest bitcoin exchange in 2014, as one cautionary tale. Due to what would ultimately be chalked up to poor management, Mt. Gox suffered multiple hacker attacks, the most fatal of which dealt a $460 million blow by adversaries who spent years fleecing the company.[17] Unlike traditional financial markets, there are no regulated agencies insuring the protection of investors in cryptocurrency exchanges. And, if illiquidity risks are insufficient to make one think twice, market volatility may do the trick. In one year alone, the value of bitcoins plunged more than 66 percent.[18]

But, perhaps the most interesting debate surrounding cryptocurrencies deals less with integrity and more with intention. Cryptocurrencies are not necessarily completely anonymous, though they do afford more privacy protection than traditional bank accounts. As such, they have become the monetary unit of exchange welcomed by bad actors online. In 2013, the FBI busted an illegal online drug exchange known as Silk

Road, seizing nearly $4 million in bitcoins.[19] In less than three years of inception, Silk Road had turned over $1.2 billion in revenue,[20] using cryptocurrency as the medium and sophisticated encryption software, Tor, to conceal the identity of its users.

Tor, originally standing for The Onion Router, was developed for the US Navy in an effort to protect government communications.[21] Tor cloaks users from Internet traffic analysis and works by encrypting and randomly bouncing communications through relay networks across the globe,[22] thereby obfuscating the user's Internet protocol (IP) address and location. With Tor muddying traffic analysis and bitcoins providing monetary freedom, sites like Silk Road operate in the shadows of the "dark web."

Yet, while these sophisticated encryption technologies can be and are used for nefarious purposes, they also provide anonymity to freedom fighters and political activists the world over. Again, like the claw hammer or lead pipe, the tool on its own is not dangerous; the intentions of the good or bad actor using the device give context to its benevolent or malevolent outcomes.

And, here is where things get even more interesting for companies defending themselves against the next major hack: threat actors know how to disguise bad intentions as perfectly normal behavior. As proverbial wolves in sheep's clothing, hackers continue to iterate and improve their tactics against their prey. Again, a brief walk down Memory Lane paints a picture of an ever-evolving threat landscape with ever-increasingly sophisticated countermeasures launched by adversaries.

"You Must Be Punished"

In a small Pakistani computer shop in the late 1980s, American tourists were presented an offer too good to refuse: top-rated commercial software starting at $1.50.[23] Buyers were in for more than a bargain when inserting the computer program in their PC's disk drive. Deposited on the disk was what is widely referred to as the first MS-DOS virus—"Brain." Brain was the creation of the Pakistani shop's owners, brothers Basit and Amjad Farooq Alvi. Back in the day, computer hard drives were precious real estate and floppy disks were used to run computer programs. Brain infected the part of the disk necessary for running programs and would contaminate computers, such that other disks were corrupted upon insertion.[24] The first of what would become known as "stealth viruses," with redirect capabilities to remain undetected from search and recovery efforts, Brain's bark was worse than its bite. According to one early victim of Brain, "It was only a floppy infector, and it was easy to copy anything off the floppy that you cared about, and just reformat the floppy or throw it away."[25] Still, those with tenacious spirits in finding Brain's hiding place within their PC were greeted with an ominous calling card from the soon-to-be-famous hackers, "WELCOME TO THE DUNGEON."[26]

The Alvi brothers claimed to have a noble intention behind the virus. Fed up with individuals who purchased or distributed pirated software, the brothers wanted to send a message, albeit in a strange way, to violators. While Brain essentially only renamed the volume label of the disk, it provided a means for the brothers to keep track of all copies made—after Basit claimed to have been a victim of piracy himself for custom software he developed.[27] In fact, the Alvis offered their personal contact information as part of their "dungeon" calling card to assist hapless victims in disinfecting their PCs (a convenient complement to the Alvis' line of business).

Interestingly, the brothers discriminated who would be exposed to their self-professed "friendly virus,"[28] having no qualms about selling bootlegged—though clean—software to Pakistani residents. Only foreigners, particularly Americans, were offered the Brain-infected bootlegged versions. The apparent hypocrisy presented no conflict for the Alvis, since Pakistani law did not prohibit piracy. When asked why they infected American buyers, Basit, the younger brother, simply replied, "Because you are pirating. You must be punished."[29]

The Alvis' Brain contagion spread so quickly, it even surprised them when they were inundated with phone calls from infected users demanding remediation. Their distinction with creating the first computer virus incited media to educate the public on a serious concern that could have been ripped from the pages of a sci-fi novel: What would happen if computers around the world were suddenly infected with much more insidious viruses? A 1988 *TIME Magazine* cover story on the topic reported that an estimated 250,000 computers had been afflicted that year alone with similar infections caused by more than 25 identified viruses, with new ones emerging nearly every week.[30]

What started as a couple of dozen strains of often nuisance-bearing viruses had reached pandemic proportions just a quarter of a century later. In the third quarter of 2016 alone, McAfee Labs reported more than 3.5 million infected files were exposed to its customers' networks and an additional 7.4 million potentially unwanted programs attempted installation or launch—each metric is what was detected *per hour* via the company's global threat intelligence capabilities.[31] Total malicious software (malware) in the McAfee Labs "zoo" approached nearly half a billion samples, with nearly 45 million new strains detected in the third quarter of 2016 alone.[32]

What many prognosticators in the late 1980s would have anticipated to be a major global collapse under such punishing volumes of malware, the world, complete with its even greater dependence on computing devices and networks, remains very much intact. Several reasons explain the unforeseen outcome.

First, anti-malware countermeasures were developed by software companies to detect and inoculate threats. Like criminals, early versions of malware carried their own modus operandi, easily observed patterns of behavior that, once identified and catalogued, could be used to spot and prevent suspicious interlopers. Anti-malware software companies provided their own remedy to a growing contagion by essentially recording, storing, and sharing a part of malicious code as a fingerprint of sorts and embedding this intelligence in their wares. Companies with this defensive software installed were inoculated from the known threat once the anti-malware software detected its presence (in essence, matched its fingerprint).

Second, technical advances beyond anti-malware software have played a critical role. For example, computing architectures have evolved through the years to better separate the operating system from applications to isolate the effects of contamination.

But, perhaps most important, the motives of threat actors themselves have changed. If a cybercriminal's goal is to abscond with sensitive information that can be exploited in some way, it benefits the adversary to remain undetected as long as possible to attain that outcome. Malware that corrupts computers is certainly destructive to a company; however, it is also readily identifiable once detected. Cybercriminals have become increasingly sophisticated in their assaults, more and more of which are designed to be inconspicuous in nature to facilitate greater damage to their victim and higher financial reward for themselves.

Such conditions have prevented a torrent of malware from upending the global digital economy. That said, remedying the volume of threats with such automated precision is fairly easy, albeit necessary, when the adversary's modus operandi is so clearly identified and understood. And, while the flood of virulent samples started with one Brain strain created by two brothers bent on "punishing" software pirates, the Alvis themselves would never be penalized for letting the malware genie out of the bottle. The same could not be said for one Donald Gene Burleson.

Enemy Within the Gates

On a September morning in 1985, company officials at USPA & IRA, a licensed life insurance agency and registered securities dealership with headquarters in Fort Worth, Texas, arrived at work to find an unusual occurrence. Approximately 75 percent of the company's commission records had been deleted. Without these records, the company would be unable to pay commissions to its roughly 450 independent agents.[33] Company investigators discovered that the files had been deleted in the overnight hours, with someone using the system to run a series of programs that resulted in the purge. Peculiarly, the malicious programs in question were developed some three weeks earlier.[34]

Three days before the incident, Donald Gene Burleson, a senior systems analyst and also the company's computer security officer, was terminated after two years of employment. A trail of computer breadcrumbs led company officials to Burleson as the perpetrator of the sabotage, who stood accused of developing the pernicious computer programs with the intention of detonating them upon voluntary or involuntary termination.[35]

In what would be a landmark case where criminal charges for computer hacking were brought against a defendant, Burleson was found guilty of burglary, harmful access to a computer with loss and damages over $2,500, and criminal mischief over $750. He was sentenced to seven years of supervised probation and ordered to pay his former company $11,800 in restitution.[36]

It may be surprising that the first prosecuted cybercrime case involved a malicious insider. Sadly, Burleson would not be the last employee to intentionally inflict harm upon his employer. Those who intend to inflict damage upon their employer for whatever the reason present a real concern for public and private organizations alike. According to a Ponemon Institute study, 35 percent of companies in 2015 suffered a cyberattack from a malicious insider.[37] While troublemaking employees ranked last among the cyberattack vectors queried (including malware, web-based attacks, and others), they took top honors as the most costly predators, imposing nearly $145,000 worth of damage with each attack.[38] As a testament to the havoc they can wreak, these insidious insiders also spawned the most complex attacks to remediate, costing their employers an average of nearly two months to resolve.[39]

Threats perpetrated by one or more of an organization's most trusted employees rank among the most difficult to detect and correct. After all, the metaphorical claw hammer wielded by an employee may be used to build up a company or bring it to its knees. Discerning the difference requires context. Unlike malware, which can often be identified by its characteristics, human behavior is far more difficult to model and understand. Perhaps that explains why even external adversaries often rely on a company's employees to do their bidding.

Gone Phishing

It was the breach that could appropriately take the moniker of *The Nightmare before Christmas*, one that would abruptly end the promising company careers of a CEO and CIO (chief information officer). Between US Thanksgiving and Christmas Day of 2013—the busiest shopping season of the year—Target, an international retailer with more than 340,000 employees worldwide, suffered a cyberattack that would compromise the bank accounts of some 40 million customers[40] and expose personally identifiable information for up to 70 million more.[41] During the quarter, the retailer saw its profits plummet by nearly half, compared to the fourth quarter of the previous year, with full-year profits declining by more than a third.[42] The breach would cost the company nearly $150 million in investigative costs,[43] $116 million in settlement costs with banks and consumers,[44] and invaluable customer trust. Casualties of the attack included CEO and Chairman Gregg Steinhafel and CIO Beth Jacobs—both of whom resigned their posts in the months following the hack.

As the public debacle of the attack made for interesting headline fodder, what many may not realize is how the hackers made their way into Target's most sensitive systems. While early reports suggested an inside job, the insider was not cut from the same malicious cloth as Burleson. In fact, the presumed insider was not even an employee of the company but a small supplier that provided heating, air conditioning, and refrigeration services to supermarkets. In this capacity, Fazio Mechanical Services of Sharpsburg, Pennsylvania, had remote access to Target's network for electronic billing, contract submission, and project management purposes.[45]

A postmortem analysis of the breach revealed that at least two months before hackers waged their attack on Target, they set their sights on Fazio Mechanical. Using spear phishing techniques, the adversaries successfully baited unwitting Fazio Mechanical employees with infected e-mails, likely with corrupted PDF or Microsoft Office attachments, which launched malware upon opening. Once the malware was deposited, the perpetrators stole Fazio Mechanical's credentials to gain entry to Target's network.[46]

Interestingly, while industry insiders and government officials debated the sophistication of the malware itself,[47] there was little argument that the adversaries had spent weeks orchestrating their attack and duping unwitting innocent employees to give them entry. To identify Fazio Mechanical as their intended mark—or sucker—in the con required the perpetrators to first do some online research on Target's suppliers. Luckily for the thieves, such information was readily available from Target itself via its supplier portal,[48] giving the threat actors enough to go on in setting the trap. From there, widely available social networking tools likely provided the adversaries with employee contact information for some working at Fazio Mechanical—requiring only one fish to take the bait.

Social engineering techniques, like phishing, are on the rise and for good reason: cybercriminals are offered multiple points of potential failure in the fabric of human beings who collectively are connected to a particular company target. Whether embedding their malware in an e-mail attachment or providing a bogus web-site address for the same, adversaries are aware that humans are often the weakest link in a company's defenses. In their semiannual survey, the Anti-Phishing Working Group (APWG) found at least 123,972 unique phishing attacks worldwide in the second half of 2014—the highest on record since the second half of 2009 (in this case, a phishing attack is defined as a phishing site that targets a specific brand or entity).[49] The study revealed that adversaries are relentless in getting their catch: The ten most-targeted companies by phishers were attacked constantly, as much as 1,000 times in a month, with this unenviable "most wanted" list sustaining more than three-quarters of all attacks worldwide.[50]

If phishing perpetrators are nothing if not tenacious in their efforts, they have good reason to be. As the old adage goes, "There's a sucker born every minute," and employees are unintentional weapons for the other side in a cyberwar most don't even realize is being waged. Verizon's 2015 Data Breach Investigations Report shows that more than one in five recipients open phishing messages, with more than one in ten clicking on attachments. Even scarier, half of these unsuspecting victims open the e-mail and click on the phishing link within the first hour.[51] If you're still not convinced that seconds really do matter in *The Second Economy*, consider that the median time to first click came in at just 82 seconds across all phishing campaigns.[52] Unfortunately, the same cannot be said for a company's speedy response, with afflicted organizations clocking in at more than ten hours to remove a phishing threat.[53] And, that figure has increased by more than one hour in one year.[54] With an average cost per phishing or social engineering incident at $86,000,[55] organizations lose more than $2 *per second*, once one of their own is hooked.

Phishing allows predators to gain quiet access to their target's most intimate areas, allowing them to stealthily pilfer valuable data, such as consumer credit card information, for eventual sale to other thugs. But, why bother with extracting data only to have to negotiate complex value chains to reap financial reward when one can simply hold it hostage from the victim himself? Indeed, holding data ransom offers predators an even faster return on their investment.

A State of Emergency

The year was 1989 and the world was worried about a different viral epidemic than one that could infect a computer—people were grappling to understand the immune disorder known as AIDS (Acquired Immune Deficiency Syndrome). Back before the Internet connected one to just about any known answer in the universe, self-education was less convenient. Accordingly, when a seemingly innocuous disk purporting to contain AIDS education software arrived at 20,000 locations across 90 countries,[56] self-edifying enthusiasts gladly booted up.

The disk made good on its promise. Users were greeted with an interactive survey that attempted to measure the risk for AIDS based on the answers provided. But, like the Brain-infected popular PC programs before it, this disk delivered more than the user wanted. Containing what would ultimately be known as the "AIDS" Trojan, the disk infected the user's PC with a virus that would eventually encrypt all files after a certain number of reboots.[57] At that time, the victim was presented with the ransom: send $189 to cover the "licensing fee" of the software to a PO Box in Panama. Only when payment was received would the user be sent instructions on how to decrypt his or her data.[58]

Long before the days of cyber laws, targeted victims of the AIDS Trojan attack—specifically hundreds of medical research institutions—panicked. Some preemptively erased their hard drive to attempt to protect the sensitive information contained therein. One AIDS organization in Italy reportedly lost ten years' work.[59]

The investigation that ensued eventually led to an evolutionary biologist with a doctorate from Harvard, Joseph L. Popp. Popp was very deliberate in targeting his victims, with many having attended the World Health Organization's (WHO) international AIDS conference in Stockholm the year before.[60] An avid AIDS researcher himself, pundits were left puzzled by his motives in pursuing colleagues with similar aspirations of eradicating the disease. Popp's attorney would later argue that the doctor intended to donate the ransom collected to fund alternative AIDS education research. Others suggested Popp may have just been seeking revenge, after recently being rejected for employment by the WHO.[61]

Whatever the reason, Popp was single-handedly responsible for setting back the global AIDS research agenda all while letting loose the first known case of ransomware. For both distinctions, one would expect some form of consequence for the doctor. In fact, he received no penalty or jail time. After the judge in the case found Popp unfit to stand trial, he was let go without so much as a slap on the wrist.[62]

With history once again repeating itself, a health organization would find itself the very public target of ransomware more than 25 years later. On the evening of February 5, 2016, staff at the Hollywood Presbyterian Medical Center (HPMC) in California noticed issues in accessing the hospital's computer network.[63] The resulting investigation revealed that HPMC was the victim of a ransomware attack, one where the cybercriminals demanded payment of about 9,000 bitcoins or just over $3.6 million.[64] After suffering nearly two weeks of disrupted operations, relegated to relics like fax machines or paper files to conduct normal business, HPMC paid $17,000 in bitcoins to have its computer systems released. When defending the decision, HPMC President and CEO Allen Stefanek stated,

> The malware locks systems by encrypting files and demanding ransom to obtain the decryption key. The quickest and most efficient way to restore our systems and administrative functions was to pay the ransom and obtain the decryption key. In the best interest of restoring normal operations, we did this.[65]

In the weeks following the public settlement, several more US hospitals found their systems hijacked, with one in Kentucky declaring an "internal state of emergency"[66] in response to the attack. The target on hospitals is no coincidence. Hackers see these targets as soft, with money in the bank and lives at stake. Seconds, let alone weeks, matter in patient care and, as in the case of HPMC, the opportunity cost of disrupted operations far exceeded the $17,000 ultimately paid in ransom. Their decision to surrender payment is validated by Ponemon's study on the cost of cybercrime, with the study's authors finding business disruption to be the highest external cost in the case of a breach— accounting for nearly 40 percent of total external costs.[67]

As is the case for kidnapping ransoms, estimates of the true cost of ransomware are hard to come by, since victims will usually not divulge how much they paid. It is such an insidious cyberattack vector that the FBI has weighed in on how victims should respond. When addressing an audience of business and technology leaders at the Cyber Security Summit 2015 event in Boston, Joseph Bonavolonta, the Bureau's Assistant Special Agent in Charge of its CYBER and Counterintelligence Program, offered this piece of advice: "To be honest, we often advise people just to pay the ransom."[68]

A Second Thought

It seems obvious today that a claw hammer or lead pipe is only as dangerous as the user wielding it——in the early 20th century, the obvious required extensive examination to prescribe legal precedents that sustains to this day. While it may be easy to wrap one's head around a physical object and its intention as a harmful weapon, the virtual world in which we increasingly dwell presents additional challenges. Cryptography, cryptocurrencies, and even the Tor network itself can be used for good or bad. Adversaries know how to disguise the use of these technologies as harmless behavior, even when malevolent outcomes are the ultimate desire. More and more, cyberattacks are becoming increasingly sophisticated, and companies are left to wonder if even their own most trusted employees are on the side, wittingly or unwittingly, of the enemy. In *The Second Economy*, there's always a second side to the story.

A SECOND HELPING OF THE CRYPTOWARS

History has coronated its kings of cryptography: Diffie, Hellman, Rivest, Shamir, Adelman, and one more name that has earned its way into cybersecurity annals: Phil Zimmermann. In the 1990s, the cryptowars had escalated. On one side: the US Government, concerned about the pervasiveness of more sophisticated encryption methods and their potential impact to national security; on the other: industry insiders and political activists espousing the benefits of cryptography in protecting privacy.

To understand the intensity of this battle, consider that cryptography had initially been the nearly exclusive province of the military and government. As such, cryptographic tools were originally classified as munitions—on the same level as nuclear technology or chemicals that could be weaponized.[69] As a result, encryption technologies found themselves on the export controls list of the US Government, essentially requiring US-based international companies to develop weaker encryption for hardware and software sold overseas versus domestically.

By the mid-1990s, the computer industry was raising its voice in opposition to these controls. Beyond forcing US computer and software firms to produce two different products for international or domestic use, industry experts feared that the weaker encryption standards on exported products would commensurately weaken American companies' ability to compete in a global market. A 1998 study by the Economic Strategy Institute put a finer point on the estimated damage, projecting as much as $96 billion in losses over the next five years as a result of encryption export controls.[70]

Zimmermann, a brilliant cryptologist in his own right and creator of Pretty Good Privacy (PGP), what would ultimately become the most widely deployed e-mail encryption software in the world, found himself in the US Justice Department's crosshairs when he uploaded his free software to the Internet. Though Zimmermann only chose sites in the United States as beneficiaries of his invention, the software found its way into international markets. The Justice Department responded with what would become a three-year investigation of Zimmermann for violating the encryption export control laws. In the end, not only was Zimmermann cleared of any wrongdoing, he had earned his place as a cryptology trailblazer, even providing expert testimony to the US Senate Committee on Commerce, Science and Transportation advocating for the repeal of encryption export controls.[71]

During the heat of his personal battle, Zimmermann couldn't help but reflect on the dichotomy his own life's work presented. In 1995, during the throes of the judicial investigation against him, the then 41-year-old Zimmermann accepted the prestigious Pioneer award from the Electronic Frontier Foundation. During his acceptance speech, the innovator acknowledged the paradox of his predicament, "I think it's ironic that the thing I'm being honored for is the same thing that I might be indicted for."[72] Realizing the value and use of cryptology is in the eyes (and intentions) of the beholder, Zimmermann went on to reflect his peace with the outcome of the then pending investigation, stating:

> I don't like to see criminals use this technology. If I had invented an automobile, and was told that criminals used it to rob banks, I would feel bad, too. But most people agree the benefits to society that come from automobiles – taking the kids to school, grocery shopping and such outweigh their drawbacks.[73]

Indeed, in *The Second Economy*, context means everything.

Notes

1. Philip R. Zimmermann, "Why I Wrote PGP," June 1991 (updated 1999), `www.philzimmermann.com/EN/essays/WhyIWrotePGP.html`, accessed April 15, 2016.

2. Bourbonnais v. State, 1912 OK CR 294, 122 P. 1131, 7 Okla. Cr. 717 (Okla. Ct. Crim. App., Case Number: No. A-865, decided Apr. 18, 1912), `http://law.justia.com/cases/oklahoma/court-of-appeals-criminal/1912/16984.html`, accessed April 8, 2016.

3. Moody v State, 11 Okla. Cr. 471, 148 P. 1055 (Okla. Ct. Crim. App., Case Number: No. A-1958, decided Jan. 30, 1915), `http://law.justia.com/cases/oklahoma/court-of-appeals-criminal/1915/21778.html`, accessed April 8, 2016.

4. Wilcox v State, 1917 OK CR 137, 166 P. 74, 13 Okla. Cr. 599 (Okla. Ct. Crim. App., Case Number: No. A-3055, decided July 10, 1917), `http://law.justia.com/cases/oklahoma/court-of-appeals-criminal/1917/22288.html`, accessed April 8, 2016.

5. Saeed Ahmed and Ralph Ellis, "Mass shooting at Inland Regional Center: What we know," CNN, December 5, 2015, `www.cnn.com/2015/12/03/us/what-we-know-san-bernardino-mass-shooting/index.html`, accessed April 11, 2016.

6. Danielle Kehl, Andi Wilson, and Kevin Bankston, "Doomed to Repeat History? Lessons from the Crypto Wars of the 1990s," Open Technology Institute Cybersecurity Initiative, June 2015, `https://static.newamerica.org/attachments/3407-doomed-to-repeat-history-lessons-from-the-crypto-wars-of-the-1990s/OTI_Crypto_Wars_History.abe6caa19cbc40de842e01c28a028418.pdf`, accessed April 12, 2016.

7. Kehl et al., note 6 *supra*.

8. Ibid.

9. Philip Elmer-Dewitt, "Who Should Keep the Keys?," *Time*, June 24, 2001, http://content.time.com/time/magazine/article/0,9171,164002,00.html, accessed April 12, 2016.

10. Kehl et al., note 6 *supra*.

11. Matt Blaze, Matt, "Protocol Failure in the Escrowed Encryption Standard," August 20, 1994, www.crypto.com/papers/eesproto.pdf, accessed April 12, 2016.

12. www.apple.com/customer-letter/, February 16, 2016, accessed April 12, 2016.

13. Romain Dillet, "Justice Department drops lawsuit against Apple as FBI has now unlocked Farook's iPhone," *Tech Crunch*, March 28, 2016, http://techcrunch.com/2016/03/28/justice-department-drops-lawsuit-against-apple-over-iphone-unlocking-case/, accessed April 12, 2016.

14. Kate Cox, "Bitcoin: What The Heck Is It, And How Does It Work?," *Consumerist*, March 4, 2014, https://consumerist.com/2014/03/04/bitcoin-what-the-heck-is-it-and-how-does-it-work/, accessed April 12, 2016.

15. "Massive Drop in Number of Unbanked, Says New Report," The World Bank, April 15, 2015, www.worldbank.org/en/news/press-release/2015/04/15/massive-drop-in-number-of-unbanked-says-new-report, accessed April 13, 2016.

16. "Do Cryptocurrencies Such as Bitcoin Have a Future?," *The Wall Street Journal*, March 1, 2015, www.wsj.com/articles/do-cryptocurrencies-such-as-bitcoin-have-a-future-1425269375, accessed April 12, 2016.

17. Robert McMillan, "The Inside Story of Mt. Gox, Bitcoin's $460 Million Disaster," *Wired*, March 3, 2014, www.wired.com/2014/03/bitcoin-exchange/, accessed April 13, 2016.

18. Market value of a bitcoin was $1,122.58 on November 30, 2013, and $379.31 on November 30, 2014, www.coindesk.com/price/, accessed April 13, 2016.

19. Andy Greenberg, "End of the Silk Road: FBI Says It's Busted The Web's Biggest Anonymous Drug Black Market," *Forbes*, October 2, 2013, www.forbes.com/sites/andygreenberg/2013/10/02/end-of-the-silk-road-fbi-busts-the-webs-biggest-anonymous-drug-black-market/#7d147d02347d, accessed April 13, 2016.

20. Ibid.

21. Techopedia, www.techopedia.com/definition/4141/the-onion-router-tor, accessed April 13, 2016.

22. Ibid.

23. Philip-Elmer Dewitt, "Technology: You Must Be Punished," *Time*, September 26, 1988b, http://content.time.com/time/subscriber/article/0,33009,968490-1,00.html, accessed April 14, 2016.

24. "The birth of the first personal computer virus, Brain," news.com.au, Jan 19, 2011, www.news.com.au/technology/the-birth-of-the-first-personal-computer-virus-brain/story-e6frfro0-1225990906387, accessed April 14, 2016.

25. Ibid.

26. Dewitt, note 23 *supra*.

27. News.com.au, note 24 *supra*.

28. Jason Kersten, "Going Viral: How Two Pakistani Brothers Created the First PC Virus," *Mental Floss*, http://mentalfloss.com/article/12462/going-viral-how-two-pakistani-brothers-created-first-pc-virus, accessed April 14, 2016.

29. Ibid.

30. Philip-Elmer Dewitt, "Technology: Invasion of the Data Snatchers," *Time*, September 26, 1988a, http://content.time.com/time/subscriber/article/0,33009,968508-3,00.html, accessed April 14, 2016.

31. Intel Security, "McAfee Labs Threats Report," November 2015, www.mcafee.com/us/resources/reports/rp-quarterly-threats-nov-2015.pdf, accessed April 14, 2016.

32. Ibid.

33. J. Thomas McEwen, *Dedicated Computer Crime Units* (Washington, DC: US Department of Justice, National Institute of Justice, Office of Justice Programs, 1989).

34. Ibid.

35. Ibid.

36. Ibid.

37. Ponemon Institute, "2015 Cost of Cyber Crime Study: Global," October 2015, https://ssl.www8.hp.com/ww/en/secure/pdf/4aa5-5207enw.pdf, accessed April 14, 2016.

38. Ibid.

39.   Ibid.

40.   Ahiza Garcia, "Target settles for $39 million over data breach," *CNN Money*, December 2, 2015, http://money.cnn.com/2015/12/02/news/companies/target-data-breach-settlement/, accessed April 14, 2016.

41.   Anthony Wing Kosner, "Actually Two Attacks In One, Target Breach Affected 70 to 110 Million Customers," *Forbes*, January 17, 2014, www.forbes.com/sites/anthonykosner/2014/01/17/actually-two-attacks-in-one-target-breach-affected-70-to-110-million-customers/#70b3dde6596e, accessed April 14, 2016.

42.   Maggie McGrath, Maggie, "Target Profit Falls 46% On Credit Card Breach And The Hits Could Keep On Coming," *Forbes*, February 26, 2014, www.forbes.com/sites/maggiemcgrath/2014/02/26/target-profit-falls-46-on-credit-card-breach-and-says-the-hits-could-keep-on-coming/#7016cd1c5e8c, accessed April 14, 2016.

43.   Samantha Sharf, "Target Shares Tumble As Retailer Reveals Cost Of Data Breach," *Forbes*, August 5, 2014, www.forbes.com/sites/samanthasharf/2014/08/05/target-shares-tumble-as-retailer-reveals-cost-of-data-breach/#6a0e0916450b, accessed April 14, 2016.

44.   Garcia, note 40 *supra*.

45.   Fazio Mechanical Services, Statement on Target Data Breach, http://faziomechanical.com/Target-Breach-Statement.pdf, accessed April 15, 2016.

46.   US Senate Committee on Commerce, Science and Transportation, Majority Staff Report for Chairman Rockefeller, "A 'Kill Chain' Analysis of the 2013 Target Data Breach," March 26, 2014, www.commerce.senate.gov/public/_cache/files/24d3c229-4f2f-405d-b8db-a3a67f183883/23E30AA955B5C00FE57CFD709621592C.2014-0325-target-kill-chain-analysis.pdf, accessed April 15, 2016.

47.   Ibid.

48.   Brian Krebs, "Email Attack on Vendor Set Up Breach at Target," *KrebsOnSecurity*, February 12, 2014, http://krebsonsecurity.com/2014/02/email-attack-on-vendor-set-up-breach-at-target/, accessed April 15, 2016.

49.   Greg Aaron and Rad Rasmussen, "Global Phishing Survey: Trends and Domain Name Use in 2H2014," *APWG*, May 27, 2015, http://internetidentity.com/wp-content/uploads/2015/05/APWG_Global_Phishing_Report_2H_2014.pdf, accessed April 15, 2016.

50. Ibid.

51. Verizon 2015 Data Breach Investigations Report, file:///C:/Users/acerra/Downloads/rp_data-breach-investigation-report-2015_en_xg%20(1).pdf, accessed April 15, 2016.

52. Ibid.

53. Aaron and Rasmussen, note 49 *supra*.

54. Ibid.

55. Ponemon Institute, note 37 *supra*.

56. Alina Simone, "Ransomware's stranger-than-fiction origin story," Unhackable, March 26, 2015, https://medium.com/un-hackable/the-bizarre-pre-internet-history-of-ransomware-bb480a652b4b#.bzn2h2nb9, accessed April 15, 2016.

57. Ibid.

58. Ibid.

59. Ibid.

60. Ibid.

61. Ibid.

62. Ibid.

63. Hollywood Presbyterian Medical Center letter signed by President & CEO Allen Stefanek, dated February 17, 2016, http://hollywoodpresbyterian.com/default/assets/File/20160217%20Memo%20from%20the%20CEO%20v2.pdf, accessed April 15, 2016.

64. Steve Ragan, "Ransomware takes Hollywood hospital offline, $3.6M demanded by attackers," *CSO*, Feb 14, 2016, www.csoonline.com/article/3033160/security/ransomware-takes-hollywood-hospital-offline-36m-demanded-by-attackers.html, accessed April 15, 2016.

65. Hollywood Presbyterian Medical Center letter, note 63 *supra*.

66. Jose Pagliery, "U.S. hospitals are getting hit by hackers," *CNN Money*, March 28, 2016, http://money.cnn.com/2016/03/23/technology/hospital-ransomware/, accessed April 15, 2016.

67. Ponemon Institute, note 37 *supra*.

68. "FBI's Advice on Ransomware? Just Pay The Ransom.," *The Security Ledger*, October 22, 2015, https://securityledger.com/2015/10/fbis-advice-on-cryptolocker-just-pay-the-ransom/, accessed April 15, 2016.

69. Kehl et al., note 6 *supra*.

70. Jeri Clausing, Jeri, "Study Puts Price on Encryption Controls," *The New York Times on the Web*, April 1, 1998, https://partners.nytimes.com/library/tech/98/04/cyber/articles/01encrypt.html, accessed April 15, 2016.

71. Testimony of Philip R. Zimmermann to the Subcommittee on Science, Technology and Space of the US Senate Committee on Commerce, Science and Transportation, June 26, 1996, www.philzimmermann.com/EN/testimony/index.html, accessed April 15, 2016.

72. Steven Levy, "The Encryption Wars: Is Privacy Good or Bad?," *Newsweek*, April 23, 1995, www.newsweek.com/encryption-wars-privacy-good-or-bad-181584, accessed April 15, 2016.

73. Ibid.

CHAPTER 2

■ ■ ■

The Second Nature of Markets

History shows that where ethics and economics come in conflict, victory is always with economics.

—B. R. Ambedkar, Indian jurist, economist, politician
and social reformer[1]

"Dear Mummy, Since Monday I have fallen into the hands of kidnappers. Don't let me be killed."[2] The ransom note could hardly be believed. The supposed victim, the 16-year-old grandson of one of the richest men in the world, had reportedly confided in a girlfriend that a simulated kidnapping would be the only way to extract money from his miserly family.[3] Thus, when John Paul Getty III, the high school dropout nicknamed the "golden hippie" by the Italian press, given his bohemian ways, vanished on July 9, 1973, after leaving a Rome discotheque,[4] some believed the kidnapping to be an orchestrated hoax by the rebellious teen to extort $17 million from his billionaire grandfather's oil fortune. If that was the plan, it fell on deaf ears, with the eldest Getty responding:

> What has happened to my grandson Paul is terrible and heartbreaking. But I know that if I become involved it will make the situation worse for all concerned. And I must think about my other grandchildren—there are 14 of them. I must think of their safety. If I show weakness to the men involved it will mean an invitation to other kidnappers to do the same thing with one of the other 14.[5]

Three months passed. No ransom paid. No sight of the wayward teen reported. Then, a Rome newspaper unexpectedly received a gruesome package: containing a human ear, purportedly Getty's, with a note promising the boy would be dismembered "piece by piece" until $3.4 million in ransom was received.[6] Subsequently, another Rome newspaper received instructions to go to a particular location along a highway near the city. There, in an empty paint can, journalists found poorly shot photos of the teen, sans a right ear, with a note in the youth's handwriting begging his grandfather to pay up.[7]

© 2016 by Intel Corp.
S. Grobman and A. Cerra, *The Second Economy*, DOI 10.1007/978-1-4842-2229-4_2

In a real-life case of truth being stranger than fiction, the Getty family contemplated the merits of the ransom for months. The boy's father would only pay a fraction of the ransom in exchange for custody of the other three children he had with the boy's mother, his ex-wife.[8] The mother attempted to negotiate higher terms with her ex-husband in exchange for their other children. Eventually, the eldest Getty paid $2.2 million, after consulting with his accountants and confirming it to be the maximum tax-deductible amount. The boy's father paid the rest of what ultimately became a nearly $3 million ransom, having borrowed it from his father at 4 percent interest.[9]

Two days later, and five months after the abduction, the then 17-year-old Getty was found shivering in freezing rain at a gas station nearly 100 miles south of Naples.[10] Bruised, distraught, and missing a right ear but otherwise unharmed, the teen provided details that, along with marked bills recovered from the ransom,[11] would help lead police to his captors. Nine men were arrested, although only two were eventually convicted and sent to prison. The remaining, including the head of the Calabrian mafia, whom police believed to be the mastermind behind the plot, were acquitted due to lack of evidence.[12] Along with their freedom, the remaining men also purportedly made off with a healthy payday—only $85,000 of the multi-million-dollar ransom was ever recovered.[13]

In the next few years, Europe would experience a spate of abductions for ransom. By 1977, abductions of the wealthy in Italy averaged one per week, giving kidnapping the derisive namesake as the country's foremost growth industry.[14] While the number of kidnappings in Italy had temporarily dropped in 1976 as courts moved to block ransom payments, the toll reached a record number in 1977 when criminals and victims' families began exploiting Swiss accounts and other undetectable means to cover their tracks.[15] Soon, other European countries began reporting abductions for ransom as the contagion spread.[16] The payment for Getty's return was at least, in part, blamed for the escalating kidnapping-for-ransom crime spree, with nearly $1 million frequently demanded per victim. Like Getty, most victims were returned upon receipt of payment, though there were at least seven confirmed deaths at the hands of kidnappers in the period 1970-1977,[17] spurring demand for bodyguards and creating an emerging industry for kidnapping and ransom insurance.

The wealthy were encouraged to vary their daily routines and avoid conspicuous behavior, such as notifying the media of travel habits. Purveyors of kidnapping and ransom insurance, including then leader in the field Lloyd's of London, offered premiums and coverage in accordance with risk. Those associated with cash-abundant industries such as life insurance firms, banks, and oil companies presented thieves with a softer target and bore higher premiums.[18] Coverage also varied by location, with certain geographies, like Europe, carrying greater risk than that of the United States, where, despite the growth in kidnappings, investigators reported a 95 percent success rate in recovering both victim and ransom.[19]

While kidnapping for ransom saw its rise in the 1970s, the number of targets with the deep pockets of oil tycoon J. Paul Getty was and still is few and far between. Organized crime syndicates, such as the Italian gang that kidnapped Getty's grandson, historically set their sights on the rich, famous, or otherwise wildly successful, providing a limited addressable market of targets. Criminals seeking to increase their take had one of two options: (1) continue aiming for lucrative victims of Getty's status with the hopes of landing fewer, bigger paydays or (2) expand their addressable market with softer, smaller targets in a more transactional fashion.

Making It Up in Volume

On June 2, 2011, Adriana Carrillo was about to start her commute to work—her family's store in a market on the outskirts of Mexico City—when she was suddenly and forcibly taken at gunpoint by three men showing police badges.[20] Her terrifying ordeal would last 37 hours, confined in the back of a Nissan, before her father would successfully arrange the drop of $12,000 in ransom to her kidnappers.[21] Upon release, the brave Carrillo would only take three days respite before returning to work. Soldiering on, she vowed, "I don't want to live as a victim."[22]

Despite her empowering and admirable assertion, two years later, Carrillo would once again find herself the target of kidnappers. This time around, her nightmare was worse, as her captors regularly beat and threatened her while awaiting an astounding $1 million payout from her father. With the help of a professional negotiator, ransom was negotiated to $24,000 before Carrillo was released.[23] The kidnappers would abscond with more than her freedom over nine days' captivity and her father's money—this time, they would also bankrupt her trust. The once resilient Carrillo cocooned in the safety of her home for a month. Upon venturing out, she regularly varied her routine and abandoned flashy jewelry that would warrant undue attention. The forever-changed Carrillo reflected on her new paradigm of the world: "I was an idealist. I thought all people were good, at first."[24]

Like Italy several decades before it, in 2015, Mexico held the unenviable position as the top country for modern-day kidnappings for ransom.[25] While the rich and famous were the preferred targets for Italian gangs, Mexican kidnappers employed a much more democratic approach, as criminals expanded the aperture of targets to include "everyday" people. Victims were increasingly cut from the same cloth as Carrillo, part of Mexico's "informal" economy of workers with quick access to cash (such as shopkeepers, taxi drivers, service employees, parking attendants, and street vendors).[26] This larger addressable market afforded thieves more targets, albeit at smaller payouts. While Carrillo was initially held for $1 million, some victims found their lives valued for as little as a couple of hundred dollars, a new microwave or refrigerator, or even a bag of groceries.[27]

It was estimated that as few as 10 percent of Mexican kidnapping cases were ever reported, making it the silent crime that affected as many as 76 victims per day.[28] Making matters worse, local law enforcement was not simply ill-equipped to address the exponential volume of attacks; corrupt officials were many times complicit in the crime, leaving victims and their families wary of whom to trust. For the targeted, the stakes couldn't have been higher: thugs would send proof of kidnapping with a severed finger or two, rape or beat their victims while in captivity, and kill as many as 20 percent of their prey.[29]

The boom in kidnapping was a result of criminals diversifying their own portfolio of activities to generate cash flow historically provided by other means. To understand it, one must think like a criminal. The goal for the financially motivated with unscrupulous intentions is to generate cash—preferably lots of it—quickly and with minimal risk. Covering one's tracks is paramount; hence the reason cash has been king for the criminal. It leaves no trace (assuming, of course, the bills aren't marked) and allows thieves to toil in the anonymity they need.

Without a Trace

Let's consider a criminal industry where cash flow has historically been abundant: drug trafficking. Illegal drugs are clearly a market traded with cash. However, if one is part of an international drug cartel, the challenge of cash becomes that of pure logistics—simply put, money is heavy and difficult to transport. The US Justice Department once estimated that a pound of cocaine sold on the street generated six pounds of cash.[30] For heroin, the ratio was worse: one pound of heroin resulted in ten pounds of currency.[31]

Let's assume, for a moment, that you are the leader of a drug cartel operating in Mexico. You employ drug dealers throughout the United States, who peddle your wares on their streets, collect their cut, and remit to you the proceeds. You'll need creative bookkeeping and an intricate supply chain to ultimately get your unfair share of the take while simultaneously averting attention from authorities. If you were fortunate enough to operate your illegal business before 1970, you would be hard pressed to find many US banking regulations deterring you from routing your illegal profits out of the country. To do so, you simply employed street couriers whose role consisted of collecting revenues from area dealers and depositing the riches in local banks. From there, wire transfers to overseas banks completed the transaction. Banks converted the cash flow to profitable, low-risk loans to community businesses and residents, unaware of and unconcerned with its true origin. According to journalist David Andelman:

> The banks turned a blind eye to the source of this wealth.
> They never questioned the propriety of fish stands or
> vegetable markets that were generating half a million dollars a
> day in cash, all in small-denomination bills.[32]

With the financial industry happy to look the other way, the US Government offered its own "incentives" to banks to report suspected offenders. In 1970, Congress passed the Bank Secrecy Act (BSA), which required banks to report cash transactions in excess of $10,000.[33] Over the next several years, the government continued to turn up the heat on banks failing to comply with the new regulations, prosecuting those that did not adhere to the BSA, along with the drug dealers they deliberately or inadvertently protected. Such regulation had little impact on cracking the drug crime problem. You, as the Mexican drug kingpin, simply innovated your supply chain to remain under the radar. If $10,000 had to be reported, you limited your couriers' deposits to $9,900.[34]

Enter the Money Laundering Control Act of 1986, which essentially upped the ante of punishments for banks failing to comply with the BSA. It also allowed banks to provide customer information to the government without violating privacy laws.[35] Rather than risk prosecution, more banks opted to adhere to the increasing regulations, placing pressure on you and your drug lord compatriots to find other solutions to evade officials. The stakes got higher after 9/11, which ushered in a new era of scrutiny for international banking transactions in the United States and elsewhere.

So, now what do you do? You face intense scrutiny for wire transfers and cash is too unwieldy and conspicuous to cart out of the country in briefcases, à la what is glamorized in the latest gangster movie. You either find other options for transporting the cash (yes, including using appliances like toasters and washing machines to smuggle your spoils[36]) or you find other means of generating the profits altogether, such as kidnapping. Ironically, some blame the booming kidnapping business in Mexico as an unintended by-product of effective law enforcement and regulation. Specifically, with the takedown of several drug cartel bosses and their rings, criminals had to diversify their "portfolio" of activities, and kidnapping for ransom readily filled the cash flow void.[37]

While kidnapping does not necessarily present the same logistical challenges of hauling money across national borders, it isn't without its own level of complexity. Physically taking a hostage presents risk in detection. Targeting the right hostage is precarious: choose a victim with self-defense skills and/or a concealed weapon and you may find yourself in harm's way. Contacting the victim's loved ones for payment is the next tricky step. If they report the incident to the authorities, you may not be able to evade their investigation. Finally, arranging the ransom drop is arguably the riskiest event in the entire sequence. Giving the family your coordinates allows law enforcement to readily descend on your location. Even if law enforcement isn't involved, where is the guarantee that the victim's relatives will actually pay up? You can't exactly meticulously account for each dollar at the drop with the victim's family (and potentially law enforcement) in close proximity. You may wind up releasing your victim, after all the effort of taking him in the first place, for little to no reward. Even worse, should your abduction go awry, you may have to take your victim's life and add murder as an offense to your rap sheet.

Indeed, crime in the physical world is fraught with risk and effort. Cybercrime offers an alternative for accelerating the return on investment for thieves, with less physical peril. Like drug trafficking, stealing personal information for profit entails its own intricate supply chain.

Follow the Money Trail

Dear Viv,

We have changed who [sic] we bank with, I forgot to inform you of the changes in the email I sent you yesterday. . .

So began the e-mail to 59-year-old Londoner Vivian Gabb from whom she believed to be her lawyer. Unbeknownst to Gabb, she was corresponding with a 14-member organized crime outfit[38]—hackers who had infiltrated her e-mail account, bent on robbing her blind. In a highly orchestrated attack, the crime syndicate studied Gabb's e-mail to learn of her pending home purchase and recent contact history. Assuming the virtual identity of her attorney, the thieves asked Gabb to transfer her deposit of nearly £50,000 ($78,000) into a different bank account, to which she dutifully complied. But, that was just the tip of the iceberg for the industrious gang. Once lured by their phishing web site, Gabb unwittingly offered her most sensitive account details, funding what would become a £1 million ($1.6 million), three-day shopping spree ranging from cheeseburgers to computers to gold bars and losing her life's savings in the process.[39] Before being busted by a police operation of 150 lawmen, each hacker had squandered at least £9,000 ($14,000) and up to £75,000 ($117,000)[40] of Gabb's treasure.

As Gabb's example so vividly illustrates, cybercrime mitigates the logistical challenges associated with laundering money when it can be siphoned off directly from a victim's bank account. That said, not all cybercrimes are created equal in terms of risk and reward. In Gabb's case, the organized crime ring triggered attention when attempting to spend her savings in record time. In a classic case of "beat the clock," the thieves were under pressure to splurge the cash faster than Gabb could realize its disappearance, all the while being inconspicuous in doing so. While deliberate planning went into hacking Gabb's e-mail account, learning her most intimate patterns and using such reconnaissance to dupe her out of her savings, the same meticulous care was abandoned in the time following the breach. In *The Second Economy*, financially motivated criminals use time to their advantage, stealthily creeping in their victim's most intimate virtual closets, attempting to avoid detection as long as is possible to collect their spoils. However, once said rewards are pocketed, cybercriminals face a time disadvantage: that is, how to balance expeditiously liquidating their take while remaining under the radar.

The cybercriminals who pulled off the Gabb heist suffered no return on their investment, despite the painstaking preparation that went into the breach. Three days of indulgent spending hardly qualifies as a handsome reward when facing the criminal prosecution to follow. What if the criminals had spent the same considerable time contemplating how to remain undetected following their breach rather than throwing caution to the wind in a reckless shopping spree? What if there were even easier ways to gain access to sensitive account information without the highly targeted attack required in Gabb's case? For the cybercriminal looking to make a quick buck at the lowest possible risk, the opportunity to do so is limited only by his imagination and access to a vibrant black market where individuals are literally up for sale.

Fueling this black market requires scale. While bigger fish the size of Gabb are certainly on the block, cybercriminals benefit from a larger total addressable market in the form of everyday people (not unlike the kidnapping rash plaguing Mexico). Central databases of proprietary customer and employee information, kept by the likes of larger companies, are attractive targets and explain why cybercriminals persist in pursuing the same unenviable companies with relentless phishing schemes.[41] Once adversaries infiltrate their target and abscond with sensitive contact or account data, the records often find their way into a sophisticated market where the laws of supply and demand are immutable.

Here, the virtual and physical worlds collide and criminals exchange their wares in a complex underground exchange where stolen account data is monetized. Among the historically more popular schemes is that of credit card theft, such as in the Target holiday breach of 2013. Once the credit card accounts are stolen, they are sold in bulk to underground third-party resellers. In this black market, victims' information is packaged up in neatly communicated value propositions to the criminally inclined. Need a credit card complete with a card verification value (that three-digit code printed on the back of a credit card or embedded on its magnetic strip)? That could cost you anywhere from $5 to $30, depending on the country. Want the accompanying bank account number along with the card? That price could run anywhere from $15 to $30. Adding date of birth to the mix increases the price up to an additional $5. And, if you want the grand prize of all-things-sensitive about the victim, including his full name, billing address, payment card number, expiration date, PIN (personal identification number), social security number, mother's maiden name, date of birth, and card verification value, you could pay anywhere from $30 to $45.[42] Even better, for an incremental charge, you can acquire the pièce de résistance—the victim's habitual shopping patterns. Armed with this seemingly innocuous information allows you to avert detection by liquidating accounts at the consumer's usual stomping grounds. Such behavior will appear normal to monitoring agencies, cloaking the criminal activity in a shroud of predictable patterns.[43]

Of course, these rates are subject to, and often do, change. Like any traditional competitive market, prices ebb and flow according to fluctuations in supply or demand. During the rash of cyberattacks on major retailers in 2014, the black market was flooded with stolen data of hapless victims. The influx of supply afforded cybercriminals more attractive deals, reminiscent of holiday discounts during peak shopping periods.[44]

From third-party resellers, the account data passes hands again to card counterfeiters, who buy the information they need, sometimes procuring it by bank or zip code, and then copying it onto fake cards using their own magnetic stripe encoding machines. They then use the cards directly to buy goods they can resell or hire others to do the work for them, in exchange for a cut of the profits.[45]

To demonstrate how dynamic this market is, in 2016, a stolen Uber account sold at up to three times a premium over personally identifiable information, including a victim's social security number or date of birth. Using the Uber account to charge "phantom" rides allowed the cybercriminal to mimic her victim's behavior, again maximizing the time to and mitigating the risk of exposure.[46] Indeed, cybercriminals adeptly react to changes in market opportunity, quickly maneuvering to more lucrative targets as historical paragons fall by the wayside. Some are even boldly predicting the demise of credit card fraud as a result of escalating risks and barriers to entry for thieves. With the advent of new point-of-sale card readers that use cryptography to interactively authenticate the card, criminals who counterfeit static magnetic stripes will find a collapsing market. In the online domain, services like Apple Pay and Visa Token Service will accomplish the same by replacing fixed credit card numbers with dynamic tokens that change with every purchase.[47]

Even after such time as credit card fraud is greatly diminished, if not obliterated, sensitive information will continue to be traded in the black market as a virtual commodity, with cybercriminals evolving to more sophisticated forms of identity theft. While they advance their tactics, these threat actors still risk exposure when attempting to monetize their payload. They are faced with the challenges of the Gabb ring, under the pressure of the clock to liquidate their spoils. But, what if the time disadvantage could be flipped on the victim, all the while giving cybercriminals an even faster and clearer path to return on investment? The era of ransomware is upon us.

Tick Tock

Imagine clicking on an e-mail or link, only to be greeted by the following ominous message:

> **Your personal files are encrypted!** Your important files were encrypted on this computer: photos, videos, documents, etc. You can verify this by clicking on the files and trying to open them.
>
> Encryption was produced using unique public key RSA-4096 generated for this computer. To decrypt the files, you need to obtain the private key.
>
> The single copy of the private key, which will allow you to decrypt the files, is located on a secret server on the internet. **The server will destroy the key within 72 hours after encryption completed.** After that, nobody will ever be able to restore files.

To retrieve the private key, you need to pay .5 bitcoins.

Click proceed to payment to obtain private key.

Any attempt to remove or damage this software will lead to immediate private key destruction by server.

Over nine months of operation, the CryptoLocker ransomware program earned its creators an estimated $3 million, while it held its victims' precious files for ransoms ranging from $100 to $500.[48] Ransomware programs like CryptoLocker are highly effective given their approach. First, they rely on the weakest and most pervasive link in any security infrastructure—the human being. Phishing scams are the conveyance through which ransomware programs are deposited and, as Gabb's case illustrates, the virtual world is awash in trusting individuals mindlessly clicking on seemingly reputable links and e-mails. Second, there is little complexity involved in extracting money from the victim once the malware is deposited. Bitcoin, as the preferred medium of exchange, offers the adversary coveted anonymity. Third, the ransom payments are typically small enough to encourage payment by the victim while remaining inconsequential to investigating authorities. Regarding the benefits of aiming low on the ransom payment, one purveyor of ransomware programs opined, "I prefer to be less expensive, more downloads and more infections."[49] Finally, ransomware shifts time to being a competitive advantage for the adversary upon breach. Rather than finding himself under the wire to quickly and discreetly cash out his reward, the criminal turns the table on the victim, forcing him or her to adhere to his schedule. Under such extreme time pressures, victims are less likely to think rationally and more likely to respond impulsively in paying the relatively insignificant ransom.

Interestingly, ransomware also solves for the other inherent problem of its counterpart in the physical world—that of the awkward and tenuous negotiation when kidnapping hostages for ransom. Consider the Getty case, where the youth found himself at the hands of his captors for several months as the ransom payment was arduously negotiated with the family. Even in Carrillo's case, ransoms were eventually settled to terms acceptable to both parties. Once ransom is decided, there is the matter of the exchange. Who gives up the exchange first—the kidnapper or the victim's family? There is an inherent level of trust required by both parties for a successful transaction. The criminal must trust the family will deliver the ransom in full, without attempting to apprehend him. The family must trust the criminal will release their loved one at the exchange and not hold out for a subsequent payment. This is an all-in game for both parties, with little opportunity to gradually build trust up to the critical moment of transaction.

Not only does ransomware lower the ante by holding files, not people, hostage, it also obviates the risk for both parties. Ironically, the "success" of such programs as CryptoLocker serves to instill trust among the afflicted that their files will be restored upon payment. If there is any doubt, cybercriminals can gradually decrypt files in batches at lower prices until all assets are restored.

This is not to suggest that ransomware is not a scourge that compromises the safety and security of netizens living in a virtual world. It simply offers a point of view as to why criminals are increasingly diversifying their interests toward a more frictionless, anonymous crime—free from the risks associated with its counterpart in the physical world and the complexities common with other forms of cybercrime, such as monetizing stolen credit card information.

For these reasons, ransomware has found its place as one of the fastest growing cybercrimes in recent history. The first targets were consumers. Next, cybercriminals set their sights on soft industry targets—hospitals, schools, and governments—institutions with a definite time disadvantage and less robust security posture. Cybercriminals will likely target larger companies next, especially as these firms are already the object of significant and repeated phishing attempts. While ransomware adversaries have steadily increased their addressable market through more and bigger targets, there is at least one more looming threat that potentially offers the richest gains and the largest attack surface.

Rise of the Machines

The decades spanning the 1970s and 1980s gave birth to popular culture media fixated on possessed vehicles and machines. The 1977 American thriller film *The Car* told the story of an automobile that terrorized residents of a small town through its mysterious murderous rampage. Master of horror Stephen King followed up in 1983 with *Christine*, a tale of a teenage boy and his beloved classic car with a mind of its own. And, 1986's *Maximum Overdrive*, also by King, imagined a world where inanimate objects, from electric signs to lawnmowers, indiscriminately kill helpless victims crossing their paths.

While interesting fodder for science fiction and horror genres, the potential for artificial intelligence giving rise to a breed of supercomputers and machines capable of taking over jobs, and more, has been a real concern for many since the computer era of the same period. The technological singularity is estimated to be the event when the aggregate artificial intelligence in the world exceeds that of human comprehension. Technology critics have long fantasized a reality more akin to that of King's imagination—one where machines dominate the humans who invented them.

Andy Greenberg found himself transported, quite literally, into such a future. While cruising at 70 miles per hour on the periphery of downtown St. Louis, his Jeep Cherokee took control over its own—and Greenberg's—destiny. Greenberg first noticed the air conditioning unit blasting frigid temperatures at maximum output, chilling him to the bone. The radio suddenly blared classic hip hop at full volume, which would undoubtedly distract even the calmest of drivers. Dispensed windshield wiper fluid blurred his view, making it increasingly dangerous to continue his commute.

As he entered the on ramp of the interstate, Greenberg lost complete control when the transmission failed. Frantically pressing on the gas pedal as he helplessly watched his speedometer decelerate, Greenberg was paralyzed as his Jeep slowed to a crawl. In his rearview mirror, he caught the image of an 18-wheeler bearing down on him as he sat immobilized on the highway.

The stuff of science fiction? Not exactly. Greenberg's Jeep did not unexpectedly become possessed by demonic forces or cross over the technological singularity to surpass the cognitive capabilities of its human driver. No, in this case, reality is much scarier than fiction. The Jeep was under complete control of humans, just not its driver.

Greenberg was the willing participant in an experiment where he subjected control of his vehicle to that of two hackers, Charlie Miller and Chris Valasek, operating the SUV from the comfort of Miller's basement some ten miles away. Greenberg knew his Jeep would be subject to any number of exploits, and while he was encouraged to remain calm through the ordeal, he had no prior knowledge of what would come next. According to Greenberg's own account, he mentally congratulated himself for remaining calm under the barrage of frigid air, punishing radio volume, and obfuscating windshield fluid. However, when the transmission cut at the time he was entering the interstate, "The experiment had ceased to be fun."[50]

Greenberg had only partially participated in the full assault of Miller and Valasek's virtual arsenal. The hackers had also identified how to affect steering when a Jeep is in reverse, track the vehicle's GPS coordinates, measure its speed, and plot the SUV's route on a map to determine driving patterns.[51]

Before 2008, drivers were encapsulated in closed systems of intricate computing circuitry, designed to get them from point A to point B in the safest way possible. At the same time, individuals were increasingly adopting smartphones, carrying computing capabilities on their hip many times more powerful than all of NASA had when it first launched astronauts to the moon.[52] Chrysler and other auto manufacturers had an idea: why not leverage that robust wireless infrastructure to enable a far better driving experience? In 2008, the company debuted WiFi connectivity in its automobiles with its Uconnect service—an infotainment system transforming any Chrysler, Jeep, or Dodge vehicle into a mobile hotspot.[53] For the bandwidth-obsessed, the 150-foot range provided high-speed connectivity for those last-minute impulses, such as sending an e-mail from the comfort of one's parked car in its garage.

While WiFi was a step forward in enhancing the vehicle experience, it certainly paled in comparison to the power and ubiquity of truly wireless networks. In 2013, General Motors raised the stakes when it announced it would partner with AT&T to outfit most of its 2014 models with wireless, high-speed Internet access, compliments of the manufacturer's OnStar 4G LTE technology.[54] The driving experience would forever be transformed—vehicles became roving entertainment systems, complete with the latest streaming movies, music, directions-on-demand, and myriad wireless applications for just about any infotainment need. Of course, the newly established network connection would mean that drivers could also enjoy a safer driving experience. Crash avoidance systems that detect proximity of objects rely on such connectivity to avert accidents. And, at the extreme, driver-assisted capabilities allow the vehicle to detect abnormalities in driving patterns—such as lane drifting—and automatically correct to protect both driver and others on the road. When considering that 90 percent of crashes are caused by human error, the opportunity to automate and correct the driving experience can literally mean the difference between life and death.[55]

Not surprisingly, auto manufacturers jumped on the wireless bandwagon. The competitive risks of providing a 1.0 driving experience when new car buyers eagerly anticipated a 2.0 reality were simply too great to ignore. In 2013, connected cars represented approximately 10 percent of all cars shipped globally; by 2020, that number is expected to increase to 75 percent.[56] Initial buyers of connected cars tended to be more sophisticated, allowing manufacturers to embed the technology in higher-end luxury vehicles for premium prices. Over the next few years, the category will eventually reach the mass market, making the technology available to a greater number of drivers. And, beyond helping manufacturers compete for the next-generation auto purchaser, such wirelessly embedded technology also provides intelligence and maintenance benefits— allowing auto companies to collect data regarding their product's performance and providing conveyance for remotely installing software patches and updates.[57]

But, there's another side to this otherwise rosy story. That same wireless connectivity offers virtual doorways through which hackers like Miller and Valasek can enter. When the duo first discovered the Uconnect flaw, they assumed it would be limited only to the vehicle's WiFi connection, containing potential damage to just a few dozen yards. Upon discovering that the vulnerability also applied to the system's wireless capabilities, they again presumed it would work only for vehicles connected to the same cell tower as their scanning phone, limiting potential attacks to a few dozen miles. Upon determining that not even that was the limit, the hackers themselves were frightened upon realizing the scope of their newly acquired power. In the words of Valasek, "When I saw we could do it anywhere, over the Internet, I freaked out. I was frightened. It was like, holy [expletive], that's a vehicle on a highway in the middle of the country. Car hacking got real, right then."[58]

Through scanning the wireless network for vulnerable automobiles and recording their vehicle identification numbers, Miller estimated there were as many as 471,000 cars with susceptible Uconnect systems on the road.[59] While pinpointing the exact location of one vehicle out of thousands is not easy, particularly when using a single phone to scan the wireless network for the intended target, harnessing the collective horsepower of multiple phones working together simultaneously makes the outcome possible. Even scarier, a skilled hacker could hijack an entire group of Uconnect systems, using the connected mesh to perform more scans—worming from one vehicle to the next over the network. In a case of life imitating art, welcome to King's *Maximum Overdrive* reality, where a wirelessly controlled automotive botnet could enslave hundreds of thousands of vehicles and the humans at their mercy.[60]

In response to Miller and Valasek's work, Chrysler recalled 1.4 million vehicles.[61] In its July 24, 2015 statement, Fiat Chrysler Automobiles stated the pair's hack of the Jeep "required unique and extensive technical knowledge, prolonged physical access to a subject vehicle and extended periods of time to write code."[62] To this point, the Jeep hack of 2015 was a journey three years in the making. In 2012, Miller and Valasek applied for a car hacking research grant from Darpa.[63] With the $80,000 that followed, the pair bought a Toyota Prius and a Ford Escape. Over the course of a year, the team painstakingly mapped each digital and physical route of the cars' electronic control units (ECUs), the computers that run practically every function of a vehicle, and learned to speak the language that controls them.[64]

At the DefCon conference the following year, one of the world's largest annual hacker conventions, the team proudly displayed the fruits of their labor, demonstrating a wired-in attack of both vehicles, after using Greenberg as their guinea pig the first time around. From the back seat of the car with Greenberg behind the wheel, the pair disabled the brakes, honked the horn, yanked the seat belt, and hijacked the steering wheel.

However, much to their chagrin, both Toyota and Ford downplayed the outcome of their research, with the former asserting its systems were "robust and secure" against wireless attacks.[65] If wireless was the new frontier, Miller and Valasek would need to aim higher for the street cred they deserved—only a remote attack of a car would suffice.

They got back to work the following year, registering for mechanics' accounts on the web sites of every major automobile manufacturer and downloading dozens of technical manuals and diagrams. From the analysis that followed, the duo meticulously ranked the vulnerability of 24 vehicles based on three factors: (1) how many and what types of radios connected the automobile to the Internet; (2) whether the Internet-capable components were isolated from critical driving systems; and (3) whether said systems had "cyberphysical" elements (which would allow digital commands to trigger physical outcomes, like activating the brakes).[66] When the Jeep Cherokee fit the bill as the most hackable model on the list, the team had their target.

It took one more year of experimentation and reverse engineering before Valasek issued a command from his laptop in Pittsburgh that engaged the windshield wipers of the Jeep in Miller's St. Louis driveway.[67] The rest will be documented in the annals of hacker history as one of the greatest demonstrations ever to be showcased at a convention (Black Hat 2015).

Fortunately for all involved, Miller and Valasek were not nefarious in their intentions. The team had been sharing the findings of their research with Chrysler for nearly nine months before its revelation, allowing the company to quietly make ready the fix that would ultimately lead to the recall of 1.4 million vehicles.[68] While the attack certainly required skill, time, and effort, the duo undoubtedly shook the auto industry with a scary wake-up call.

This looming threat puts automobile manufacturers in an especially unenviable position. The closed automobile systems of yesteryear were not designed for open communications networks and the risks they bring with them. At the same time, the need for constant innovation is outpacing the speed at which these manufacturers can shore up security vulnerabilities. According to Josh Corman, cofounder of I Am the Cavalry, a security industry organization dedicated to protecting the Internet of Things, "If it takes a year to introduce a new hackable feature, then it takes them [automobile manufacturers] four to five years to protect it."[69]

Modern-day cars get most of the attention when discussing the potential hack of any number of Internet of Things given we can all relate to being drivers or passengers. While many are vocalizing consumer concern for this unprecedented threat, auto manufacturers are hardly standing still, nor do they face a nontrivial task as they race to bolster potential vulnerabilities. To put the challenge in perspective, consider that the space ship that put humans on the moon had 145,000 lines of computer code. Today's Android operating system has 12 million. In the typical connected car, there are easily 100 million lines of code.[70]

And, threat actors have more motivation than simply harassing, if not distracting, drivers with their efforts. If cash is the ultimate pursuit for some, one can easily envision a case where any connected device, and that includes a car, is up for ransom. As Miller and Valasek noted through their experiment, "It's much easier to hack all the Jeeps than a certain one."[71] Upping the stakes, resourceful cybercriminals with the time, talent, and incentive could hack all vehicles with a particular software vulnerability, embedding a ransomware program that demands payment in bitcoin before the ignition will start. Taking a page from what has successfully worked when the same playbook is used for encrypting computer files, the adversaries will likely ask for "nominal" payment, say anywhere from $100 to $200, to encourage the victim to readily pay up. Again, the time advantage shifts to the attacker. How badly does the victim need her car for work, an emergency, or daily errands? Is it worth the hassle of calling a dealership in the hopes of resolution or better to simply give in to the ransom? Adversaries will bet on the latter and, by attacking thousands of vehicles simultaneously in a given radius, will prevent other viable solutions. Such a coordinated attack would not only paralyze thousands of victims but also make it nearly impossible for a limited number of local dealers to resolve the problem without being brought to their own labor capacity constraints. With thousands impacted, cybercriminals could cripple the underlying economic infrastructure of a geographic area.

The outlook is bleaker still when considering just about anything and everything is or will be equipped with a convenient connection to the Internet. Want to open your connected refrigerator for some food? You may need to pay a threat actor for access. Find yourself on an especially cold night and need to turn up your connected thermostat? That may cost you as well. One can even envisage something as innocuous as a connected coffee machine suddenly being used as a weapon against its owner with a scrolling message that almost writes itself:

> I have been hacked. If you ever want coffee from me again,
> you will need a private key. **To retrieve the private key, you**
> **need to pay .025 bitcoins.** Click proceed to payment to obtain
> the private key.

As they have done in the lucrative black market where victims' account information is shamelessly traded, cybercriminals will find the optimal market price based on the item in question. Known to share openly among themselves, they will readily exchange this market intelligence (sometimes for a price, of course) to optimize their collective return on investment for any conceivable ransomware attack. In this new world order, everyday machines will serve as drone armies to the criminal masterminds orchestrating their every move—an outcome few of the most imaginative science fiction or horror writers would have conjured up in their popular stories just some decades ago.

A Second Thought

As financially motivated criminals have taught us through the ages, their probability (P) for attempting a crime comes down to a formula that can best be expressed as follows:

$$P = (Incentive \ x \ Opportunity) / Risk$$

Incentive is the financial reward, net of efforts, available to the adversary. The more effort involved in coordinating an attack, the bigger the incentive required to make the investment of time and resources worth the potential reward. Opportunity refers to the criminal's addressable market potential. The greater the potential attack surface, the higher the motivation for attempting an attack, particularly for campaigns requiring significant effort. Finally, the risk of apprehension mixed with the potential degree of prosecutorial punishment acts as a deterrent when evaluating motivation. Riskier ventures require more incentive or opportunity to increase the probability of attack.

The stories in this chapter elucidate the case. Kidnapping for ransom is an extremely risky crime, leaving criminals targeting the uber-wealthy (like Getty) or dramatically increasing their addressable market with less affluent, though still cash-rich, targets (like Carrillo). Highly targeted phishing schemes require more orchestration, and therefore require a bigger payout (like Gabb) while more pervasive ransomware schemes significantly increase the addressable market of victims. But, of all these, ransomware of everyday connected devices—including cars, thermostats, refrigerators, and more—offers cybercriminals perhaps the most attractive probability, providing an attack surface exponentially larger in size, with comparable risks to today's increasingly popular ransomware programs. In *The Second Economy*, financially driven criminals follow the playbook of their predecessors, methodically balancing risk and reward like black market entrepreneurs. The path to the next big cybercrime trend clearly follows the money.

A SECOND HELPING OF THE SILENT CYBERCRIME

"Hey, you want to free your data? Pay us." As Charles Hucks, technology director of Horry County, South Carolina's school district read the on-screen ransom note that affected some 60 percent of his school district's computers, he realized he was the latest victim of ransomware.[72] In 2015 alone, the FBI received nearly 2,500 complaints about ransomware incidents, costing victims more than $24 million.[73] Yet, this estimate is likely largely understated, particularly since many victims are reluctant to come forward. According to Paul Roberts, founder of the Internet newsletter *Security Ledger*, "Most people aren't talking. Companies don't want their customers, or governments don't want their citizens, to think, they're not protecting their computer systems."[74]

And so, victims quietly pay the ransom, hoping to avoid their number being called again in the next attack. To establish a level of trust with their attackers, some may even negotiate the release of one file or system at a time, as Hucks did against his adversaries. He paid to release one machine first and, after verifying all was in working order, transferred the equivalent of $10,000 in bitcoins to get his school system back up and running.[75] It's the mind-set ransomware cybercriminals rely on when leveraging time as their competitive weapon. As Hucks put it,

"You get to the point of making the business decision: Do I make my end-users—in our case teachers and students—wait for weeks and weeks and weeks while we restore servers from backup? Or do we pay the ransom and get the data back online more quickly?"[76]

In the end, Horry County School District and so many others just pay up, many without so much as reporting it. This silence serves as further motivation to cyberthugs to continue unabated in their ransomware pursuits. The year 2015 saw a more than 5-fold annual increase in new ransomware strains.[77] Just one, CryptoWall, cost users and businesses more than $325 million in damages, according to the Cyber Threat Alliance, a group of leading cybersecurity solution providers committed to sharing threat intelligence in the interest of their collective customers.[78]

While ransomware attacks rely on the helplessness of victims to leave the crime unreported, strains like CryptoWall also traverse completely anonymous networks, further muddying the waters in finding the perpetrators. Beyond using the Tor network to obfuscate traffic origination, CryptoWall also cloaked itself through an additional anonymity network known as the Invisible Internet Project (I2P). In a virtual spider's web that is incredibly complex to untangle, some suggest the malware used a Tor gateway to pass the user's traffic to a hidden service first, which would then connect the user through the I2P network to retrieve the web site housing the decryption key made available upon payment. This double layer of anonymity demonstrates the resourcefulness of adept cybercriminals in covering their tracks—made even easier by victims who remain silent in the process.

Hucks, for one, is ready to give a voice to ransomware. He publicly shares his story to raise awareness of this silent cybercrime, in the hopes of preventing other victims from suffering the same fate. "We got hit, the hospital in California [Hollywood Presbyterian Hospital] got hit. Virtually every day you hear of a virus such as this." Indeed, some have boldly labeled 2016 as the "year of ransomware."[79] And, it would seem that cybercriminals have only scratched the surface of what is possible when just about any connected device can be commandeered against one's will in *The Second Economy*.

Notes

1. www.brainyquote.com/quotes/keywords/economics.html, accessed April 29, 2016.

2. Bruce Weber, "J. Paul Getty III, 54, Dies; Had Ear Cut Off by Captors," *The New York Times*, February 7, 2011, www.nytimes.com/2011/02/08/world/europe/08gettyobit.html?_r=1, accessed April 21, 2016.

3. "Girlfriend Says Getty May Have Arranged His Kidnap," *San Rafael Daily Independent-Journal*, July 14, 1973, p. 3, http://newspaperarchive.com/us/california/san-rafael/san-rafael-daily-independent-journal/1973/07-14/page-3, accessed April 24, 2016.

4. "Paul Getty's Mother Awaits Ransom Note," *Naples Daily News*, July 18, 1973, p. 48, http://newspaperarchive.com/us/florida/naples/naples-daily-news/1973/06-18/page-44, accessed April 24, 2016.

5. John Wood, Women's News Service, "Richest Man in the World Curses His Vast Wealth," *Burlington (N.C) TIMES-NEWS*, November 30, 1973, p. 5A, http://newspaperarchive.com/us/north-carolina/burlington/burlington-daily-times-news/1973/11-30/page-17, site accessed April 24, 2016.

6. "Getty Case: Strange Kidnapping or Hoax?," *Fort Walton Beach Playground Daily News*, December 9, 1973, p. 6B, http://newspaperarchive.com/us/florida/fort-walton-beach/fort-walton-beach-playground-daily-news/1973/12-09/page-18?tag=ear+kidnapping+getty&rtserp=tags/ear-kidnapping-getty?ndt=by&py=1973&pey=1973, accessed April 24, 2016.

7. Ibid.

8.	John Wood, "Tragedy Laces Family: Gettys Await Kidnapping News," *The Lima News*, December 9, 1973, p. B1, http://newspaperarchive.com/us/ohio/lima/lima-news/1973/12-09/page-19, accessed April 24, 2016.

9.	Weber, note 2 *supra*.

10.	"Young Getty Released After 5-Month Captivity," *Madison Capital Times*, December 15, 1973, p. 2, http://newspaperarchive.com/us/wisconsin/madison/madison-capital-times/1973/12-15/page-2?tag=getty+kidnapping+ransom+found&rtserp=tags/getty-kidnapping-ransom-fo und?ndt=by&py=1970&pey=1979&ndt=ex&py=1973, accessed April 24, 2016.

11.	"Three charged in Getty kidnapping," *Mason City Globe Gazette*, January 16, 1974, p. 13, http://newspaperarchive.com/us/iowa/mason-city/mason-city-globe-gazette/1974/01-16/page-14, accessed April 24, 2016.

12.	Weber, note 2 *supra*.

13.	Charles Fox, "Oh, what a crazy kidnap: Police thought Paul Getty had staged his abduction to steal his family's billions. Then a severed ear turned up. New book reveals how case has become even more bizarre. . .," DailyMail.com, April 12, 2013, www.dailymail.co.uk/news/article-2308367/Oh-crazy-kidnap-Police-thought-Paul-Getty-staged-abduction-steal-familys-billions-Then-severed-ear-turned-New-book-reveals-case-bizarre-.html, accessed April 25, 2016.

14.	Mario Deaglio "Virtual Anarchy Driving Italy Toward Chaos," *Florence Morning News*, July 10, 1977, p. 5-A, http://newspaperarchive.com/us/south-carolina/florence/florence-morning-news/1977/07-10/page-5, accessed April 24, 2016.

15.	"Wealthy Europeans living in kidnapping fear," *Jacksonville Courier*, Jacksonville, Ill, November 9, 1977, http://newspaperarchive.com/us/illinois/jacksonville/jacksonville-courier/1977/11-09/page-25, accessed April 24, 2016.

16.	Ibid.

17.	Ibid.

18.	Lisa Berger, "The Insurance Policy No One Will Talk About," *Cedar Rapids Gazette*, January 8, 1978, http://newspaperarchive.com/us/iowa/cedar-rapids/cedar-rapids-gazette/1978/01-08/page-130, accessed April 24, 2016.

19. Ibid.

20. Joshua Partlow, "Kidnappings in Mexico surge to the highest number on record," *The Washington Post*, August 15, 2014, www.washingtonpost.com/world/the_americas/kidnappings-in-mexico-surge-to-the-highest-number-on-record/2014/08/15/3f8ee2d2-1e6e-11e4-82f9-2cd6fa8da5c4_story.html, accessed April 25, 2016.

21. Ibid.

22. Ibid.

23. Ibid.

24. Ibid.

25. "Kidnapping in Mexico Increased by 30% in June," *Telesur*, July 16, 2015, www.telesurtv.net/english/news/Kidnapping-in-Mexico-Increased-by-30-in-June-20150716-0003.html, accessed April 25, 2016.

26. Partlow note 20 *supra*.

27. Ibid.

28. Ibid.

29. Ibid.

30. Stephen Mihm, "Are Bitcoins the Criminal's Best Friend?," *Bloomberg View*, November 18, 2013, www.bloombergview.com/articles/2013-11-18/are-bitcoins-the-criminal-s-best-friend-, accessed April 26, 2016.

31. Ibid.

32. David A. Andelman, "The Drug Money Maze." 73(4) Foreign Affairs 94–108.

33. Mihm, note 30 *supra*.

34. Ibid.

35. Ibid.

36. Ibid.

37. Partlow, note 20.

38. Matt Liebowitz "Phishing gang steals victim's life savings of $1.6M," nbcnews.com, March 19, 2012, www.nbcnews.com/id/46789454/ns/technology_and_science-security/t/phishing-gang-steals-victims-life-savings-m/#.VyIlwVYrLX7, accessed April 28, 2016.

39. Tom Espiner, "Dawn raids net 14 suspects in £1m phishing theft," ZDNet, March 15, 2012, www.zdnet.com/article/dawn-raids-net-14-suspects-in-1m-phishing-theft/, accessed April 28, 2016.

40. Ibid.

41. Greg Aaron and Rad Rasmussen, "Global Phishing Survey: Trends and Domain Name Use in 2H2014," APWG (Anti-Phishing Working Group), May 27, 2015, http://internetidentity.com/wp-content/uploads/2015/05/APWG_Global_Phishing_Report_2H_2014.pdf, accessed April 15, 2016.

42. Charles McFarland, Francois Paget, and Raj Samani, "The Hidden Data Economy: The Marketplace for Stolen Digital Information," *Intel Security*, www.mcafee.com/us/about/news/2015/q4/20151015-01.aspx, accessed April 28, 2016.

43. Theresa Payton and credit.com, "What Really Happens After Your Credit Card Is Stolen," ABC News, September 20, 2014, http://abcnews.go.com/Business/credit-card-stolen/story?id=25633648, accessed April 28, 2016.

44. Raj Samani, "New Year's Sales; Big Discounts on Stolen Data," McAfee Labs Blog, January 29, 2014, https://blogs.mcafee.com/mcafee-labs/new-years-sales-big-discounts-stolen-data/, accessed April 28, 2016.

45. Kevin Poulsen, "Why the Heyday of Credit Card Fraud Is Almost Over," *Wired*, September 25, 2014, www.wired.com/2014/09/emv/, accessed May 2, 2016.

46. Harriet Taylor, "Stolen Uber accounts worth more than stolen credit cards," CNBC, January 19, 2016, www.cnbc.com/2016/01/19/stolen-uber-accounts-worth-more-than-stolen-credit-cards.html, accessed April 28, 2016.

47. Poulsen, note 46 *supra*.

48. Lucian Constantin, IDG News Service, "CryptoWall ransomware held over 600K computers hostage, encrypted 5 billion files," PCWorld.com, August 29, 2014, www.pcworld.com/article/2600543/cryptowall-held-over-halfamillion-computers-hostage-encrypted-5-billion-files.html, site accessed April 28, 2016.

49. Steve Ragan, "New Ransomware business cashing in on CryptoLocker's name," CSO, November 12, 2015, www.csoonline.com/article/3004594/cyber-attacks-espionage/new-ransomware-business-cashing-in-on-cryptolockers-name.html, accessed April 28, 2016.

50. Andy Greenberg, "Hackers Remotely Kill a Jeep on the Highway–with Me in It," *Wired*, July 21, 2015, www.wired.com/2015/07/hackers-remotely-kill-jeep-highway/, accessed April 29, 2016.

51. Ibid.

52. Matt Rosoff, "Your Phone Is More Powerful Than The Computer In The Spaceship NASA Launched This Week," *Business Insider*, December 6, 2014, www.businessinsider.com/your-phone-is-more-powerful-than-the-orion-computer-2014-12, accessed April 29, 2016.

53. Lindsay Martell "Got WiFi? Cars with WiFi Hot Spots Keep Drivers Connected," *Autotrader*, June 2014, www.autotrader.com/car-tech/got-wifi-cars-with-wifi-hot-spots-keep-drivers-connected-226747, accessed April 29, 2016.

54. Ibid.

55. "Avoiding crashes with self-driving cars," *Consumer Reports*, February 2014, www.consumerreports.org/cro/magazine/2014/04/the-road-to-self-driving-cars/index.htm, accessed May 2, 2016.

56. John Greenough, "THE CONNECTED CAR REPORT: Forecasts, competing technologies, and leading manufacturers," *Business Insider*, January 7, 2016, www.businessinsider.com/connected-car-forecasts-top-manufacturers-leading-car-makers-2015-3, accessed April 29, 2016.

57. Ibid.

58. Greenberg, note 51 *supra*.

59. Ibid.

60. Ibid.

61. Ibid.

62. John Villasenor, "Five Lessons On The 'Security Of Things' From The Jeep Cherokee Hack," Forbes.com, July 27, 2015, www.forbes.com/sites/johnvillasenor/2015/07/27/five-lessons-on-the-security-of-things-from-the-jeep-cherokee-hack/#b6b9047204a6, accessed April 29, 2016.

63. Greenberg, note 51 *supra*.

64. Ibid.

65. Ibid.

66. Ibid.

67. Ibid.

68. Ibid.

69. Ibid.

70. Jose Pagliery, "Your car is a giant computer—and it can be hacked," CNN Money, June 2, 2014, http://money.cnn.com/2014/06/01/technology/security/car-hack/, accessed May 2, 2016.

71. Alex Drozhzhin "Black Hat USA 2015: The full story of how that Jeep was hacked," *Kaspersky Lab Daily*, August 6, 2015, https://blog.kaspersky.com/blackhat-jeep-cherokee-hack-explained/9493/, accessed April 29, 2016.

72. David Fitzpatrick and Drew Griffin, "'Ransomware' crime wave growing," *CNN Money*, April 4, 2016, http://money.cnn.com/2016/04/04/technology/ransomware-cybercrime/, accessed May 2, 2016.

73. Ibid.

74. Ibid.

75. Ibid.

76. Ibid.

77. McAfee Labs Threat Report, March 2016, http://www.mcafee.com/us/resources/reports/rp-quarterly-threats-mar-2016.pdf, site accessed September 29, 2016.

78. Cyber Threat Alliance, "Lucrative Ransomware Attacks: Analysis of the CryptoWall Version 3 Threat," October 2015, http://cyberthreatalliance.org/cryptowall-report.pdf, accessed May 2, 2016.

79. Michael Hiltzik, Michael, "2016 is shaping up as the year of ransomware—and the FBI isn't helping," *Los Angeles Times*, March 8, 2016, www.latimes.com/business/hiltzik/la-fi-mh-2016-is-the-year-of-ransomware-20160308-column.html, accessed May 2, 2016.

CHAPTER 3

■ ■ ■

Seconding the Cause

What is the use of having right on your side if you have not got might?

—Henrik Ibsen, *An Enemy of the People[1]*

It was billed as simply "The Fight." It sold out Madison Square Garden's nearly 21,000-seat capacity a full month in advance and featured premium tickets at then record-setting prices of $150.[2] It left some A-list celebrities, like former vice president of the United States Hubert Humphrey and best-selling recording artist of the 20th century Bing Crosby relegated to the "cheap seats" or out in the cold, respectively.[3] It featured two undefeated boxing icons, each guaranteed $2.5 million—setting another record at the time as the largest purse for any entertainer or athlete.[4] And, on March 8, 1971, the much anticipated matchup between former heavyweight champion Muhammad Ali and current titleholder Joe Frazier drew a worldwide audience of 300 million viewers, glued to radio and television broadcast networks that offered updates between each of the 15 rounds[5]— among them security guards at an FBI satellite office in Media, Pennsylvania, distracted by the perfect smokescreen for a nondescript team of eight to execute the perfect crime.

Months of meticulous planning had preceded their moment, set into motion by a pivotal question that would alter the direction of each of their lives and that of one of the world's largest intelligence agencies: "What do you think of burglarizing an FBI office?"[6] When the group's leader, an unassuming physics professor named William Davidon, began selectively floating the controversial question in late 1970 amidst a backdrop of a politically and racially charged America, with mounting opposition to the Vietnam War and civil rights injustices reaching a fever pitch, it was outrageous, even for the most committed activists of the time. The FBI was untouchable, widely regarded as the touchstone for integrity. It was also under the direction of its original leader of nearly 50 years, J. Edgar Hoover, who held the rare distinction of retaining his position as bureau chief when presidents of both political parties extended his service, regardless of his growing age and tenure.[7] Despite his lauded public persona, Hoover also had a private reputation of extreme intolerance toward any threat, foreign or domestic, against his agency's existence. His own boss, Attorney General Nicholas Katzenbach, resigned in 1966 due to Hoover's resentment of being told to operate his agency within the limits of the law. According to Katzenbach, Hoover

S. Grobman and A. Cerra, *The Second Economy*, DOI 10.1007/978-1-4842-2229-4_3

> ruled the FBI with a combination of discipline and fear and
> was capable of acting in an excessively arbitrary way. No one
> dared object. . . . The FBI was principality with absolutely
> secure borders, in Hoover's view.[8]

While Hoover governed with an iron fist behind closed doors, Katzenbach admitted, "There was no man better known or admired by the general public than J. Edgar Hoover."[9] So, any intelligent human being with regard for his personal freedom would have rebuked Davidon's question outright—burglarizing the nation's prime federal law enforcement agency and challenging the dominating force at its helm would come at the certain price of prison, if not ruin the lives of those involved.

But Davidon had weighed these consequences carefully. He and his band of cohorts had followed the prescription for activism of their day: peaceful protests, picketing, marching, and petitioning, to name just a few. Exasperated by their seeming lack of results, Davidon and his cadre faced a crisis of conscience. They believed the government, specifically the trusted and revered FBI, was spying on Americans and trampling their sacred constitutional right to dissent.[10] If they were right, this was a crime they were morally compelled to stop—at any cost. And, they knew that simply asserting their allegations without tangible proof would be met with disbelief and reproach. As Keith Forsyth, one of the eight, would reveal decades after the crime,

> When you talked to people outside the movement about what
> the FBI was doing, nobody wanted to believe it. There was
> only one way to convince people that it was true, and that was
> to get it in their [the FBI's] handwriting.[11]

And so, the group of eight initiated their audacious plan, each playing to their unique strengths. In addition to leader Davidon, there was Bonnie Raines, who, weeks before the crime, cased the location by posing as a college student seeking to interview the agent in charge about job opportunities for women in the FBI. She took great care to conceal her identity through her reconnaissance mission, removing any physical trace of her existence through extreme measures: "What (the agent) didn't notice during the whole interview was that I never took my gloves off."[12] Her investigation proved fruitful, emboldening the group's confidence they had the right target in the Media, Pennsylvania, office when no trace of a security system was found inside.[13]

There was Forsyth, the designated locksmith, who had developed a skill of picking locks by taking a correspondence course, and remained calm under pressure upon diverting the team's break-in to a side entrance when confronted with an impenetrable deadbolt at the planned main entry.[14] Also among them was Raines' husband, John, a professor of religion at Temple University at the time and the chosen getaway driver, transporting the group and the more than 1,000 FBI documents they scored in their heist to a Quaker farm outside of town.[15] There, the team painstakingly pored over their bounty, carefully inspecting each document for evidence that would confirm their suspicions.

In examining the contents, the group, which would ultimately self-identify with the anonymous yet descriptive moniker of the "Citizens' Commission to Investigate the FBI," claimed only one percent of the files involved investigation of organized crime.[16] In contrast, 40 percent of the documents dealt with some form of political surveillance, according to the team's analysis. With deliberate scrutiny, the group selected 14 of the most incriminating documents and mailed them to several newspapers and two congressmen.[17]

This was a watershed moment in media history. Journalists were presented with an interesting dilemma: does one publish papers that proved the nation's domestic intelligence and security agency was targeting political groups—particularly antiwar and civil rights activists—beyond justifiable means of surveillance, even if the proof in question was itself illegally obtained? With mounting pressure from Attorney General John N. Mitchell urging publications in receipt of the pilfered copies to refrain from publishing them on grounds that "disclosure of this information could endanger the lives or cause other serious harm to persons engaged in investigative activities on behalf of the United States,"[18] one journalist, Betty Medsger of *The Washington Post*, disregarded the warning and ran the story. Other news organizations, including *The New York Times*, followed suit.[19]

The damning evidence provided a rare and chilling behind-the-scenes glimpse of Hoover's FBI. As proof of Hoover's disdain for dissidence, one 1970 memorandum recovered in the raid encouraged agents to intensify interview efforts of antiwar activists and black student groups, stating:

> [Doing so] will enhance the paranoia epidemic in these circles
> and will further serve to get the point across there is an FBI
> agent behind every mailbox.[20]

But, it would be an internal routing slip, dated in 1968, with simply one mysterious word, "Cointelpro," that would serve as the most incendiary proof of how far Hoover's FBI would go to maintain the peace. At the time, there was no further context to Cointelpro to give the term meaning. It wasn't until several years later, when a journalist obtained more files from the FBI under the Freedom of Information Act, that the American people would fully understand what the agency's Cointelpro—short for Counterintelligence Program—entailed. The program, initiated in 1956, was an extensive campaign to surveil civil rights leaders, suspected Communists, and political organizers. Among the most reprehensible revelations was the agency's blackmail intimidation of Dr. Martin Luther King, Jr., threatening to expose the civil rights leader's extramarital affairs if he did not commit suicide.[21]

In the aftermath, an investigation into the FBI's surveillance efforts led by Senator Frank Church, Democrat of Idaho, resulted in greater congressional oversight of the FBI and other US intelligence agencies. The Church Committee's final report did not mince words when describing the extent of the FBI's abuses, "Too many people have been spied upon by too many government agencies, and too much information has been collected."[22]

Hoover's FBI would never be the same, and it all stemmed from the act of one group, completely fed up with the overreach of a government they believed needed to be held to account. Hoover's maniacal focus on locating the perpetrators absorbed hundreds of agents' time but, with thousands of potential suspects, the agency was overwhelmed to find the proverbial needles in the haystack within the five-year statute of limitations.[23] All eight walked free, never speaking of the crime again, and carrying on downright ordinary lives, some writing books, others driving the kids' carpool.[24] They maintained their silence for decades, choosing to come out of the shadows at a time when the US Government would once again find itself in the maelstrom of a shocking scandal and history would repeat itself.

Déjà vu

On March 13, 2013, Edward Snowden came across a news story that hardly appeared newsworthy at all. But, one comment in the piece would sufficiently incense Snowden to a point of making his own headlines the world over. The report recounted James Clapper's testimony in front of a Senate committee in which the director of national intelligence asserted that the National Security Agency (NSA) did "not wittingly" collect information on millions of Americans.[25] Snowden, a 29-year-old infrastructure analyst, with NSA contractor Booz Allen was afforded unique security clearance in his position of cyberwar espionage, namely, in accessing the NSA's surveillance capabilities both domestically and abroad. In his role, Snowden was exposed to the inner workings of the NSA and Clapper's comment struck an uncomfortable chord. Increasingly, the once staunch government advocate who joined the armed forces as the war in Iraq was heating up in 2004 had become disillusioned by what he perceived to be the government's overreach into the privacy of its citizens. Clapper's public assertion to the contrary was the flint that lit the spark that would reveal, if not permanently alter, the complexion of national security once again.

Over his short tenure with both the CIA and the NSA, Snowden had quickly risen through the ranks as an adept technology specialist, acquiring more exclusive security rights with each move and holding a privileged backstage pass to the government's most sensitive secrets and plans. He first began questioning his government on the very cause that excited him to enlist—that is, he had difficulty rationalizing the government's conduct in the Iraq War. According to Snowden,

> This was the Bush period, when the war on terror had gotten really dark. We were torturing people; we had warrantless wiretapping.[26]

He contemplated becoming a whistleblower but opted against the controversial move when Barack Obama entered office. Snowden believed the new president would change course on the war and correct other mistrusts he had about his employer and government. Instead, his disenchantment grew. He witnessed drone attacks obliterate human beings into human body parts. He became privy to controversial NSA practices, including the regular passing of raw private communications, to Israeli intelligence—complete with the personally identifiable information from e-mails and phone calls of millions of Arab and Palestinian Americans.[27] He learned that his employer would spy on the pornography-viewing habits of targeted political radicals, with the intent to use these "personal vulnerabilities" to destroy the reputations of government critics who were not otherwise involved in terrorist plots.[28]

Snowden was increasingly reaching his breaking point as his cyberwarfare gig with Booz Allen revealed the US Government's overstep in hacking civilian infrastructure, such as foreign universities and hospitals, in addition to select government and military targets. The last straw came when he gained access to a new cyberwar program under development, codenamed MonsterMind, which would automate the process for discovering and responding to foreign cyberattacks. To do so, MonsterMind would look for traffic patterns to identify and thwart potential foreign cyberattacks—a dated and readily defensible practice for even Snowden himself. However, MonsterMind offered the additional capacity to automatically retaliate against a suspected threat with a commensurate cyberstrike, a much more difficult feature for the information technology (IT) guru to accept, particularly given his understanding of how such cyber exploits can mask the true enemy behind an innocent target. The possibility for an unfettered game of chicken among the world's superpowers, with blameless nations as potential collateral damage, gave Snowden considerable pause.

> These attacks can be spoofed. You could have someone sitting in China, for example, making it appear that one of these attacks is originating in Russia. And then we [the US government] end up shooting back at a Russian hospital. What happens next?[29]

And, to be effective in detecting patterns of possible attack, MonsterMind would require government surveillance of virtually all private communications between overseas and domestic connection points. Like the Citizens' Commission to Investigate the FBI before him, Snowden was confronted with a crisis of conscience. In his mind, such extreme monitoring by the US Government would necessarily trample the constitutional rights to privacy endowed to every American. And so, it was no longer a matter of *if* Snowden would become the next whistleblower to expose misgivings about his employer but *when*. That moment of truth coincided with Snowden's outrage at Clapper's assertion that the NSA did not knowingly collect information on millions of Americans.

Of course, Snowden had flirted with the possibility of exposing his employer before. Much the same way the Media plot was set in motion by a question, Snowden's explosive scandal initiated with a suggestion to *Guardian* reporter Glenn Greenwald, in which the whistleblower simply offered, "I've got some stuff you might be interested in."[30] Greenwald initially ignored the message, given such suggestive proposals are par for the course in the life of a journalist. But, Snowden was persistent, engaging Greenwald and documentary filmmaker Laura Poitras several more times before unloading the thumb drives he had surreptitiously collected. The trio rendezvoused in Hong Kong where the secret exchange was made. It wasn't until Greenwald and Poitras were on the flight home, in air space they were confident was free from potential government spying, that the duo realized the extent of Snowden's disclosure. Combing through the many thousands of top secret files, Greenwald was overwhelmed by the evidence of the NSA's eavesdropping practices and sensed yet another watershed moment in American journalism history.

> I couldn't sleep one second for the next 16 hours because the adrenaline made that impossible. We essentially couldn't believe what it was that we had. And that was really the first time, I think, I fully understood that this was going to be unlike any other story—really ever—in American journalism or politics.[31]

The Guardian exposed Snowden's government secrets in an explosive story that revealed a court order requiring communications provider Verizon to release information on all telephone calls in its system, both within the United States and between the United States and other countries, to the NSA on an "ongoing, daily basis."[32] In an effort to look less Orwellian, White House spokesperson Josh Earnest stressed the limits of the order, clarifying that it did not "allow the government to listen in on anyone's telephone calls."[33]

President Obama resurrected an age-old debate in defending the government's actions, emphasizing that the United States would have to "make some tough choices between balancing privacy and security to protect against terror."[34]

In what would ensue as a case of death by a thousand paper cuts, one story after another followed, revealing more secrets from Snowden's stash. While the Verizon court order didn't entail the government "listening in" on private conversations, another top-secret data mining program codenamed Prism offered NSA access to e-mails, chat logs, and other data directly from the servers of nine Internet companies—including the contents of their messages.[35] The American public would learn of all the moral conflicts with which Snowden wrestled as he learned of what his government was capable: the attacks on civilian infrastructure, the spying on government radicals, and the virtually limitless monitoring of just about any form of domestic communication—all without warrants or probable cause—an outcome assured never to happen when the government was reeled in during the Media investigation, yet forewarned by Church in his committee's final report:

> The NSA's capability at any time could be turned around
> on the American people, and no American would have any
> privacy left, such is the capability to monitor everything:
> telephone conversations, telegrams, it doesn't matter.[36]

The media blitzkrieg reignited decades-old concerns of government overreach. The man at the center of the storm, Snowden, was simultaneously extolled as a hero by privacy advocates and vilified as a traitor by government supporters. Greenwald found himself in the heat of the conflict, drawing criticism from Clapper for accused "hyperbole" and a "rush to publish" when leaking the initial documents.[37] As if channeling Attorney General John N. Mitchell more than four decades earlier, Clapper offered the following sentiment:

> For me, it is literally—not figuratively—literally gut-wrenching
> to see this happen because of the huge, grave damage it does
> to our intelligence capabilities.[38]

The similarities between the Media break-in and the Snowden leaks more than 40 years later are uncanny. Both cases involved individuals acting in accordance with their consciences, despite personal or national consequences. Both tested the boundaries of ethics in journalism, making history by putting the very US Government on trial in the court of public opinion. Both exposed shocking evidence of the pervasiveness of the government's reach. Both ignited vociferous debate about the balance of personal privacy against national security. And, both made heroes and villains of the perpetrators and the journalists who broke their stories.

Of course, there were also striking differences between the cases. The Media heist involved a group of outsiders making history in a few precious hours under the shroud of a boxing match. Snowden was an insider who meticulously and clandestinely absconded with evidence over a prolonged period of time. The Media team lived in the shadows of their crime for decades before revealing their identities. Snowden brazenly came forward as the NSA leaker soon after Greenwald broke the story. And, while each case involved the theft of more than a thousand government documents, the Media gang was relegated to extracting their haul the old-fashioned way—in suitcases lugged in the back of a getaway car. Snowden's method was decidedly technical in its approach. He claims to have left a trace of digital breadcrumbs in his wake to reveal to his former employer the extent of his theft and, in so doing, attempt to prove his motive entailed adhering to his principles rather than exposing government secrets to national enemies.[39] This last point is particularly important to avoid one of the most serious offenses available to government prosecutors, that of "aiding the enemy," of particular concern to Snowden who had witnessed an eerily similar case of a government official leaking sensitive documents and barely dodging this bullet himself.

Leaking Secrets

On October 1, 2007, a 19-year-old new recruit of diminutive 5'2" stature named Bradley Manning stepped on the scene of Maryland's Fort Meade military base. Manning joined the military for several reasons—to escape a troubled upbringing, to qualify for scholarships that would fund his education, even to attempt to rid himself of a gender identity disorder.[40] He could hardly have imagined that six years to the day of arriving as an idealistic recruit, he would find himself once again on the same base, donned in fatigues, this time awaiting sentence for the biggest leak in US military history.[41]

Like Snowden, Manning had grown increasingly disenchanted with the military's actions in Iraq. In what his defense claims was an effort to expose what he perceived as wrongdoings and save lives as a result, Manning deliberately leaked some 250,000 State Department cables and another 470,000 Iraq and Afghanistan battlefield logs to WikiLeaks,[42] a nonprofit journalist organization that provides a platform for secret information, news leaks, and classified media from anonymous sources. Among the most shocking pieces of evidence in Manning's arsenal was a video showing a US helicopter attack on what was later discovered to be an unarmed group of civilians in Iraq, killing 11, including two Reuters journalists.[43] He was arrested in May 2010, after being sold out to the FBI by a hacker who had conversed with Manning in online chats.[44]

Manning would receive a 35-year prison sentence for his crime. Although the most extreme charge of "aiding the enemy" was ultimately dropped, Snowden witnessed the aftermath of consequences thrust upon the soldier as he contemplated a leak of his own. Though the parallels between Manning and Snowden are obvious, Snowden was hardly billed as a Manning also-ran. Instead, his crime drew more outrage from government officials claiming that while Manning offered a behind-the-scenes glimpse of "what" the government does when assuming no one to be watching, Snowden offered the far more valuable "how" of the government's secret sauce in its surveillance practices, giving enemies the formula to alter their behavior and remain under the radar.

In light of the very public fate of Manning and given the extent of knowledge released in his own leak, Snowden immediately sought asylum from US law enforcement in other sympathetic countries. But, it would be more than the parallel paths that would link Manning and Snowden to an elite, if not infamous, club of government leakers. Snowden's eventual safe harbor in Russia came at the advice of WikiLeaks founder Julian Assange, who had crossed paths with Manning just a few years prior, when he provided the army leaker with the global stage upon which to divulge the military secrets he had acquired. And, in another strange twist that demonstrates just how far ideologues will go to protect a cause, another group of hacktivists made their voices known when WikiLeaks inspired adversaries of its own.

A Legion Joins the Fight

It's difficult to fight an army that can't be identified, especially when the enemy has no named soldiers, let alone established leaders calling the shots. There is only a headless, amorphous group of mask-donning fighters, committed to taking on any establishment that threatens the values the collective holds dear. How does such an army wield its power? First, allow anyone to join the ranks, without requiring those pledging their allegiance to also disclose their identity. Next, let the group of unnamed volunteers democratically determine their next target through an Internet Relay Channel (IRC), where conversations can be obfuscated and anonymity of participants protected. If the group is feeling especially charitable toward its next victim, it may come out with a declaration of war—anonymously, of course—to compel the target to repent from its undesirable ways. If the prey ignores the warning or if the behavior is so objectionable that a warning is undeserving altogether, launch the attack through software that allows each fighter to volunteer his or her computer's processing power toward the cause— and strike with unforgiving and concerted force to take down the target's web sites via distributed denial of service (DDoS) attacks, essentially paralyzing its web properties under the crushing volume of repeated requests via the volunteer army of drone computers. Lather, rinse, repeat, and you have one of the most punishing and effective hacktivist groups of our day, known fittingly and only as "Anonymous."

When Senator Joe Lieberman, chairman of the Senate Homeland Security Committee, called on Visa, MasterCard, and PayPal to withdraw support for WikiLeaks by refusing to process donations to Assange's nonprofit journalist organization, Anonymous unleashed its fury in a mission known as "Operation Payback"—a campaign that initially targeted the recording industry for its antipiracy stance but was expanded to include WikiLeaks detractors adhering to the government's request to thwart further dissemination of Manning's leaks. In an effort to galvanize its volunteer troops and issue fair warning to possible targets, Anonymous posted the following message to broaden the scope of Operation Payback:

> We will attack any organization which seeks to remove
> WikiLeaks from the internet or promote the censorship of the
> masses. Join us. TARGET THESE IP's [List of IP addresses for
> targeted WikiLeaks critics followed][45]

Anonymous spokespeople are few and far between—after all, anonymity is at the core of the group's identity. However, at least one representative of the collective, known only as Coldblood, clarified that Anons (as individual members of the group are known) did not necessarily support the data that was distributed by WikiLeaks but vehemently disagreed with any form of censorship on the Internet.[46] Targeted organizations that found themselves crosswise with this ideology found their web sites disabled under Anonymous' punishing surge—some for minutes, others for hours—with one victim, PayPal, reporting losses of £3.5 million (more than $5.5 million).[47]

It may be reassuring to assume that the "typical" company would largely be immune from some hacktivist takedowns. After all, how many companies were even remotely engaged in something as sensational as the WikiLeaks scandal? Assuming a hacktivist attempt as an isolated occurrence destined for the Goliath-sized firms that inadvertently find themselves on a hacktivist group's hit list is a comforting thought. Unfortunately, hacktivists are expanding their aperture of targets to wreak havoc more indiscriminately.

Take web site defacement as a tried-and-true attack vector—a form of virtual vandalism that seizes control of and manipulates a company's web site. As an example, the entire site can be taken down and replaced with one of the hacker's choosing. Or, the hacker may inject code to add images or messages to the page, hijacking a company's loyal online followers to promote a message of one's own.

Web site defacement dates back to the early days of the Internet. In 1995, Attrition. org, a nonprofit Internet security site staffed by volunteers committed to exposing the latest cybercrime trends, began displaying web site defacements as fair warning to early businesses putting out their virtual shingles. By 2001, the group announced it would no longer report on web defacements due to their crippling volume on the organization's altruistic volunteers. Upon releasing its statement in 2001, Attrition.org reported:

> What began as a small collection of Web site defacement
> mirrors soon turned into a near 24/7 chore of keeping it up
> to date. In the last month, we have experienced single days
> of mirroring over 100 defaced web sites, over three times the
> total for 1995 and 1996 combined.[48]

At the time, the group's decision was met with little fanfare from the industry. After all, the hackers behind web site defacements were criticized as having too much time on their hands to launch benign attacks, all for personal ego. With Attrition.org no longer reporting on these pranksters' efforts, there would be less limelight for their self-serving interests. Today, web site defacement is far more popular-according to firms that track such vandalism (much the way Attrition.org did back in the day), there have been well over one million reported incidents per year since 2010. No longer the work of pranksters, hacktivists readily use defacement as a weapon in their arsenal. In the most insidious cases, web defacement moves beyond publicly embarrassing a company to covertly inserting malicious code to infect the site's unsuspecting visitors.

Still think the bell won't toll for thee? In 2015, the FBI warned of Islamic State of Iraq and al-Shams (ISIS) hacktivist sympathizers exploiting a vulnerability for web sites using WordPress.[49] WordPress was easily the most popular blogging and content management system used by web sites at the time. How popular? By 2015, 25 percent of all web sites across the Internet used WordPress[50]-a huge target for hacktivists looking to deface digital properties on a massive scale, small and large organizations alike.

A Second Thought

Perhaps the quintessential story of the heart of an activist comes from a 19th-century Norwegian playwright named Henrik Ibsen. Ibsen literally used the stage through his plays in exposing what he believed to be the moral hypocrisy of his time. Using the pen as his sword, he debuted his seminal play *An Enemy of the People* in 1882, where the protagonist is an activist who takes on the most threatening adversary of all-his entire community. Thought to be Ibsen's metaphorical middle-finger salute to critics who excoriated the playwright for his previous works where controversial topics like incest, marital infidelity, and sexually transmitted diseases were brazenly dramatized on the theatrical stage, *Enemy* took the audience on a very different excursion where fighting on the side of "right" could result in very "wrong" consequences. In the fictional play, Ibsen's "hero," Dr. Thomas Stockmann, blows the whistle on his town's source of tourism-its natural springs, widely promoted as healing waters, which Stockmann comes to discover are actually toxic. Believing he would be exalted for his discovery, our hero is ceremoniously ostracized by his community, left to stand alone in his principles, and facing an uncertain, if not perilous, future as the curtain falls.

So describes the fate awaiting most activists. While some are applauded for exposing a wrongdoing, the vast majority find themselves in an uphill battle, defending their actions to those they intended to protect. Perhaps that explains why almost all internal activists-the whistleblowers, for example-say they would not do it again.[51] But, whether the shape of activism comes in the form of these internal whistleblowers compelled to turn on their employers in spite of personal ramifications or a nameless, faceless legion of hackers bent on punishing organizations that act against the collective's moral compass, the mind-set of the activist is core to his value structure. In some cases, the values are readily understood. In others, the ideology may be diametrically opposed to one's own cultural values, landing the target directly in the crosshairs of one or many crusaders prepared to take decisive and, in their minds, corrective action.

Whether the cause in question for an activist is noble or malicious is up for debate in every case. Our point is not to evaluate the merits of an activist's principles but to understand the incentives driving his actions. Activists believe their efforts will inspire change for the better (in this case, "better" is in the eyes of the activist himself). However, what has been fairly clearly communicated through cultural examples dating as far back as Ibsen's *Enemy* is that heroes are rarely born from such efforts, providing cautionary tales to other motivated individuals willing to take on a fight that the mission must be worth the consequence. It's one of the reasons hacktivism is such an insidious threat to unsuspecting organizations-in some cases, the hacktivists are on the right side of the fight, even if their ends cannot justify their means. And, given that hacktivists seek glory for their cause, not themselves, they will relentlessly pursue any target which they believe to be on the wrong side of the battle in their ideological war.

Since self-bravado and financial greed are not their end pursuits, hacktivists follow a decidedly different playbook than the "traditional" hacker. Look no further than the examples of activists cited in this chapter for individuals professing unwavering commitment to their cause-even at the potential expense of personal freedom. Each chose to shine the spotlight of fame upon their mission, rather than stand in it for their own glory. The Citizens' Commission remained in the shadows for decades before coming forward. In the words of John Raines, "We didn't need attention, because we had done what needed to be done."[52] Despite Snowden's controversial choice to reveal his identity, he has gone on record as saying, "I don't want the stage. I'm terrified of giving these talking heads some distraction, some excuse to jeopardize, smear, and delegitimize a very important movement."[53] And, Anons deliberately conceal their identity, not simply to avert personal repercussions but as a part of their movement to showcase causes, not celebrate individuals. According to Gabriella Coleman, an anthropologist at McGill University and avid researcher of Anonymous, "There are surprisingly few people [within Anonymous] who violate the rule [against attention-seeking]. Those who do . . . are marginalized."[54]

When the cause is worth more than personal sacrifice and change is the ultimate reward, the probability (P) for a hacktivist attack can be summed up with the same familiar equation, though with a very different interpretation:

$$P = (Incentive \ x \ Opportunity) / Risk$$

Incentive is the amount of change the hacktivist hopes to mobilize. The stronger the ideological principle, the greater the incentive for attack. Incentive also pertains to the notoriety available in the planned attack, but, in this case, the glory is for the cause itself, not for individual fame. Larger targets, such as the multiple leaks for the US Government by both insiders and outsiders, afford a much bigger stage for hacktivists to share their message. Importantly, the availability of pervasive media vehicles, whether in the form of traditional journalists like Betty Medsger or nontraditional outlets like WikiLeaks, provides hacktivists the audience through which to make their cause known.

Opportunity deals with how accessible, or vulnerable, the target is. While the Media break-in offered tremendous incentive for eight determined activists, the opportunity to easily penetrate such an office required months of measured planning. Likewise, some targets online will be more accessible than others-whether in vandalizing sites or readying more effective DDoS strikes against weaker defenses.

Finally, risk is the potential for being discovered and reprimanded. The higher the risk, the lower the probability; however, hacktivists arguably have the highest risk tolerance of all cybercriminal breeds. When principles are in play, personal motives fall by the wayside, causing the fiercest and most committed hacktivists to take extreme risks in support of their philosophies. Where the financially motivated criminals are driven by the dollar, hacktivists are compelled by change. Where "typical" cybercriminals dwell in the shadows, leveraging time to their advantage as they surreptitiously steal from their victims, hacktivists welcome the bang, not the whimper, when outright promoting their crusades. And, while cyberthieves focus their energy on deriving maximum profit along the path of least resistance, hacktivists seek the loudest microphone to vocalize their principles regardless of effort in finding it, creating a very different public relations challenge for their victims.

While activist causes are certainly nothing new, hacktivism brings with it unbelievable leverage in the hands of a motivated few. Consider the analogy of protesting in the streets for a cause. A dozen highly spirited people would do little more than attract fleeting attention from passersby for their mission. The chance of long-term reform with such practices is possible, but also potentially lengthy and exhausting as the Media activists found with their own traditional methods of petitioning and protesting. Before hacktivism, those same motivated individuals would be forced to resort to extreme lengths (and risk) to effect radical change, if their patience for traditional activist methods ran dry. Today's hacktivist movements do not require armies of thousands. While it's true that groups like Anonymous rely upon others to volunteer their computers to a botnet army, enlistees can more readily donate idle compute processing power to a cause than engage in more time-consuming pursuits of traditional activism, like marching in the streets. In the end, it only takes a few hacktivists to topple a target in a highly asymmetrical battle. As Tim Rogers, a reporter who took an inside look at Anonymous, describes:

> As with the animals on Orwell's farm, all Anonymous are equal, but some are more equal than others. It's hard, obviously, to get a reliable estimate on the number of those elite Anons who are channel operators . . . it could be a few dozen. When those—don't call them leaders—change the topic of an IRC channel, all the LOIC [Low Orbit Ion Cannon]-armed computers [volunteer computers in the botnet army] linked to that channel will automatically fire at the target. That's when embarrassing things happen to ill-prepared companies (and governments, too).[55]

Yes, activism is as old as organized government itself. But radicals have been losing steam, if not inspiration, in recent decades. Recruiting the masses to one's cause is time-consuming and requires significant commitment. Hacktivism puts the power back in the hands of a few, with the ability to quickly enlist sympathizers to their purpose, for significantly less time and trouble. As one former Anonymous member and spokesperson for the group puts it,

> The full-time professional activists from the '80s and '90s
> didn't really have a strategy. I don't think there's been
> anything effective or worth taking part in since the late '60s.[56]

But, thanks to the Internet and social media and the borderless capabilities they afford, a new kind of activist, no longer content to sit on the sidelines, is connecting to movements that otherwise may have suffered the same apathy that plagued those nonstrategic missions in the latter decades of the first millennium. Indeed, any inspired person can join a cause to expose a perceived wrongdoing, freely, anonymously, and easily-either in lending her coding talents or volunteering her computer's processing power to a botnet army-all in the fight for principles in *The Second Economy*.

A SECOND HELPING OF ANONYMOUS

How does one begin to explain a nameless, faceless society of online vigilantes committed to the cause of their "hive mind"? It helps to start at the beginning, in the origins of how a hacktivist group known as Anonymous would rise in rank and power to strike fear into governments, corporations, or other potential ne'er-do-wells that cross its path. Specifically, let's go back to 2003 and to a then 15-year-old insomniac from New York City named Christopher Poole. Poole launched a discussion board for fans of anime that would soon evolve as the birthplace of some of the most popular Internet memes in history, including cats doing outrageous things, the soulful sounds of an unknown singer performing an equally unknown, yet infectious "Chocolate Rain," or the annoying popup of Rick Astley's "Never Gonna Give You Up" music video when one found himself the latest dupe of "Rickrolling." Users opined on these and other topics on Poole's board 4chan. Those who chose not to use a screen name were given the moniker default, "Anonymous." With an underground culture all their own and a penchant for identifying the next hilarious Internet meme, 4chan users pursued the thrill of "lulz"—a term derived from acronym LOL (laugh out loud)—in an attempt to showcase the irreverent nature of the discussion board's topics. Around 2004, some 4chan discussion groups began referring to Anonymous as an independent entity.

To be clear, Anonymous does not refer to itself as a group (though many others do since attempting to describe the shadowy collective any other way is confusing at best). Researchers and spokespeople have likened it to a "shapeshifting subculture" or "series of relationships," respectively.[57] Given the fluidity of the "subculture," it can be difficult to reconcile Anonymous' pursuits, with some causes sympathetic (such as their relentless targeting of pedophiles) and others disturbing (including some Anons posting photos of pipe bombs or threatening violence at public venues).

Arguably, Anonymous' major coming-out party involved the Church of Scientology in 2008, when Gawker Media posted a video of notable Scientologist Tom Cruise enthusiastically espousing the benefits of his religion. The Church of Scientology sent a cease-and-desist to Gawker, demanding the copyrighted video be removed. This perceived act of censorship angered at least one Anon, who posted, "I think it's time . . . to do something big. I'm talking about 'hacking' or 'taking down' the official Scientology website."[58] Anonymous had its first established target. It sent its warning via a YouTube video, which would ultimately be viewed more than two million times within a few weeks of posting, in which a computerized voiceover warned, "We shall proceed to expel you from the Internet and systematically dismantle the Church of Scientology in its present form. You have nowhere to hide."[59]

The Church, fortified with more than a billion dollars of assets, found itself outmatched by Anonymous' relentless, if not annoying, attacks—in paralyzing the Church's web site intermittently over a period of days with successive DDoS attacks, in launching a "Google bomb" that rendered the Church's web site the top result when users searched for "dangerous cult," in drowning certain Church physical locations with hundreds of unwanted pizzas, or in sapping the Church's fax machines of ink by sending all-black transmissions.[60]

On March 15, 2008, the "face" of Anonymous was finally revealed, when thousands of Anons systematically marched past Scientology churches in more than 100 global cities. Anons reportedly deliberated what face they would choose, considering caped crusader Batman before settling on the Guy Fawkes mask worn in the 2005 movie "V is for Vendetta" after finding it to be in plentiful (and cheap) supply in designated protest markets.[61] In the end, the Tom Cruise video remained on the Internet. Anonymous had made its point and "identity" known. Like any deserving marketing brand, it also developed its own slogan to strike fear in the hearts of potential targets, "We are Legion. We do not forgive. We do not forget. Expect us."

Anonymous started from unassuming roots on a community board dedicated to the lulz. It has since grown into a seemingly unstoppable juggernaut fixing its gaze and its wrath against those who do not share its ideological principles. Yet, it doesn't take itself too seriously in every case, reminiscent of the lulz that started it all. In the words of Barrett Brown, former Anon and loose spokesperson for what has also been metaphorically described as a flock of birds with ever-changing leadership:

> *Anonymous is a process more than it is a thing. I can't speak on behalf of Anonymous, because there's no one who can authorize me to do that. You have to remember, we're the Freemasons. Only, we've got a sense of humor. You have to wield power with a sense of humor. Otherwise you become the FBI.*[62]

Notes

1. www.goodreads.com/work/quotes/2307067-en-folkefiende, accessed May 24, 2016.

2. International Boxing Hall of Fame, "The Fight of the Century," www.ibhof.com/pages/archives/alifrazier.html, accessed May 19, 2016.

3. Michael Silver, "Where Were You on March 8, 1971?," ESPN Classic, November 19, 2003, http://espn.go.com/classic/s/silver_ali_frazier.html, accessed May 19, 2016.

4. Ibid.

5. Carrie Johnson, "The Secret Burglary That Exposed J. Edgar Hoover's FBI," NPR Oregon Public Broadcasting, January 7, 2014, www.npr.org/2014/01/07/260302289/the-secret-burglary-that-exposed-j-edgar-hoovers-fbi, accessed May 19, 2016.

6. Betty Medsger, *The Burglary: The Discovery of J. Edgar Hoover's Secret FBI* (New York: Vintage Books, 2014).

7. Federal Bureau of Investigation, www.fbi.gov/about-us/history/directors/hoover, accessed May 20, 2016.

8. Medsger, note 6 *supra*.

9. Ibid.

10. Ibid.

11. Mark Mazzetti "Burglars Who Took On F.B.I. Abandon Shadows," *The New York Times*, January 7, 2014, www.nytimes.com/2014/01/07/us/burglars-who-took-on-fbi-abandon-shadows.html?_r=2, accessed May 20, 2016.

12. Michael Isikoff, "After 43 years, activists admit theft at FBI office that exposed domestic spying," NBC News, January 6, 2014, http://investigations.nbcnews.com/_news/2014/01/06/22205443-after-43-years-activists-admit-theft-at-fbi-office-that-exposed-domestic-spying?lite, accessed May 20, 2016.

13. Mazzetti, note 11 *supra*.

14. Ibid.

15. Isikoff, note 12 *supra*.

16. Betty Medsger, "Stolen FBI Documents Analyzed," *The Washington Post*, May 9, 1971, p. 5, https://media. proquest.com/media/pq/hnp/doc/157384922/fmt/ai/rep/ NONE?ic=1&hl=fbi&_s=oxwFIxEsu3ieyd5Lc5258iwEyUM%3D, accessed May 20, 2016.

17. Betty Medsger and Ken W. Clawson, "Thieves Got Over 1,000 FBI Papers," *The Washington Post*, March 25, 1971, p. A1, https://media.proquest.com/media/pq/hnp/ doc/144553582/fmt/ai/rep/NONE?ic=1&hl=fbi&_s=dA7dL8i i17JkoeGPKrXmkbFQRNs%3D, accessed May 20, 2016.

18. Ibid.

19. Mazzetti, note 11 *supra*.

20. Ibid.

21. Ibid.

22. Ibid.

23. Johnson, note 5 *supra*.

24. Ibid.

25. James Bamford, "Edward Snowden: The Untold Story," *Wired*, August 22, 2014, www.wired.com/2014/08/edward-snowden/, accessed May 21, 2016.

26. Ibid.

27. Ibid.

28. Ibid.

29. Ibid.

30. Jason M. Breslow, "How Edward Snowden Leaked "Thousands" of NSA Documents," *PBS Frontline*, May 13, 2014, www.pbs.org/wgbh/frontline/article/how-edward-snowden-leaked-thousands-of-nsa-documents/, accessed May 21, 2016.

31. Ibid.

32. Glenn Greenwald, "NSA collecting phone records of millions of Verizon customers daily," *The Guardian*, June 6, 2013, www. theguardian.com/world/2013/jun/06/nsa-phone-records-verizon-court-order, accessed May 21, 2016.

33. Dan Roberts and Spencer Ackerman, "Anger swells after NSA phone records court order revelations," *The Guardian*, June 6, 2013, www.theguardian.com/world/2013/jun/06/obama-administration-nsa-verizon-records, accessed May 22, 2016.

34. Ian Black, "NSA spying scandal: what we have learned," The Guardian, June 10, 2013, www.theguardian.com/world/2013/jun/10/nsa-spying-scandal-what-we-have-learned, accessed May 21, 2016.

35. Ibid.

36. Greenwald, note 32 *supra*.

37. Barton Gellman, Aaron Blake, and Greg Miller, "Edward Snowden comes forward as source of NSA leaks," *The Washington Post*, June 9, 2013, www.washingtonpost.com/politics/intelligence-leaders-push-back-on-leakers-media/2013/06/09/fff80160-d122-11e2-a73e-826d299ff459_story.html, accessed May 22, 2016.

38. Ibid.

39. Bamford, note 25 *supra*.

40. Paul Lewis, "Bradley Manning trial revealed a lonely soldier with a troubled past," *The Guardian*, August 21, 2013b, www.theguardian.com/world/2013/aug/21/bradley-manning-lonely-soldier-childhood, accessed May 22, 2016.

41. Ibid.

42. Paul Lewis, "Bradley Manning given 35-year prison term for passing files to WikiLeaks," *The Guardian*, August 21, 2013a, www.theguardian.com/world/2013/aug/21/bradley-manning-35-years-prison-wikileaks-sentence, accessed May 22, 2016.

43. Brad Knickerbocker, "Bradley Manning trial closing arguments ask: Why did he do it?," *The Christian Science Monitor*, July 25, 2013, www.csmonitor.com/USA/Justice/2013/0725/Bradley-Manning-trial-closing-arguments-ask-Why-did-he-do-it, accessed May 22, 2016.

44. Lewis, note 42 *supra*.

45. Ronny Kerr, "4Chan-supported Anonymous takes down PayPal," *Vator*, December 9, 2010, http://vator.tv/news/2010-12-09-4chan-supported-anonymous-takes-down-paypal, accessed May 23, 2016.

46. Josh Halliday and Charles Arthur, "WikiLeaks: Who are the hackers behind Operation Payback?," *The Guardian*, December 8, 2010, www.theguardian.com/media/2010/dec/08/anonymous-4chan-wikileaks-mastercard-paypal, accessed May 23, 2016.

47.   Sandra Laville, "Anonymous cyber-attacks cost PayPal
       £3.5m, court told," *The Guardian*, November 22, 2012, www.
       theguardian.com/technology/2012/nov/22/anonymous-
       cyber-attacks-paypal-court, accessed May 23, 2016.

48.   Sam Costello, Sam, "Attrition.org stops mirroring hacked Web
       sites," CNN.com, May 23, 2001, www.cnn.com/2001/TECH/
       internet/05/23/attrition.mirroring.idg/, accessed June
       1, 2016.

49.   Brian Krebs, "FBI Warns of Fake Govt Sites, ISIS Defacements,"
       KrebsonSecurity, April 7, 2015, http://krebsonsecurity.
       com/2015/04/fbi-warns-of-fake-govt-sites-isis-
       defacements/, accessed June 1, 2016.

50.   Matt McGee, "WordPress Used On 25 Percent Of All Websites,"
       Marketing Land, November 9, 2015, http://marketingland.
       com/wordpress-used-on-25-percent-of-all-websites-
       report-151115, accessed June 1, 2016.

51.   Richard Lacayo and Amanda Ripley, "Persons of The
       Year 2002: The Whistleblowers," *Time*, December 30,
       2002, http://content.time.com/time/subscriber/
       article/0,33009,1003998-3,00.html, accessed May 24,
       2016.

52.   Mazzetti, note 11 *supra*.

53.   Bamford, note 25 *supra*.

54.   David Kushner, "The Masked Avengers," *The New
       Yorker*, September 8, 2014, www.newyorker.com/
       magazine/2014/09/08/masked-avengers, accessed May 24,
       2016.

55.   Tim Rogers, "Barrett Brown Is Anonymous," *D Magazine*, April
       2011, www.dmagazine.com/publications/d-magazine/2011/
       april/how-barrett-brown-helped-overthrow-the-
       government-of-tunisia?page=2, accessed June 1, 2016.

56.   Ibid.

57.   Kushner, note 54 *supra*.

58.   Ibid.

59.   Ibid.

60.   Ibid.

61.   Ibid.

62.   Rogers, note 55 *supra*.

CHAPTER 4

■ ■ ■

No Second Chance

"States have an inherent right to self-defense that may be triggered by certain aggressive acts in cyberspace. . . . When warranted, the United States will respond to hostile acts in cyberspace as we would to any other threat to our country."

—International Strategy for Cyberspace, The White House, 2011

"Plain, deliberate, contemplated murder is dwarfed in magnitude by comparison with the crime you have committed."[1] With a sentence more biting than his parting words, Federal Judge Irving Kaufman condemned Julius and Ethel Rosenberg to death. Despite multiple appeals and objections by famous celebrities and protesters alike, the Rosenbergs faced the electric chair, and their demise, at New York's Sing Sing prison at sundown on June 19, 1953. Up until their final breaths, they both maintained their innocence. Up until this day, their names remain indelibly etched in history's annals as the first American civilians to be executed for espionage.

The Rosenbergs' story would be set in motion by an event in 1938, when German Otto Hahn and his assistant Fritz Strassman discovered nuclear fission. Global tensions were building at the time, with Adolf Hitler's Nazi Germany striking alliances with Italy and Japan. The Axis, as the trio of nations would come to be called, were united in their ambitions to expand their territories through military conquest and overthrow the post-World War I international order.[2] Less than a year after Hahn made his discovery, Germany dropped bombs on Poland in a series of air raids,[3] and an epic world war that matched the Axis alliance against the Allied Powers of Great Britain, the United States, and the Soviet Union had begun.

With Germany's aggressions building, concerns mounted that Hitler may have the goods to produce an atomic bomb, particularly given the head start afforded through Hahn's breakthrough. Those suspicions were confirmed in 1942, when British volunteer commandos discovered Germans hard at work building a nuclear weapon during a raid in German-occupied Norway. When the United States learned through its British ally how far their enemy had advanced in its nuclear endeavors, the race was on to build the world's first weapon of mass destruction.[4]

On May 12, 1942, President Franklin D. Roosevelt, previously forewarned by none other than Albert Einstein in a personal letter explaining the new field of physics that could give rise to the world's first nuke, signed into order a secret project to develop one for the United States. In its top secret Manhattan Project, the United States would spend $2 billion (equivalent to more than $26 billion in 2016) and employ 125,000 people[5] to become the first nation (and the only one to date) to detonate an atomic bomb against an enemy. On August 6, 1945, President Harry Truman, who himself was unaware of the Manhattan Project's existence when serving as vice president under Roosevelt, took less than ten minutes to expose years of stealthy progress to the American people in an address:

> Sixteen hours ago an American airplane dropped one bomb on Hiroshima and destroyed its usefulness to the enemy. That bomb had more power than 20,000 tons of TNT... With this bomb we have now added a new and revolutionary increase in destruction to supplement the growing power of our armed forces. . . . It is an atomic bomb. It is a harnessing of the basic power of the universe. . . . Before 1939, it was the accepted belief of scientists that it was theoretically possible to release atomic energy. But no one knew any practical method of doing it. By 1942, however, we knew that the Germans were working feverishly to find a way to add atomic energy to the other engines of war with which they hoped to enslave the world. But they failed. . . . The battle of the laboratories held fateful risks for us as well as the battles of the air, land, and sea, and we have now won the battle of the laboratories as we have won the other battles. . . . With American and British scientists working together we entered the race of discovery against the Germans. . . . We have spent two billion dollars on the greatest scientific gamble in history—and won.[6]

Four months after that historic day, the US Army published a secret report on the security surrounding the Manhattan Project. The findings would remain classified until 2014. The study's authors called the Manhattan Project "more drastically guarded than any other highly secret war development."[7] Citing the fact that Germany was never successful in deploying a nuclear weapon of its own, the report deemed the covert operation of the Project a success. In an ironic twist, while the United States kept its gaze firmly fixed on thwarting its enemy Germany from building a nuke, it missed a threat looming from within its inner circle of Allied Powers seeking the same ambition—that of the Soviet Union. And, despite the authors' lauding of the Manhattan Project's success in keeping a lid on the US nuclear development mission, they also admitted to thousands of leaks over the Project's span—specifically, to more than 1,500 discovered cases in which classified information was transmitted to unauthorized persons, approximately 200 events of sabotage, and roughly 100 suspected incidents involving espionage.[8] The Rosenbergs, devoted to the Soviet Union's Communist movement, would find themselves in disreputable company in this last category.

When Julius and Ethel Rosenberg married in 1939, their union simultaneously fused an opportunistic group of Communist sympathizers with unprecedented access to the United States' most sacred national secret. Julius, the leader of the group, developed a passion for radical politics early in life, after abandoning an early calling for religion in exchange for a membership card to the Young Communist League.[9] While attending City College in his pursuit of an electrical engineering degree, Julius met Morton Sobell, who would become another puzzle piece in the Rosenbergs' spy story. But, it was Ethel's brother, David Greenglass, who played the most significant part in uniting the Rosenbergs to their Communist mission. Greenglass, a member of the US Army, was stationed at a remote base in Los Alamos, New Mexico—a primary site for the Manhattan Project's research and where the bomb, known in government code language as "the gadget" at the time, was under development. Julius, notorious for his active proselytizing in converting family members to the Communist Party, convinced his brother-in-law David to hand over secrets of the Project.

In a real-world case of cloak and dagger, each member of the Rosenberg spy ring played a part in accelerating the political and military ambitions of the Soviet Union. Julius, the mastermind, used couriers to pick up the classified documents from Greenglass, exploiting code phrases and discarded Jell-O box tops as the auditory and visual signals through which to identify the mules.[10] Sobell had a hand in stealing military secrets from Langley Field, at the time one of the nation's preeminent centers for military design.[11] And there was Ethel, Julius' faithful wife and Greenglass' sister, who was accused and convicted of typing Greenglass' notes about the bomb, testimony provided by Greenglass himself against his sister when he turned state's witness. In exchange for his testimony, Greenglass received a lesser sentence of 15 years' imprisonment.

For decades after the Rosenbergs' execution, doubts remained about the extent of their war crimes. Of the four, only Greenglass had confessed and incriminated his fellow cohorts in the espionage, particularly his sister and brother-in-law. Many suspected the Rosenbergs to be scapegoats in a postwar America where anti-Communist sentiments were escalating. Though also convicted, Sobell vehemently maintained his innocence up until 2008, when he unexpectedly offered a confession that corroborated the espionage had, in fact, occurred. However, according to Sobell's confession, one of the most famous American spies in history was hardly a spy at all. Sobell confirmed that Ethel knew of the crime but was not actively involved. Those typewritten notes of her brother's atomic secrets? All fabricated by her brother under testimony in an attempt to garner a lighter sentence for his wife and himself. Greenglass himself admitted to the fabrication decades after his sister had been put to death.[12]

The Soviet Union exploded its own atomic bomb four years after the US attack on Japan—a surprise to many who believed the Soviets to be far behind in the nuclear race. Soon after, the Cold War would commence, pitting two superpowers against one another for nearly five decades as nuclear tensions rose. The Rosenberg leaks were, at least in part, blamed for the seemingly questionable leapfrogging of the Soviets in their nuclear capabilities. In hindsight, it appears the Soviets were much closer to a nuclear weapon than the Americans gave them credit—some argue that the Rosenbergs' secrets advanced the Soviet mission by no more than a year.[13] Even if the caliber of the traded secrets were less valuable in retrospect, the Rosenberg ring had intentions of enabling an ideological adversary against their country. They paid a handsome price for their crime. And, with the nuclear genie out of the bottle and other nations readying their own defenses with weapons of mass destruction, worldwide stability would never be the same. In a case of history once again repeating itself, in 2016, the United States would find itself at odds with a political adversary in Iran with nuclear ambitions of its own. The question that persisted for decades remained: how to deal with the unending threat of a nuclear arms race that showed no signs of abating?

Somebody Crossed the Rubicon

The year is now 2006, more than 60 years after the United States' first nuclear attack. President George W. Bush is in office. He has suffered political shrapnel associated with accusing Saddam Hussein of harboring weapons of mass destruction—an allegation that has yet to be fully proven, though it was serious enough to lead the United States into the highly controversial Iraq War. Bush saw another adversary building its nuclear war chest—this time, it was Iran. The president couldn't exactly stand on conviction in accusing another nation of nuclear pursuits after the Iraq debacle. He also couldn't rely on his European allies in imposing sanctions against Iran, with many divided on the potential impact of doing so to their own economies.[14]

Iran was emboldened by US impotence, doubling down on its nuclear path. Iranian President Mahmoud Ahmadinejad hosted a press tour of a site in Natanz. He marveled at the country's goal to install upward of 50,000 centrifuges.[15] Bush administration officials balked at the claim that such an increase in supply would singularly provide power to Iranians. They feared another reason for the enormous output—that of creating a stockpile for future nuclear weapons.

If the United States' suspicions were accurate, a nuclear weapon in Iran's hands would further destabilize an already fragile Middle East and potentially lead to the next cataclysmic war. Spurred by his administration, Bush considered a military strike to thwart Iran. But, after contemplating several scenarios, the uncertain outcome of such an attempt—particularly in lighting a match to Middle East tensions—gave Bush pause. The CIA had already engaged in sabotage attempts by tampering with Iran's imported power supplies such that they would explode. All attempts proved futile in causing significant damage and Iran remained undeterred.[16]

If the United States lacked the appetite to engage in another war, couldn't rely on tamer economic sanctions to dissuade Iran, and had already exhausted physical sabotage measures, perhaps there was another alternative to slow its adversary's nuclear mission. Much like the Manhattan Project, it would require the utmost in secrecy. It would also require the United States to break new ground—going back to the "laboratory battle" that Truman referenced when revealing the Manhattan Project for the first time. This time, the laboratory fight would be waged on a virtual battlefield.

Enter project Olympic Games. The initiative, greenlit by Bush after exhausting all other options, sought to take cyberwarfare to another level. Its weapon would not be a nuclear bomb but a computer worm, capable of propagating itself and infecting targeted machines in the Natanz plant. The goal of the program was to find a way to disrupt the centrifuges at the heart of Iran's nuclear pursuits. If the United States could sabotage the centrifuges with its worm, it stood to disrupt, if not temporarily halt, Iran's mission.

The worm, code-named "the bug," that would ultimately be unleashed on Natanz was 50 times larger than the typical computer worm,[17] demonstrating the scale and sophistication of Olympic Games. However, before the US menace could be let loose on its target, the Bush administration first had to collect reconnaissance of the plant itself. In olden times, such investigating would come at the hands of spies physically transferring blueprints and evidence between themselves—much like the Rosenberg ring aided the Soviets with extensive designs of the United States' first nuclear weapon over a shadowy courier network of affiliates. But, when one is releasing a worm and not an A-bomb, it only seems fitting that the initial spying would come at the hands of another sophisticated computer code in its own right, called a beacon, to surreptitiously collect sophisticated mappings of Natanz's inner workings. The beacon would provide US officials with a virtual blueprint of the Natanz facility, supplying details of how the nuclear centrifuges were connected across an extensive labyrinth of industrial controls. It would ultimately "phone home" in transmitting the files back to the National Security Agency (NSA) command center for Olympic Games. Even Bush himself was doubtful the reconnaissance mission would work. His skepticism was vanquished when the maps of Natanz's virtual connections were in US hands.[18]

Joining forces with a secret Israeli unit respected for its cyberskills, the NSA went to work in developing the worm to attack Natanz. "The bug" was sophisticatedly engineered to ravage Natanz with clandestine military precision:

1. First, the bug had to be implanted, no small feat given the Natanz "air gap" that virtually separated the facility from connections to the outside world. The architects settled on a USB memory stick as the means of infiltration.

2. The bug would then check whether a given machine was part of the targeted industrial control system made by Siemens. Such systems were known to be in the network that controlled the high-speed centrifuges that helped enrich nuclear fuel.

3. If the system was not a targeted machine, the bug did nothing further. If it was, the bug would attempt to access the Internet to update itself.

4. Using a combination of zero-day exploit attacks, the bug compromised software vulnerabilities in the target system's logic controllers. One of the zero-days exploited a fundamental vulnerability in the Windows operating system that, during the time it remained unreported and unpatched, left millions vulnerable. The moral conflict of the US government engaged in leveraging discovered zero-day vulnerabilities rather than reporting such weaknesses to software companies and their customers is just one of Olympic Games' many gray areas. Even more troubling, such zero-days can be purchased on the market, arguably from at least a few black hatters in the mix, for anywhere from $10,000 to $500,000 or more.[19] Snowden's leaks revealed that the NSA paid $25 million for zero-days in 2013 alone.[20]

5. Once inside, the bug spied on the operations of the targeted system. It ultimately used the information it had gathered to take over the centrifuges, making them spin themselves to failure.

6. Finally, in what has been hailed as one of the more brilliant elements of the code, the bug sent faulty feedback to outside controllers, reporting business-as-usual functionality. Beyond concealing the mission, this part of the code also intended to overwhelm Natanz plant operators with false information, leaving them bewildered as to the cause of centrifuge burnout and, it is hoped, doubting their capabilities in managing the facility as a result.

Once the Olympic Games coders believed they had the stuff of cyberwar legend, they needed a test subject. Launching a worm to detect its effectiveness in such a narrow case as sabotaging nuclear centrifuges isn't exactly the equivalent of releasing it to a few test computers. The industrial equipment in play was highly specialized. Only finding the same Siemens controllers for a validated test would suffice. Fortunately for the United States, it had just such a stockpile from former Libyan dictator Colonel Muammar el-Qaddafi, when he surrendered his nuclear program in 2003 and handed over the nuclear centrifuges he had procured from Pakistan. Those centrifuges were now property of the US Government, shelved in a weapons laboratory in Tennessee. Borrowing the stockpile for "destructive testing" the Olympic Games planners built a virtual replica of the Natanz plant and went to work evaluating the effectiveness of their creation.

On a day near the end of Bush's term, the rubble of a centrifuge from Qaddafi's test pile was spread out before the president in the Situation Room. The experiment was a success. Former chief of the CIA Michael Hayden summed up the meaning of the historic moment:

> Previous cyberattacks had effects limited to other computers. This is the first attack of a major nature in which a cyberattack was used to effect physical destruction [rather than hamper a computer's performance or steal data]. Somebody crossed the Rubicon.[21]

Olympic Games was ready to move from dress rehearsal to opening night. To cross the air gap that separated Natanz from the outside world, a highly targeted series of attacks that used soft targets, including contractors,[22] and at least one Iranian double agent[23] implanted the bug via its conveyance of a corrupt USB memory stick. According to one of the plan's architects, "That was our holy grail. It turns out there is always an idiot around who doesn't think much about the thumb drive in their hand."[24]

Slowly, the plan began to work. When the first centrifuges began spinning out of control in 2008, the Iranians were stumped by the cause. Part of the confusion rested in another element of the code's genius—no two attacks were exactly alike. This, coupled with the covert nature of the code to lurk in its environment for weeks before striking and the faulty messages it conveyed to plant operators of seemingly normal operations, led to the Iranians' bewilderment. Frustrated and confused, they took drastic measures, including deploying operatives in the plant to watch the equipment and report on their observations and even terminating some who were suspected of incompetence to resolve the issue. According to one insider, "The intent was that the failures should make them feel they were stupid, which is what happened."[25] Confusion, paranoia, and wrongful terminations notwithstanding, Olympic Games had not dealt the lethal blow to Iran's nuclear program that its architects had intended. Success had come, but slowly and modestly. The program would need to be continued and even ramped up to see the full extent of its destructive capabilities. In much the same way that the Manhattan Project torch was passed from Roosevelt to Truman, Bush briefed President-elect Barack Obama on Olympic Games and urged him to continue the cause. The new president accepted the challenge.

A Cyber Pearl Harbor

In 2009, Iran was in the middle of political upheaval. It had just completed one of its most contentious presidential elections in some time, leading to a disputed landslide reelection for Ahmadinejad. As protesters threw the streets of Tehran into chaos, things at Natanz were going swimmingly. By February of that year, workers had installed 5,400 centrifuges—very close to the 6,000 target that Ahmadinejad had issued the previous year.[26] By June, the figure had jumped to 7,052 centrifuges, although not all were enriching gas.[27] Daily throughput of the centrifuges was on the rise as well. Iran's daily production of low-enriched uranium was up 20 percent.[28] At its current pace, the country would have enough enriched uranium to make two nuclear weapons within a year. It had begun installing newer versions of its centrifuges, each with the capacity to more than double its daily output of uranium.[29] Olympic Games was in serious danger of leaving Iran's nuclear ambitions unchecked.

A new version of the bug was soon unleashed, this one with even greater power to spread more efficiently to designated targets. Between June and August, the number of centrifuges enriching uranium gas at Natanz began to decrease. By August, only 4,592 centrifuges were enriching at the plant, a decrease of more than 300 units since June.[30] By November, the precipitous freefall had continued, with only 3,936 uranium-enriching centrifuges in production, down 984 in five months.[31] And, while the Iranians raced to install more machines, none of them was being fed gas. In essence, Iran's race had slowed to a measured crawl. Olympic Games was finally having an impact.

While production at Natanz was facing speedbumps, a control engineer at one of the plant's contracted suppliers emerged on a Siemens user forum complaining about problems employees at his company were having with their machines. All PCs at the company were having issues with a Siemens dynamic link library (DLL), a shared library file. The problem only occurred when transferring files from an infected machine via a USB drive—the method of transport for Olympic Games' bug. It had escaped the perimeter of Natanz and was now in the wild wreaking havoc.

It fell to three Olympic Games insiders to break the news to Obama and Vice President Joe Biden. They cited an error with the code, blamed on the Israelis, which spread to an engineer's computer when it was connected to the centrifuges and ultimately passed to the Internet when the engineer left the confines of Natanz. Failing to recognize its environment had changed, it was now replicating itself across the World Wide Web. Though the extent of the bug's damage when infecting nontargeted machines remained to be seen, no one could deny that the US weapon was now on the loose. When Obama allegedly learned of the creation gone awry, he asked the obvious question, "Should we shut this thing down?"[32] Convinced that the bug was still undetected by the Iranians and was doing its part in disrupting Iran's nuclear pursuits, Olympic Games continued course.

It would take nearly a year before the bug, which came to be known as "Stuxnet" by the industry, was discovered. By then, internal Obama administration estimates suggested Iran's nuclear ambitions were set back 18 to 24 months. (However, some experts were more skeptical, suggesting that Iran had steadily recovered from the attack, enhancing production to develop multiple nuclear weapons within a couple of years of the attack.)[33] Olympic Games was estimated to cost between $5 million and $10 million to create—a downright bargain when compared with the billions of dollars invested in the Manhattan Project. Plus, Stuxnet required no fatalities to inflict its harm. By most accounts, it temporarily achieved its mission with little consequences, including the spilled blood and treasure that may have been contemplated with a more drastic military strike.

Yet, unlike an atomic bomb that detonates on impact, leaving no remnant for enemies to reverse engineer its design, Stuxnet was more like the proverbial Frankenstein, who escaped his confines to wreak havoc on his villagers, including his creator. In October 2012, US Defense Secretary Leon Panetta warned that the United States was vulnerable to a "cyber Pearl Harbor" that could derail trains, poison water supplies, and cripple power grids.[34] According to insiders, Obama was familiar with the risks he assumed in waging cyberwar against his country's enemies, repeatedly expressing concerns that any acknowledgement of the United States engaging in such tactics would give justification to other nations, hackers, or terrorists to launch the same—an irony that was discussed "more than once."[35] While the United States may not flinch at a few million dollars investment to engineer one of the most advanced computer worms ever released, the black hat community of hackers would otherwise experience a considerable barrier to entry in pursuing the same. Thanks to its unintended release, the code could now be reverse engineered by any motivated criminal with intentions of his own—be they for profit, principle, or province. And, there was no nation's infrastructure more dependent on computer infrastructure than the United States, leaving it the most vulnerable to an attack that may use some of the secret sauce initially developed by itself in Stuxnet.[36]

Cyberwarfare ushered in another set of crucial conversations yet unexplored in this latest arms race. In May 2010, the US Cyber Command was officially activated, taking over cyberwarfare initiatives from each of the branches of the US armed forces. With the lines between physical and virtual worlds all but obliterated, the question of when to use traditional military force as opposed to cyberforce had become murky at best. The Cyber Command's chief, Army General Keith Alexander, raised the controversial point in 2010 in a hearing before the Senate Armed Services Committee. Specifically, how would a nation formulate the right response based on nothing more than a rough inkling of a hacker's true intent? Further, when would a nation move from merely defending itself against cyberwarfare to initiating an offensive war to advance its pursuits or neutralize its enemies? As Alexander opined,

> These are tough issues, especially when attribution and neutrality are brought in, and when trying to figure out what's come in. [We don't have] the authority . . . to reach out into a neutral country and do an attack. And therein lies the complication. . . . What do you do to take that second step?[37]

Of course, cyberwarfare remains serious business for any reasonable citizen concerned about his welfare when institutional underpinnings, like transportation systems, power grids, and financial exchanges, are under threat. But, this threat vector is unique in that it pits one nation against another. Private organizations may find themselves caught in the crossfire but would not expect to be the intended target of such an attack in the first place, leading some companies to believe they are immune from nation-state threat actors. Of course, this assumption has already been disproven in at least one case.

Fun with a Dash of Smarts

The week of US Thanksgiving is typically slow for most companies. Employees are busy making holiday arrangements for the condensed three-day workweek, as they ready family festivities of feasting, shopping, and fellowship with loved ones. Thus, when the Monday before Thanksgiving rolled around in 2014, employees at Sony Pictures were expecting a rather uneventful week. At around 8:15 that morning, the uneventful turned unexpected, when a "black screen of death" savaged employees' computers, accompanied by the sound of gunfire and the gruesome image of a fiery skeleton looming over the tiny zombie heads of the studio's top two executives, with this chilling warning:

> We've already warned you and this is just a beginning.
>
> We continue till our request be met.
>
> We've obtained all your internal data including your secrets and top secrets.
>
> If you don't obey us, we'll release data shown below to the world.
>
> Determine what will you do till November the 24th, 11:00 PM (GMT)...
>
> And even if you just try to seek out who we are, all of your data will be released at once.[38]

Unaware of what was happening, the company promptly shut down its network, paralyzing any hopes of productivity for the already abbreviated workweek. But, before its cyber professionals had pulled the plug, hackers had already contaminated half of Sony's network, erasing everything stored on 3,262 of the company's 6,797 personal computers and 837 of its 1,555 servers. To ensure the data remained unrecoverable, the hackers took an extra step in installing a special deleting algorithm that overwrote the data seven different ways.[39]

At first, employees were in the dark on the gravity of the attack, chalking it up to just an innocuous run-of-the-mill prankster hack. At least one employee's account speaks of the lightheartedness that was first experienced when the assault happened (in spite of the grisly message), joking that it might take "a while" to get her work life back before wrapping up another calendar year.[40] However, by the beginning of the following week, after the Thanksgiving dust had settled and employees returned to their normal grind, it had become apparent this was no ordinary hack. By Wednesday of that week, employees were told to hurriedly change bank, insurance, and other online passwords. They were provided with a complimentary identity protection service, courtesy of the company, a nice token but also a stark reality check that this was serious. Desperate for answers and relegated to the dark ages of working with pen and paper, employees scoured online blogs to find out what had occurred. The answer would send shockwaves well beyond the studio lot of Sony Pictures.

Over the next three weeks, the hackers posted nine batches of confidential files exfiltrated from Sony's network. As if someone were rummaging through the company's underwear drawers, everything from unfinished movie scripts to embarrassing e-mails to more than 47,000 social security numbers of employees (many of whom had not worked for Sony in some years) were fair game in public domain.[41] Unfortunately, this wasn't the first time Sony found itself the victim of a major breach. In 2011, in what would become known as the company's "war on hackers," the company fought back against a well-known hacker, George Hotz, for jailbreaking his Sony PlayStation and making his methods known to his counterparts the world over when he posted instructions on the Internet. The company's lawsuit against Hotz drew the ire of hackers who idolized the 21-year-old as one of their own. In April of that year, they successfully penetrated Sony's network and exposed the personally identifiable information for 77 million customers and credit card information for 10 million of them.[42] Sony was caught flat-footed and was forced to shut down its PlayStation network for more than three weeks, incurring a cost of $171 million. Before 2011 was over, Sony would fall victim to another 20 cyberattacks. Sony Pictures itself was the target of one such breach perpetrated by Anonymous splinter group LulzSec, whose stated intentions were simply to reveal how vulnerable the company was to such "easy" infiltration: "From a single injection, we accessed EVERYTHING. Why do you put such faith in a company that allows itself to become open to these simple attacks?"[43] With Sony on the ropes and its cyberdefenses questionable at best, a new term entered the blogosphere lexicon, "Sownage," as in "being totally owned like Sony."[44] With the stinging memory of the 2011 hacks likely still fresh in the minds of Sony Pictures executives, they may have been left to wonder if this latest breach was a repeat performance from Anonymous (which publicly targeted Sony during the Hotz trial) or LulzSec. But, if hacktivists were to blame, what was their reason this time around?

Long before the 2014 hack, Sony Pictures was suffering from a string of disappointing ventures. What was supposed to be a hero project for the studio, *Amazing Spider-Man 2*, left executives disillusioned by worldwide ticket sales of $709 million—far below the expected $865 million take. That same summer, the comedy *Sex Tape* added to the studio's pressures, offering an unequivocal flop at the box office. Studio head Amy Pascal needed a hit. A longtime industry professional, Pascal's rolodex was a veritable *Who's Who* of Hollywood stars. Among those with whom she had cultivated close relationships were comedian Seth Rogen and his collaborator Evan Goldberg, who had given Pascal a string of profitable movies dating back to 2007's *Superbad*. The two had recently finished their latest production, *The Interview*, which was ultimately set for wide release on Christmas Day.[45]

The Interview featured a controversial plot, wrapped in comedic devices. The main stars, one of whom is Rogen, are a host and producer of a tabloid talk show that has earned the admiration of North Korea leader Kim Jong-un—a fan of the program who invites the pair to his country for an interview. The CIA enlists the duo to assassinate Kim. In the final climactic scene, Kim goes down in flames in a helicopter gunned down by the twosome from a commandeered tank.

In test screenings, response to *The Interview* was strong. Sony Pictures invested big in their next venture, keen to keep the profitable relationship with Rogen and Goldberg on good terms. With a $44 million production budget and $32 million set aside for marketing expenses, the studio expected great returns from the project—at least $100 million to $135 million at the box office.[46] Undeterred by the questionable decision to feature a real-life world leader as the target of an assassination in a fictional movie, studio executives greenlit the venture with enthusiasm. Dwight Caines, Sony's president of theatrical marketing, wrote Rogen in May with his accolades,

The movie is doing something bold that I'm not sure any other movie has done before—taking on as its subject matter a real persona of this notoriety. This is the kind of angle that makes this notable . . . fun with a dash of smarts.[47]

The media began linking the controversial film to Sony's hack within four days of the attack. By December 8, the group responsible for the attack, known as only "Guardians of Peace" (GOP), demanded that Sony "stop immediately showing the movie of terrorism."[48] Upping the ante, the GOP vowed to unleash physical acts of terrorism to movie theaters showing the film, equating the potential violence to another 9/11-style attack. With tensions reaching a boiling point, Sony Pictures relented, shelving the project and drawing criticism from fans and President Obama alike for surrendering to terrorist pressures. On December 19, the FBI blamed the hack on North Korea and Obama imposed economic sanctions as a result. Obama's response was measured as he had promised reporters at an end-of-year press conference, "We will respond proportionally, and we'll respond in a place and time and manner that we choose."[49]

As for Sony Pictures, the hack would see the ousting of studio chief Pascal, who was unable to recover from the spectacle of a highly doomed project and scandalous personal e-mails that were leaked in the breach. Though *The Interview* would go on to set a new record of $40 million in video-on-demand revenues, the highest grossing digital seller in Sony's history at the time,[50] it would fall drastically short of the once lofty expectations for a dream team that was the studio's money-printing machine. And, for companies the world over that once thought themselves immune to such an assault, Sony Pictures offered a cautionary tale of an adversary cut from a different cloth—this time, that of a nation-state.

A Second Thought

Ask a company executive where the next hacker threat could be looming and you would be hard pressed to find "nation-state" rise anywhere near the top of the list. The reason is perfectly understandable, as drawing the fury of an entire country bent on destroying one's private company seems to be a far-fetched possibility. Yet, as the Sony Pictures example reminds us, though nation-state attacks may be rare, they pack a powerful punch. And, even if not the direct target of a nation-state attack, companies may find themselves casualties in the crossfire. Take Siemens, the manufacturer of the industrial control systems inflicted by the Stuxnet worm. Though Siemens was not the intended victim of Stuxnet, the company found itself doing damage control after the worm broke free in the wild. Within a few quarters of outbreak, Siemens reported at least 14 plants infected,[51] creating noise in the public discourse over the security of the company.

In revisiting our formula to better understand the incentives available to nation-state actors and the probability (P) behind such an attack:

$$P = (Incentive \ x \ Opportunity) / Risk$$

Incentive in this case goes to the nation's political ambitions, such as thwarting an enemy's nuclear ambitions or shelving a politically insensitive film. How easily such a mission can be fulfilled, the opportunity, is evaluated differently when cyberwarfare is involved. No longer forced to operate within extensive spy networks that physically transfer secrets via covert audio and visual signals, cyberwarfare has the potential to infiltrate enemy networks and wreak havoc on industrial control systems, be they nuclear centrifuges, electrical power grids, or any myriad examples in between. Finally, the risk involved speaks not only to a nation being outed in its pursuits but to the chance that its own creation (as the Stuxnet case so vividly illustrates) becomes open intellectual property to its enemies. Furthermore, nations must carefully measure the proportional response from their targeted victim based on how the threat is perceived—whether as intelligence gathering, espionage, or an act of war.

Much like the nuclear race before it, this is a dangerous game in which nations engage, largely because they feel they have no choice. The best way to prevent absolute power is to ready one's own capabilities to rule absolutely. As cyberwarfare missions become more exposed, proportional force will become the delicate fulcrum through which responses are balanced. Hack a major movie studio in the United States? You may find yourself the recipient of economic sanctions. Attempt to take out the financial underpinnings of an economy? The result may be a far more severe countermeasure, potentially even drifting into "traditional" military campaigns to address the most insidious virtual attacks. And, when does one play offense in striking first versus defensively protecting oneself? Further, how does one properly attribute the motive and identity of hackers with code that can so easily be obfuscated even upon detection? If not properly identified, the target may be a hapless scapegoat, as Ethel Rosenberg found herself, or, worse, may retaliate in kind with retribution of its own. Each of these questions and more will plague the next generation of leaders—both of governments and of private organizations which may find themselves the targets or casualties of unprecedented assaults. Only one certainty persists—in *The Second Economy*, the rules of engagement will continue to be rewritten in this fifth plane of warfare.

A SECOND HELPING OF THE SONY PICTURES HACK

Sony Pictures CEO Michael Lynton found himself at the center of the storm when his company was hacked in 2014. In a December interview with National Public Radio, the executive defended his company's cyberdefenses, asserting it was "extremely well prepared for conventional cybersecurity," but fell victim to "the worst cyberattack in US history."[52] At the time, Lynton reported no plans to fire any of his cybersecurity team over the breach. Rationalizing his position, Lynton claimed the full force of a nation-state was simply too much for any privately run organization to bear. Citing evidence from the FBI and security forensics consultant Kevin Mandia, whom Sony retained to deconstruct the threat, the malware would have slipped through 90 percent of traditional defenses used by private industry and potentially even the government. Further, the exfiltration method employed a sophisticated trickle approach to inconspicuously abscond with large amounts of information slowly and deliberately to evade detection.[53]

Still, public interviews with Sony Pictures' head of cybersecurity, Jason Spaltro, paint a different picture of the company's conservative approach to cybersecurity, long before the 2014 breach or even the multiple attacks of 2012. In a 2007 interview with *CIO* magazine, Spaltro relayed the story of a Sarbanes-Oxley auditor who found several security weaknesses in a 2005 review. Among other items, the auditor cited that password compliance was virtually nonexistent, with employees failing to conform to the rules of setting more hardened passwords. Putting a finer point on his findings, the auditor warned Spaltro, "If you were a bank, you'd be out of business," to which the exasperated cybersecurity chief retorted, "If a bank was a Hollywood studio, it would be out of business."[54] Arguing that nonintuitive passwords would likely be accompanied by employees using Post-It notes stuck to screens and other devices with the passwords written in plain sight for any to abuse, Spaltro successfully convinced the auditor to ignore the weak password finding in the final report.

In his later recalling of the event to *CIO*, Spaltro offered the following balance that must be taken by any cybersecurity professional in a for-profit enterprise:

> There are decisions that have to be made. We're trying to remain profitable for our shareholders, and we literally could go broke trying to cover for everything. So, you make risk-based decisions: What're the most important things that are absolutely required by law?... Legislative requirements are mandatory, but going the extra step is a business decision.[55]

Speculating whether Spaltro effectively weighed these risks in light of the 2014 hack is as unfair as playing Monday morning quarterback after the weekend's big game. Who can anticipate if additional measures would have sufficiently thwarted a highly motivated nation-state adversary from penetrating Sony's perimeter, in this case through the use of a spear phishing campaign? The only certainty from the breach is the indescribable fallout for the company— particularly for executives like Pascal, who equated seeing her most intimate thoughts transmitted over private e-mails now plastered in the public arena for all to criticize as the metaphorical equivalent of being "raped"[56] or for the tens of thousands of current and former employees who must constantly look over their shoulders, lest they become victims of identity theft.

Anyone can have perfect vision in hindsight. And, facing a nation in an attack is certainly more complex than battling other types of adversaries. But, in looking at the Sony case, companies would be wise to reexamine the balance between protection and profit. As cybersecurity expert James Lewis, senior fellow at the Center for Strategic and International Studies, puts it, "The fact that it's a nation-state and is hard to defeat doesn't mean you have to leave the doors wide open and put out the welcome mat."[57]

Notes

1. "Espionage: Still Defiant," *TIME*, January 12, 1953, http://content.time.com/time/subscriber/printout/0,8816,817678,00.html, accessed May 29, 2016.

2. United States Holocaust Memorial Museum, "Axis Alliance in World War II," www.ushmm.org/wlc/en/article.php?ModuleId=10005177, accessed May 29, 2016.

3. TIME Staff, "World War: Grey Friday," *TIME*, September 11, 1939, http://time.com/3195322/world-war-grey-friday/, accessed May 29, 2016.

4. "US at War," *TIME*, August 13, 1945, p. 19, http://time.com/vault/issue/1945-08-13/page/19/, accessed May 29, 2016.

5. Harry S. Truman Library, "Army press notes," box 4, Papers of Eben A. Ayers, August 6, 1945, www.pbs.org/wgbh/americanexperience/features/primary-resources/truman-hiroshima/, accessed May 29, 2016.

6. Ibid.

7. Manhattan District History, Book I, Volume 14, *Intelligence and Security*, http://fas.org/sgp/library/mdhist-vol14.pdf, accessed May 29, 2016.

8. Ibid.

9. Biography.com Editors, "Julius Rosenberg Biography," A&E Television Networks, www.biography.com/people/julius-rosenberg-21168439, accessed May 30, 2016.

10. Rebecca Onion, "The Jell-O Box That Helped Convict the Rosenbergs," *Slate*, February 20, 2013, www.slate.com/blogs/the_vault/2013/02/20/ethel_and_julius_rosenberg_how_a_jell_o_box_helped_convict_them.html, accessed May 30, 2016.

11. Ronald Radosh and Steven Usdin, "The Sobell Confession," *The Weekly Standard*, March 28, 2011, www.weeklystandard.com/the-sobell-confession/article/554817, accessed May 30, 2016.

12. Sam Roberts, "Figure in Rosenberg Case Admits to Soviet Spying," *The New York Times*, September 11, 2008, www.nytimes.com/2008/09/12/nyregion/12spy.html?_r=0, accessed May 30, 2016.

13. Jennifer Latson, "One of America's Most Famous Spies Didn't Do Any Spying," *TIME*, March 6, 2015, http://time.com/3720514/rosenberg-execution/?iid=sr-link1, accessed May 30, 2016.

14. David Sanger, "Obama Order Sped Up Wave of Cyberattacks Against Iran," *The New York Times*, June 1, 2012, www.nytimes.com/2012/06/01/world/middleeast/obama-ordered-wave-of-cyberattacks-against-iran.html?pagewanted=1&_r=2&hp, accessed May 30, 2016.

15. Ibid.

16. Ibid.

17. Ibid.

18. Ibid.

19. Kim Zetter, "US Used Zero-Day Exploits Before It Had Policies for Them," *Wired*, March 30, 2015, www.wired.com/2015/03/us-used-zero-day-exploits-policies/, accessed May 30, 2016.

20. Brian Fung, "The NSA hacks other countries by buying millions of dollars' worth of computer vulnerabilities," *The Washington Post*, August 31, 2013, www.washingtonpost.com/news/the-switch/wp/2013/08/31/the-nsa-hacks-other-countries-by-buying-millions-of-dollars-worth-of-computer-vulnerabilities/, accessed May 30, 2016.

21. Sanger, note 14 *supra*.

22. Kim Zetter, "An Unprecedented Look at Stuxnet, the World's First Digital Weapon," *Wired*, November 3, 2014, www.wired.com/2014/11/countdown-to-zero-day-stuxnet/, accessed May 30, 2016.

23. Richard Sale, "Stuxnet Loaded by Iran Double Agents," *ISS Source*, April 11, 2012, www.isssource.com/stuxnet-loaded-by-iran-double-agents/, accessed May 30, 2016.

24. Sanger, note 14 *supra*.

25. Ibid.

26. Zetter, note 22 *supra*.

27. Ibid.

28. Ibid.

29. Ibid.

30. Ibid.

31. Ibid.

32. Sanger, note 14 *supra*.

33. Ibid.

34. David Kushner, "The Real Story of Stuxnet," *IEEE Spectrum*, February 26, 2013, http://spectrum.ieee.org/telecom/security/the-real-story-of-stuxnet, accessed May 30, 2016.

35. Sanger, note 14 *supra*.

36. Ibid.

37. Seymour M. Hersh, "The Online Threat," *The New Yorker*, November 1, 2010, www.newyorker.com/magazine/2010/11/01/the-online-threat, accessed May 30, 2016.

38. Peter Elkind, "Inside the Hack of the Century," *Fortune* (Part 1), July 1, 2015a, http://fortune.com/sony-hack-part-1/, accessed May 30, 2016.

39. Ibid.

40. Sheila Marikar, "I work at Sony Pictures. This is what it was like after we got hacked.," *Fortune*, December 20, 2014, http://fortune.com/2014/12/20/sony-pictures-entertainment-essay/, accessed May 30, 2016.

41. Elkind, note 38 *supra*.

42. Peter Elkind, "Inside the Hack of the Century," *Fortune* (Part 2), July 1, 2015b, http://fortune.com/sony-hack-part-two/, accessed May 30, 2016.

43. Ibid.

44. Ibid.

45. Elkind, note 38 *supra*.

46. Ibid.

47. Ibid.

48. Peter Elkind, "Inside the Hack of the Century," *Fortune* (Part 3), July 1, 2015c, http://fortune.com/sony-hack-final-part/, accessed May 30, 2016.

49. Gregory Korte and David Jackson, "Obama sanctions North Korea for movie hacking," *USA Today*, January 2, 2015, www.usatoday.com/story/news/politics/2015/01/02/obama-north-korea-sanctions-interview-movie/21195385/, accessed May 30, 2016.

50. Elkind, note 48 *supra*.

51. Robert McMillan, "Siemens: Stuxnet Worm Hit Industrial Systems," *PC World*, September 14, 2010, www.pcworld.com/article/205420/article.html, accessed June 2, 2016.

52. Elkind, note 38 *supra*.

53. Ibid.

54. Allan Holmes "Your Guide To Good-Enough Compliance," *CIO*, April 6, 2007, www.cio.com/article/2439324/risk-management/your-guide-to-good-enough-compliance.html, accessed May 30, 2016.

55. Ibid.

56. Elkind, note 48 *supra*.

57. Elkind, note 38 *supra*.

CHAPTER 5

■ ■ ■

Second-Guessing the Obvious

Trust takes years to build, seconds to break and forever to repair.

—Unknown

It's the equivalent of a tombstone for a company that once was. When a company goes bust, its web site disappears almost overnight, often replaced by a seemingly cheery "For Sale" sign that the domain is available for the next buyer. Currently, that "For Sale" sign is prominently displayed at the former virtual address of Code Spaces. It, along with some news stories of the company's demise, is all that remains of a small business that met its untimely end. Code Spaces was hardly a household name. Its specialty was in lending its expertise to software developers with tools offered via Amazon Web Services (AWS). It did so using Amazon's vast infrastructure of computer processing power in the public cloud to elastically scale its business and grow with its customers. It was a bona fide business model that sustained the company for seven years. Unfortunately, its run ended with one hack that made a casualty rather than headlines.

In the postmortem, it appears a hacker found his way into Code Spaces' AWS control panel, likely through a phishing scheme. Getting access to the AWS control panel is akin to entering the data center for the company; in essence, the hacker could use his stolen credentials to manipulate or otherwise destroy any of Code Spaces' data. He was motivated by profit, demanding Code Spaces pay a ransom to bid him adieu without further harm. Given Code Spaces' expertise in the information technology (IT) field, it attempted to quickly lock down its data and assets before he had the chance. Unfortunately, its efforts were futile. When the hacker realized that his intended victim was not paying up, he punished Code Spaces severely, destroying its virtual assets and records with a few keystrokes and mouse clicks.

If there really was a virtual resting place for Code Spaces' remains on the Internet, it could come with this epitaph to memorialize its victim, based on the company's final statement the day it closed up shop:

> Code Spaces will not be able to operate beyond this point, the cost of resolving this issue to date and the expected cost of refunding customers who have been left without the service they paid for will put Code Spaces in an irreversible position both financially and in terms of ongoing credibility.[1]

77

S. Grobman and A. Cerra, *The Second Economy*, DOI 10.1007/978-1-4842-2229-4_5

With 52 words, the seven-year-old going concern was no more. Code Spaces found itself in the graveyard with nearly 60 percent of other small business victims that fold within six months of experiencing a cyberattack.[2] Despite the crushing blow cyberattacks have on small businesses, in particular, one would think there would be far more outrage over the Wild Wild West that has become the World Wide Web. Adversaries are ever increasingly incentivized by profit, principle, or province. A commensurate level of motivation appears lacking on the part of most businesses and consumers who continue along, business-as-usual, as hacks become more commonplace. It begs two questions: Is there really a lack of motivation on the part of these potential victims? And, if so, why?

Consider one of the first major breaches to make headlines: TJX, parent company to merchants TJ Maxx, Marshalls, Home Goods, and A. J. Wright and the leading off-price retailer of apparel and fashions worldwide. In 2007, hackers virtually entered the retail conglomerate's central database in Framingham, Massachusetts, through two Marshalls stores in Miami.[3] There, using a telescope-shaped antenna pointed at their targets, the thieves intercepted the bits of data streaming through the air between the merchant's hand-held price-checking devices, cash registers, and computers.[4] Once in, the hackers made off with 45.7 million credit and debit card numbers along with personally identifiable information (social security numbers, military identification, and driver's license numbers) for more than 450,000 customers.[5] The intruders remained undetected within the retail giant's most sensitive systems for two years.[6]

Upon news breaking on the largest breach in history at the time, TJX once again found itself a victim as it faced excoriation in the court of public opinion. Investigators criticized the company for collecting too much information about its customers, such as driver's license and social security numbers, and retaining such sensitive data interminably. The company took heat for purportedly using weaker wireless security than what was available in many home-based networks at the time, making the attack "as easy as breaking into a house through a side window that was wide open," according to a source familiar with the investigation.[7] Class-action lawsuits followed[8] and future losses seemed inevitable, with more than 20 percent of the company's customers indicating they were "much less inclined" to shop at its stores.[9] Compromised victims, including Marilyn Oliver of San Marcos, California, who was alerted that her Visa account had been used to buy 40 $400 gift cards at a single Florida Walmart location, were sufficiently frightened to take precautions: "It sort of unnerves you. I'm very cautious, I shred everything."[10] Affected banks, both large and small, were consumed in the aftermath. According to the chief executive officer (CEO) of a small Louisiana savings bank that had sustained $23,000 in fraudulent losses from the incident, "All bankers are talking about these days is the TJX situation."[11] One analyst speculated total damages to TJX would exceed $1 billion over a five-year period[12]—a somber warning to purveyors of reputable businesses wary of being the next poster child victim. In short, consumer and industry outrage were palpable.

One year passed. TJX acknowledged the breach had been costly, setting aside about $250 million in breach-related costs, including all claims, lawsuits, fines, and security fixes associated with the attack.[13] Still, with more than $17 billion in net sales at the time[14] and the hysteria that accompanied the event, TJX seemed to have dodged a bullet in suffering a less than 2 percent impact to the top line. But, looking at only the costs of the breach ignores the impact to future revenues from all those customers who lost trust in the retailer following the massive incursion—particularly the more than one in five indicating they were much less inclined to continue doing business with the brand as a result. There again, the results may be surprising. In the 48-week period that followed, the company saw its comparable store sales *increase* 4 percent. But, what about shareholders? Surely, investors would vote with their wallets after seeing the vulnerability of their investment fall to such an audacious attack. Again, not so. TJX's stock was worth about $30 at the time the breach was announced. One year later, Wall Street appeared largely unshaken by the incident, keeping the company's stock more than afloat at $29.[15]

TJX would be followed by other major companies in a hit parade of major cybercrime victims—each experiencing market fire from media and customers when the breaches occurred followed by similar market recoveries soon thereafter. Target suffered a very public breach of more than 100 million customer records that carried with it more damaging consequences, including the unceremonious exits of both its CEO and CIO (chief information officer). Yet, even though Target's breach was orders of magnitude more significant than that of TJX, its stock quickly recovered from a nearly 14 percent drop after the attack,[16] rebounding with a five-year record high in percentage regain a few months later.[17] The Home Depot, which would lose even more credit and debit card records than Target to cybercriminals, saw its stock price decrease minimally one week after going public with the incident and posted a 21 percent increase in earnings per share the same quarter.[18] Adobe, eBay, and JPMorgan Chase all found themselves in the public eye for major breaches. All were granted forgiveness from Wall Street with stock prices that were higher one year following the attacks.[19]

Enough, Already!

While investors may have short memories, one could reasonably assume the average consumer would not suffer such amnesia. Remember the great concern following the TJX hit from those like Marilyn Oliver, shaken enough to shred "everything" to prevent themselves from falling prey to the next predator? Indeed, by 2014, cybercrime's rash had spread to nearly 50 percent of consumers who reported their personally identifiable information (such as social security, driver's license and credit card numbers, and medical records) had been compromised in similar breaches.[20] Among the afflicted, more than three-quarters claimed stress as the most significant consequence,[21] highlighting the often underestimated emotional aftermath of such attacks. That same year, the top 20 organizations worldwide that went public with their own cybercrime account of hijacked data would collectively represent nearly 600 million compromised customer records.[22] Cybercriminals in pursuit of financial gain found their exploits the fodder for countless front-page headlines. Corporate victims could do little more than hope that consumers would be as forgiving as investors and not dispense their own punishment of revoked loyalty over time.

As it turns out, companies didn't have to rely on the generosity of consumers after all. In fact, while many organizations likely loathed being raked over the coals by journalists seeking their next big byline article, such media buzz may have actually benefited the corporations under scrutiny. Consumers were simply overwhelmed by the media onslaught of what seemed to be the never-ending story of entities victimized by the next major cyberattack. As the noise increased, consumer attention decreased. While 70 percent of consumers were aware of the Target hack in 2014, only 58 percent knew of the even larger The Home Depot breach.[23] Eight other notable cyberattacks, including eBay and JPMorgan Chase, found no more than 23 percent of consumers mindful of the incident.[24] Perhaps worse, in a case of mistaken identity, some consumers ascribed cybertheft incursions to other targets entirely. For instance, 15 percent of consumers mistakenly assigned JPMorgan Chase's breach to Bank of America.[25] Similarly, nearly 20 percent assumed Facebook had suffered an attack, rather than actual victim AOL.[26]

With a new epidemic sweeping the market, aptly termed "breach fatigue," consumers simply tuned out the negative press and reverted to their banal, habitual behaviors. Unisys' annual survey measuring concerns around personal data security recorded a 2014 US Security Index score of 123 out of a possible 300.[27] Putting this number into context, it was the second lowest score since Unisys began conducting the study in 2007.[28] When asked to explain the counterintuitive results in the wake of so many exposed breaches in 2014, Unisys Chief Information Security Officer Dave Frymier could only offer the following:

> Despite highly publicized data breaches and hacker attacks, the majority of people have not been personally harmed by cyber-crimes because the losses are absorbed by businesses and financial institutions. This is bad news for businesses, because the average consumer has little incentive to avoid risky online behavior.[29]

Indeed, nearly one in two consumers admitted that the spate of cyberattacks had not affected their use of credit or debit cards, with one out of every three Americans using the same one or two passwords for all their online accounts.[30] Perhaps most alarming, a 2014 Ponemon Institute study found that when consumers received data breach notifications, nearly one-third *ignored the notifications and did nothing.*"[31]

It's somewhat shocking to consider that nearly one-third of breached customers would ignore a data breach warning and continue about their merry way. We may criticize consumers for such reckless behavior, holding ourselves to a much higher standard. And, one could assume business leaders to be immune from such apparent apathy, as they take the mantle of cybersecurity much more seriously for their firms. Certainly, if you received a warning of a cyberthreat sweeping the world, even perhaps impacting your personally identifiable information or that of your customers, you would take immediate and decisive action to protect yourself and your company. *Or, would you?*

Before you answer with conviction, consider that human nature has an interesting way of responding to potential threats. First, one would need to properly measure the degree of risk involved to effectively respond. Our human brain is a highly complex organ that is pre-programmed with instinctual capabilities to keep us alive. It can almost instantaneously register risk for known dangers (think snakes, axe murderers, or extreme heights) and immediately trigger the body's natural fight-or-flight response. However, our brains haven't sufficiently evolved to properly assess more nuanced threats common in a modern world (think pollution, obesity, and, yes, cybercrime). As such, one's natural ability to properly calculate risk can be, and often is, impaired.

There are several documented ways we misinterpret risk that are germane to our topic.

1. *We tend to underestimate threats that creep up on us.* We're more likely to engage in behaviors that don't produce immediate negative consequences. Eating a cupcake won't suddenly cause death. Eating thousands of them over a lifetime can lead to serious consequences, some life-threatening, such as heart disease. Yet, humans continue to rationalize bad habits given the long-term consequences are hard to define, if not difficult to imagine. Our inability to properly measure the cumulative effects of seemingly minor risks has been attributed to such things as unplanned

pregnancies. At most points during the menstrual cycle, the odds of pregnancy are low; however, after a full year of unprotected sex, some 85 percent of couples experience an unplanned pregnancy.[32] In cybersecurity terms, it's easy to conceive how habitual behaviors, such as using the same password for multiple sites over a long period of time, become defensible to consumers who can't calculate the snowballing risk of doing so or fathom the thought of a cyberpredator waiting for just one of these defenses to fall.

Let's use a mathematical example to illustrate. Suppose the probability of a major cyber breach on any given day is 1 in 450. We would represent this as 1/450 or 0.0022. We could also then say that the probability of a major event not happening on any particular day is 1-0.0022 or 0.9977 —well that looks pretty good right? A 99.77 percent chance of not having a major event is pretty good odds, or is it? We can calculate the odds that we will not have a major event every day for a year by calculating $(0.9977)^{365} = 0.4315$, so only a 43 percent chance that, in a year, we will not have at least one event. Or, said another way, we have a 57 percent chance that there will be at least one major incident during the year. All of a sudden, the odds seem a lot less appealing.

2. *We mistakenly overcompensate to avoid risks, thereby putting ourselves in harm's way of a new threat entirely.* After 9/11, people were justifiably fearful of flying. Some 1.4 million people changed their travel plans to avoid planes altogether, opting to drive to their holiday destinations. Unfortunately, driving is far more dangerous than flying, as countless statistics prove year after year. As such, an additional 1,000 automobile accident fatalities occurred in 2001[33]—roughly one-third the death toll of the 9/11 attacks—casualties that could have been prevented had the individuals opted for safer plane travel instead. In the cybersecurity world, consumers may restrict behaviors they believe to be dangerous, such as online shopping, only to increase patronage at brick-and-mortar establishments. Yet, as we have already discussed, these retailers are themselves increasingly the target for major breaches,[34] in particular for thieves looking to abscond with massive hauls of credit card or personally identifiable information.

3. *We believe our risks decrease in situations where we have the illusion of control.* The post-9/11, ill-fated automobile victims had more confidence in their own ability to safely drive an automobile with no threat of terrorist attack than relinquish control on a plane where a hijacking could happen. When we believe we are in control of the risks around us, we tend to underestimate them as a result. According to one risk consultant,

Many people report that when they move from the driver's seat to the passenger's seat, the car in front of them looks closer and their foot goes to the imaginary brake. You're likely to be less scared with the steering wheel in your hand, because you can do something about your circumstances, and that's reassuring.[35]

Such psychology helps explain why we fear drivers distracted by cell phones, all the while remaining completely confident in our own abilities to slip in that impulsive text behind the wheel. It also helps clarify why some 50 percent of IT security decision makers surveyed in a 2016 McAfee study were more confident in their own team's ability to address the next cybersecurity threat, rather than the expertise of a partner with presumably more credentials.

4.   *We replace one risk for another.* Initially, drivers in the UK who purchased cars with safer brakes were offered insurance discounts. That has since changed, since these drivers didn't experience fewer accidents, just different ones. It's the same reason that vehicles with four-wheel drive are also the ones most likely to go out of control in snowy conditions. It's called risk substitution and it involves our natural tendency to modulate behavior to keep risk at a constant level. Automobile features designed to increase safety, such as air bags and antilock brakes, create a false sense of security that unintentionally leads to unsafe driving. As such, while risk may be mitigated in one case, it is compensated by substitutionary behavior in another. Putting this in perspective, Paul Slovic, president of Decision Research, quipped, "If I drink a diet soda with dinner, I have ice cream for dessert."[36] Relating this to cybersecurity, consumers with antivirus protection may mistakenly assume they are immune from all threats—including complex, zero-day attacks that bypass antivirus defenses—and engage in more hazardous online behaviors as a result. Further, companies deploying a specific cybersecurity product that may defend one aspect of their environment, such as the network or the cloud, may find themselves exposed when employees with a false sense of confidence engage in risky behaviors using unprotected devices, such as mobile clients.

Let's assume consumers and businesses have an accurate measure of risk and don't succumb to any of these vulnerabilities seemingly wired in our human nature. The next challenge now requires individuals to be accountable for the risks they take—rather than passing the consequences off to someone else entirely.

Passing the Buck

Economists call it moral hazard. It occurs when one party gets involved in a precarious situation knowing that another party bears the brunt of the risk. Large companies aren't exactly incentivized to prevent the next major cyberattack, given that the most public breaches of our day have resulted in little more than a temporary loss of profits and shareholder value (the exception to this rule involves company executives protecting their jobs and reputations, but, even then, organizational reward structures around cybercrime defense are often misdirected, as we will discuss in the next chapter). Small businesses are much more likely to be casualties in the fight, yet headlines don't exactly cover the sensational stories of the Code Spaces lost along the way. American consumers aren't on the hook as, at the time of this writing, losses are limited to $50 upon timely reporting of fraudulent charges.

While large companies and consumers appear less incentivized to care, there is one constituency with sufficient motivation to combat the next threat. Banks and credit card companies have historically suffered the most when cybercrime rears its head. Even still, JPMorgan Chase's CEO Jamie Dimon acknowledged an annual budget of $250 million on cybersecurity —at the time, roughly .35 percent of the company's annual expenses.[37] If a company with the weight of cybercrime risk on its shoulders allocated less than a half of a percent of its expense budget on the topic, one can justifiably assume the average firm would spend even less.

In 2015, legislation sought to balance risk between card issuer and merchant. The United States was the last of the G20 nations to move to more secure chip-based cards, otherwise known as the EMV (Europay, MasterCard, and Visa) standard. Chip-based cards were believed to be safer than traditional debit and credit cards since account information stored on cards is encrypted uniquely each time it is accessed. On October 1, 2015, new MasterCard and Visa rules shifted the liability of fraudulent purchases to merchants in cases where the customer presented a chip-based card and was not asked or able to "dip the chip"[38] (a case where the customer inserted the chip-based card in a special point-of-sale terminal). With the burden of risk shifting to retailers that did not honor the chip-based card, one would have expected a mass rush to deploy and utilize chip-based point-of-sale devices with every transaction. Again, this assumption underestimated powerful inertia in reverting to old habits.

In January 2016, Visa CEO Charles W. Scharf reported in the company's earnings call that 17 percent of US brick-and-mortar locations were enabled to handle chip-based transactions.[39] Stated less positively, more than four in five face-to-face merchants had failed to deploy chip-based readers several months after the legislative deadline. Smaller retailers blamed the delay on the prohibitive costs of deploying the new terminals, estimated at up to $2,000 each.[40] Larger establishments had a different take on the challenge—that is, chip-based cards seemed to fly in the face of an instant-gratification culture. The processing time involved in reading a dipped chip card could take up to 20 seconds longer than a simple magnetic swipe transaction.[41] One consumer summed up the sentiment that caused so many like her to revert back to what was comfortable, familiar, and convenient: "Most retailers don't even have the chip reader turned on. When they do, it takes way too long. I always opt to just run it through the old way [via magnetic stripe swipe]."[42] And so, some retailers competing on every dimension of customer experience, including speedy checkout lines, opted to shift the cost and inconvenience of retraining consumers to their competitors, particularly before the busy holiday shopping season when the new liability rules went into effect.

As Visa and its cohorts attempted to compel reluctant US retailers to move to the chip-based standard, they found themselves defending their case against other retailers claiming chip-based cards did not go far enough in preventing fraud. As liability rules shifted, a new era of litigation dawned. At the time of this writing, Walmart, a retail juggernaut with close to 12,000 stores across the world,[43] was suing Visa for not moving more swiftly to more secure standards. Specifically, the retailer claimed that Visa's mandate of chip-and-signature (where a chip-based card is presented with only a customer's signature required to complete the transaction) to be less stringent than chip-and-PIN (where the card must be accompanied by a PIN (personal identification number), presumably only known by the authorized cardholder). The suit claimed chip-and-signature to be inadequate in retarding fraud rates, as it failed to account for stolen debit cards where a signature could be easily forged. In making its case, Walmart argued that its data showed that 91 percent of fraudulent debit purchases were completed with signatures.[44] The retailer further asserted that Visa's policy was designed to generate more revenues for the credit card company, given that chip-and-signature transactions were routed across signature debit networks for approval—commanding higher fees than corresponding PIN debit networks. One can expect more litigation between ecosystem players as liabilities shift and legislations morphs, yet one more telltale sign of *The Second Economy*.

Perhaps legislation that balances the scales of risk between merchant and card issuer is necessary but not sufficient in compelling more vigilant behaviors against cybercrime. In 2015, law enforcement from at least one major global city proposed to shift even more responsibility to those consumers who willfully ignored breach warnings and did nothing to change their habits. A report commissioned by the City of London Police and the City of London Corporation provocatively concluded that forewarned victims who failed to take precautions against cyberattacks should be treated with lower priority than those who acted to improve their own security.[45] With the seemingly endless rise in cyberattacks, the study argued that limited law enforcement resources could be more optimally prioritized, placing greater accountability with individuals who would otherwise benefit from moral hazard inequalities, stating:

> For some individuals . . . it is arguable that they should not
> receive scarce policing resources because they have not
> exercised due diligence on their own behalf.[46]

If we suppose such proposed legislation found a wider audience of supporters around the globe, it does little to mitigate the risk companies face among their most vulnerable security component—their own employees. Sure, one could theoretically imagine legislation that assigns cybercrime losses commensurately across breached companies, issuing cardholders and potentially negligent consumers, but how does a CEO stop an attack in the first place when her own employees shirk responsibility for keeping their company safe? Even if corporate data is leaked or lost by the employee, one-fourth of American workers claimed it would not be their problem.[47] Again, moral hazard may be a bit to blame, as consequences rarely follow and ascription of risks are misaligned. Case in point: 59 percent of US employees estimated the value of the corporate data on their mobile phones to be less than $500 (a far cry from the actual value should such data lead to a massive breach of company systems). Further, of those employees who actually lost their mobile phone, 34 percent escaped punishment outright and 21 percent simply received a reprimand.

And so, in a never-ending saga of passing the buck, consumers, employees, and businesses alike perpetually kick the cybersecurity can down the road, relying on someone else to solve the problem or taking their chances with any consequences that may follow. Legislation may help but will take considerable time to enact and enforce. All the while, cybercriminals rely on this seemingly incurable, contagious apathy as they ready their next attack.

The Long Game

While the realities of moral hazard and breach fatigue certainly paint a sobering picture as to why cybersecurity presents such an enigma for larger companies—on one hand, no one wants to suffer the costs associated with a major breach; on the other, those who have endured such mainstream attacks have more than lived to fight another day shortly thereafter. But, perhaps the answer becomes much clearer when exploring a longer-term horizon than a few quarters following a major breach. In other words, what can history teach us about the value of corporate brand and reputation on long-term shareholder value?

Examining the question requires a view into the value of a large firm. In 1975, more than 80 percent of a firm's value on the S&P 500 consisted of tangible assets,[48] things like machinery, buildings, land, and inventory. By 2010, the inverse prevailed—80 percent of that same average corporation's value was based on intangible assets.[49] Within just a few decades, wide variations between a company's stock price and its underlying book value could only be described by what shareholders attributed to assets like patents, trademarks, copyrights, and brand equity. This last point is especially tricky. After all, when one introduces brand into a conversation of long-term shareholder value, it is often met with skeptical eye rolls about the true financial impact associated with the brand itself. Critics question how one can meaningfully disentangle brand from any other interdependent function of the enterprise, including products, quality, and innovation. Luckily, history provides more than enough evidence to understand how something as esoteric as brand—an asset developed and sustained over multiple years—can deliver real financial benefits to a company.

The goodness of a strong brand creates a virtuous circle, where each advantage builds on the one before it to create a situation where the whole is greater than the sum of its parts:

1. *Evidence supports that stronger brands command higher premiums* (read: higher margins) in market, all else being equal. While the finding prevails across multiple categories, consider one that is familiar to most, if not all, consumers—the automobile. In a practice known as "badge engineering," car manufacturers leverage the same factories, workers, and production lines to essentially produce identical cars, sans tiny cosmetic distinctions, with very different price tags depending on the logo stamped on the vehicle. These price premiums can be significant—as much as $31,000 for two similarly produced cars, albeit with different brand names.[50]

2. *Higher premiums create the perception of higher quality.* A 2008 study by Antonio Rangel of the California Institute of Technology found that if people are told a wine is expensive while drinking it, they really do think it tastes better than a cheap wine, rather than just saying they do. Dr. Rangel and his associates measured the neurological patterns of 20 volunteers to measure changes in the brain associated with registering pleasant experiences. Of course, the researchers used the same wines in the test and simply manipulated price points to determine the effect on respondents' evaluation and physiology.[51] Perceived quality has been linked to higher prices, in part, due to the brain's impulsive nature of finding shortcuts to decipher meaning.[52] Higher prices and higher quality naturally seem to go together, producing a convenient timesaver for overtaxed brains.

3. *Perceived quality has been shown to positively affect customer usage and loyalty.* Management consultant firm Bain & Company has found an undeniable linkage between customer loyalty and company growth. Specifically, its Net Promoter Score measures the likelihood of customers to refer a brand to their friends, less those who are not at all likely to do so. Firms with leading Net Promoter Scores grow at more than twice the rate of their competitors. And, companies that achieve long-term profitable growth have Net Promoter Scores two times higher than the average firm.[53]

The virtuous circle is complete: higher prices produce the perception of greater quality which creates more loyalty. But, this chain reaction starts with a strong brand. And, although distinctly different, brand equity and corporate reputation are inextricably linked, at least according to nearly three-quarters of US managers and executives.[54] Further, more than 90 percent of these leaders believe that privacy and data protection are important in protecting the organization's reputation and brand value. To this latter point, brand value is worth preserving, as powerful brands outperform their peers on the stock market.

For ten years, Millward Brown, a leading global research agency with a specialty in brand equity research, has studied and ranked the most valuable global brands. Their research covers three million consumers and more than 100,000 different brands in over 50 markets to determine what makes brands meaningful (including appeal of the brand, emotional connection, and how well the brand meets expectations), different (how well the brand sets trends that benefit consumers), and salient (including top-of-mind reference as the brand of choice for key needs). The firm then compares the most valuable brands, based on consumer evaluations, and evaluates their share price performance against that of their peers.

Companies with brands that made Millward Brown's cut as being in the distinguished class of 100 most valuable worldwide significantly delivered more shareholder value than their peers. Specifically, Millward Brown's achievers offered greater returns to their shareholders, growing 102.6 percent in value over ten years, from

2006 to 2015, outperforming the S&P 500, which grew 63 percent. Additionally, these brand superstars beat the MSCI World Index, a weighted index of global stocks, which grew at just 30.3 percent over the same time frame. In its 10th Anniversary Edition, Millward Brown CEO Travyn Rhall answered the obvious question posed to the firm so many times over its multiple years of brand rankings:

> One of the first questions that people ask on seeing the latest BrandZ™ results is how do brands build such value? We know from over 40 years of research that a successful brand is made up of three key components. How relevant or Meaningful a brand is to our lives; how Different it is to competitors and; how well we know and *trust* the brand, whether it is Salient.[55]

Trust provides interesting benefits beyond adding to a brand's tangible value (and subsequent stock performance). It also creates a fascinating halo effect in making firms more resilient to negative information. Consider the following: When a company is distrusted, 57 percent of consumers will believe negative information about it after hearing it just a couple of times. In contrast, only 15 percent of consumers will believe positive information about a distrusted company after hearing it a couple of times. For trusted companies, the outlook is much brighter: 51 percent of consumers will believe positive information after hearing it a couple of times; only 25 percent will believe negative information after hearing it a couple of times.[56] As such, breach fatigue notwithstanding, a ceaseless drumbeat of negative media attention associated with repeated breaches is a curse to those companies with already low customer trust scores.

So, we are left to question: Did the temporary rebound of sales and profitability after those widely publicized company breaches ensue due to the brands in question already benefiting from high brand equity, including underlying positive trust scores among consumers? If so, how many more breaches can be sustained before trust is capsized and those same companies find themselves on the other end of the media maelstrom? And, would other large companies with lower starting trust scores find such a certain and swift rebound? It's worth noting that several large companies cited in this chapter for major cybersecurity breaches only to ultimately find redemption were ranked on Millward Brown's list shortly before each of their hacks, suggesting they each had the advantage of a powerful brand resilient to negative media attention. Among them: Target, JPMorgan Chase, and The Home Depot.[57]

A Second Thought

So, back to the original questions. Is there really a lack of motivation on the part of these potential victims? It would appear so, but the reasons are far more complex than a simple shrug of the shoulders on the part of consumers and businesses hoping their number isn't the next up. A perfect storm of breach fatigue, moral hazard, and risk miscomprehension creates sufficient fog to paralyze unsuspecting victims from acting with the same motivation their adversaries seem to have in spades.

If one isn't careful, one could wrongly conclude from the data that consumers and businesses aren't motivated since the risks don't appear all that severe. Consumers can default to the financial institutions to cover their losses. Larger companies in some of the most publicized breaches have more than weathered the storm. But, suggesting that cybercrime risks are overblown flies in the face of the obvious. While short-term losses of large companies suffering highly publicized breaches are few and far between, the subjects of many of these attacks came from a strong position of brand equity, arguably making the companies more resilient to negative hype and finding a more forgiving consumer audience as a result. Only time will tell how the equation changes as attacks become more frequent and insidious and as developing legislation assigns responsibility where it belongs. Further, when companies that are not even in the cybersecurity debate today land themselves in the public eye for a different kind of breach—think of an attack on a connected device, like a medical monitor or automobile—we may find a different response from consumers, no longer overwhelmed by apathy but overcome by fear. Of course, small businesses increasingly need no convincing of the obvious threat, with more than half of them meeting their demise a few months after an attack. It's only a matter of time before larger businesses and consumers realize the same.

We won't be as bold as to attempt to predict the future. We will only offer that there is one constituency that is absolutely determined to debate the otherwise obvious consequences of cybercrime—the threat actors who multiply their efforts and intensity with every passing day. Indeed, breach fatigue, moral hazard, and risk miscomprehension are the silent weapons in their arsenal, lulling their victims to sleep as they carefully coordinate their next attack. As the enemy continues to multiply in both number and type, motivated by profit, principle, or province, the threats will mutate over time. While one can find no long-term damage for the notorious black swan incidents in recent years, perhaps the reason is we have yet to witness a real black swan attack. Maybe, just maybe, the bad guys have yet to target a company to unequivocally inflict long-term irreparable harm, not merely theft of customer records, however many millions may be purloined. Perhaps we have yet to see what is truly possible when we rest on our laurels and allow the perfect poison of breach fatigue, moral hazard, and risk miscomprehension to get the better of us. Indeed, companies that second-guess the obvious may find a slower demise than Code Spaces, but a demise nonetheless. When the intangible currency of trust is slowly eroded over a long period of time, the cemetery of fallen companies stands ready to welcome its next resident in *The Second Economy*.

A SECOND HELPING OF THE IRRATIONAL MIND

We are a species of optimists. Research has shown that people hugely underestimate future negative outcomes. We don't anticipate divorcing our spouse, losing our job, or contracting a terminal disease. We expect our children to be superior in talents and abilities. We imagine ourselves to be far more successful than our peers. We even overestimate our life expectancy, sometimes by 20 years or more.[58]

This condition of the human psyche—the tendency to imagine the future as being better than the past—is known in psychology parlance as optimism bias. It transcends divisions that typically exist in culture—universally present across race, geography, gender, and age. As evidence of our tendency to operate paradoxically, we can create a pessimistic view of collective concerns (such as the state of the economy or world), while at the same time preserving an overly optimistic view of our own personal circumstances. A 2007 study found that while 70 percent thought families in general were less successful than in their parents' day, 76 percent were optimistic about the future of their own family.[59]

We can criticize optimism bias as weakness or mental delusion. It certainly creates blind spots in our daily behaviors that enable senseless risk taking, whether in our health and lifestyle habits, financial prudence, or other tendencies. But, it is also credited for preserving the very existence of humanity.[60] It keeps us moving forward as a species, rather than retreating in defeat. It may be the fuel that inspired our ancestors to push new boundaries and keeps us testing new possibilities each day. It also feeds the tenacity that drives us to try again when we do fail. Yes, optimists are equally likely to divorce, but they are also more likely to remarry, proving that hope springs eternal.

Recent scientific evidence is turning what we thought we knew about our brain on its head (pun intended). Optimism may in fact be hardwired by evolution into the human mind. Accumulating research suggests we are not merely products of our past, but works-in-progress toward our future. What ostensibly invisible force could otherwise explain why we toil each day for a brighter future, despite the unequivocal fact that death awaits us all (a macabre thought, but one that captures the extreme of why optimism bias exists)?

And, yes, while optimism bias keeps us marching forward, looking toward a brighter future, it also seduces us to minimize the probability of bad events in our path. Couple this hardwired bias with our natural tendencies to miscalculate risk, and you have a powerful concoction that prevents the most reasonable, rational behaviors from prevailing—an outcome welcomed by threat actors the world over. It bears repeating: human beings are not rational so much as they rationalize in *The Second Economy.*

Notes

1. Steve Ragan, "Code Spaces forced to close its doors after security incident," CSO, June 18, 2014, www.csoonline. com/article/2365062/disaster-recovery/code-spaces-forced-to-close-its-doors-after-security-incident. html, accessed June 1, 2016.

2. D. J. Jordan and Joel Hannahs, "Collins Subcommittee Examines Small Business Cyber-Security Challenges With New Technologies," March 21, 2013, http://smallbusiness. house.gov/news/documentsingle.aspx?DocumentID=325034, accessed June 1, 2016.

3.   Jaikumar Vijayan, "Canadian probe finds TJX breach followed wireless hack," *Computerworld*, September 25, 2007b, www.computerworld.com/article/2541162/security0/canadian-probe-finds-tjx-breach-followed-wireless-hack.html, accessed May 6, 2016.

4.   Joseph Pereira, "How Credit-Card Data Went Out Wireless Door," *The Wall Street Journal*, May 4, 2007, www.wsj.com/news/articles/SB117824446226991797?mg=id-wsj, accessed May 6, 2016.

5.   Ibid.

6.   Vijayan, note 3 *supra*.

7.   Pereira, note 4 *supra*.

8.   Jaikumar Vijayan, "TJX offers settlement deal in wake of massive data breach," *Computerworld*, September 24, 2007a, www.computerworld.com/article/2541220/security0/tjx-offers-settlement-deal-in-wake-of-massive-data-breach.html, accessed May 8, 2016.

9.   Vijayan, note 3 *supra*.

10.   Pereira, note 4 *supra*.

11.   Ibid.

12.   Ibid.

13.   Jaikumar Vijayan, "One year later: Five takeaways from the TJX breach," *Computerworld*, January 17, 2008, www.computerworld.com/article/2538711/cybercrime-hacking/one-year-later--five-takeaways-from-the-tjx-breach.html, accessed May 8, 2016.

14.   TJX 2009 Annual Report, http://thomson.mobular.net/thomson/7/2968/3980/, page 21, accessed May 8, 2016.

15.   Vijayan, note 13 *supra*.

16.   Trefis Team, "Home Depot: Could The Impact Of The Data Breach Be Significant?," *Forbes*, September 24, 2014, www.forbes.com/sites/greatspeculations/2014/09/24/home-depot-could-the-impact-of-the-data-breach-be-significant/#6ebd0da8237f, accessed May 8, 2016.

17.   Doug Drinkwater, "Does a data breach really affect your firm's reputation?," *CSO*, January 7, 2016, www.csoonline.com/article/3019283/data-breach/does-a-data-breach-really-affect-your-firm-s-reputation.html, accessed May 8, 2016.

18. Ibid.

19. Ibid.

20. Ponemon Institute Research Report, "The Aftermath of a Mega Data Breach: Consumer Sentiment," April 2014, www.experian.com/assets/p/data-breach/experian-consumer-study-on-aftermath-of-a-data-breach.pdf, accessed May 8, 2016.

21. Ibid.

22. Josh Bradford, "2014 by the numbers: record-setting cyber breaches," Advisen Cyber Risk Network, December 31, 2014, www.cyberrisknetwork.com/2014/12/31/2014-year-cyber-breaches/, accessed May 8, 2016.

23. Software Advice, "Public Awareness of Security Breaches IndustryView 2014," www.softwareadvice.com/security/industryview/public-awareness-breaches-2014/, accessed May 8, 2016.

24. Ibid.

25. Ibid.

26. Ibid.

27. Samuel Greengard, "Is Data Breach Fatigue Making Us Careless?," *Baseline*, June 6, 2014, www.baselinemag.com/security/slideshows/is-data-breach-fatigue-making-us-careless.html, Accessed May 8, 2016.

28. Ibid.

29. Ibid.

30. Diane Moogalian, "Data Breach Fatigue: The New Identity Theft Risk," Equifax Finance Blog, May 11, 2015, http://blog.equifax.com/credit/data-breach-fatigue-the-new-identity-theft-risk/, accessed May 8, 2016.

31. Ibid. (emphasis added).

32. Maia Szalalvitz, "10 Ways We Get the Odds Wrong," Psychology Today, January/February 2008, http://jaydixit.com/files/PDFs/Risk.pdf, accessed May 11, 2016.

33. Ibid.

34. NPR, Oregon Public Broadcasting, "Brick-And-Mortar Shops: Safer Than Online Stores?," April 27, 2011, www.npr.org/2011/04/27/135778733/why-do-online-security-breaches-happen, accessed May 11, 2016.

35. Szalalvitz, note 32 *supra*.

36. Ibid.

37. Benjamin Dean, "Sorry consumers, companies have little incentive to invest in better cybersecurity," *Quartz*, March 5, 2015, http://qz.com/356274/cybersecurity-breaches-hurt-consumers-companies-not-so-much/, accessed May 8, 2016.

38. "The Great EMV Fake-Out: No Chip For You!," *KrebsOnSecurity*, February 16, 2016, http://krebsonsecurity.com/2016/02/the-great-emv-fake-out-no-chip-for-you/comment-page-3/, accessed May 8, 2016.

39. Ibid.

40. Bob Sullivan, "Chip & PAIN? Some Cardholders Frustrated With Slow Transition," Credit.com, November 2, 2015, http://blog.credit.com/2015/11/chip-pain-some-cardholders-frustrated-with-slow-transition-128576/, accessed May 8, 2016.

41. Ibid.

42. Ibid.

43. Walmart Company Facts, http://corporate.walmart.com/newsroom/company-facts, accessed May 11, 2016.

44. Chris Isidore, "Walmart sues Visa over chip debit card rules," *CNN Money*, May 11, 2016, http://money.cnn.com/2016/05/11/news/companies/walmart-sues-visa-chip-card/, accessed May 11, 2016.

45. David Barrett, "Victims of cyber crime should be 'low priority' if they fail to take security steps, says report," *The Telegraph*, October 15, 2015, www.telegraph.co.uk/news/uknews/crime/11931958/Victims-of-cyber-crime-should-be-low-priority-if-they-fail-to-take-security-steps-says-report.html, accessed May 9, 2016.

46. Ibid.

47. Tom Kaneshige, "CIOs Battle Worker Apathy Towards Lost or Stolen Mobile Phones," *CIO*, March 5, 2014, www.cio.com/article/2378170/cio-role/cios-battle-worker-apathy-towards-lost-or-stolen-mobile-phones.html, accessed May 9, 2016.

48. Roger Neville Sinclair and Kevin Lane Keller, "A case for brands as assets: Acquired and internally developed," *Journal of Brand Management*, February 28, 2014, www.palgrave-journals.com/bm/journal/v21/n4/full/bm20148a.html, accessed May 9, 2016.

49. Ibid.

50. Eamonn Fingleton, "Same Car, Different Brand, Hugely Higher Price: Why Pay An Extra $30,000 For Fake Prestige?," *Forbes*, July 4, 2013, www.forbes.com/sites/eamonnfingleton/2013/07/04/same-car-different-brand-hugely-higher-price-why-pay-an-extra-30000-for-fake-prestige/#6cf704b49ee6, accessed May 9, 2016.

51. "Hitting the spot," *The Economist*, January 17, 2008, www.economist.com/node/10530119, accessed May 9, 2016.

52. Ibid.

53. Bain & Company, "Measuring Your Net Promoter Score," www.netpromotersystem.com/about/measuring-your-net-promoter-score.aspx, accessed May 9, 2016.

54. Ponemon Institute, "Reputation Impact of a Data Breach," November 2011, www.experian.com/assets/data-breach/white-papers/reputation-study.pdf, accessed May 9, 2016.

55. Millward Brown, "BrandZ Top 100 Most Valuable Global Brands 2015," file:///C:/Users/acerra/Documents/2015_BrandZ_Top100_Report.pdf, report accessed May 9, 2016 (emphasis added).

56. Edelman Trust Barometer, as reported in the World Economic Forum's "The Evolution of Trust in Business: From Delivery to Values," January 2015.

57. Millward Brown, "BrandZ Top 100 Most Valuable Global Brands 2013," www.millwardbrown.com/brandz/2013/Top100/Docs/2013_BrandZ_Top100_Report.pdf, accessed May 9, 2016.

58. Tali Sharot, "The Optimism Bias," *Time*, May 28, 2011, http://content.time.com/time/health/article/0,8599,2074067-2,00.html, accessed May 11, 2016.

59. Ibid.

60. Ibid.

PART II

■ ■ ■

A Second Look at Conventional Wisdom

There is always a well-known solution to every human problem—neat, plausible, and wrong.

—H. L. Mencken
American journalist

CHAPTER 6

■ ■ ■

Playing Second Fiddle

I'm attracted to computers, and some people can't understand that. But some people are attracted to horses and I can't understand that.

—Dan Nydick, Electrical Engineering major at Carnegie-Mellon, 1983[1]

In 2016, CareerCast, an online job search site, evaluated 200 jobs on 11 stress factors and published a report ranking the most and least stressful careers of the year. Those in high-strung positions faced punishing deadlines, physical demands, hazardous conditions, and even life-threatening risks to themselves and others. Deservingly, enlisted military personnel, firefighters, airline pilots, and police officers topped the company's list for occupying the most stressful jobs.[2] And, while the most nerve-racking occupations came as no surprise, the study's calculation of the least stressful job raised at least a few eyebrows. Those enjoying the most enviable combination of low-stress and high-salary positions were none other than information security analysts.[3]

The finding seemed to defy logic. After all, information security analysts are on the frontline of an escalating battle between malevolent hackers and the organizations in their crosshairs. Perhaps the criteria was partly to blame. While cyberattacks can carry personal risk (think of nation-state attacks against civil infrastructure, for example), information security analysts don't exactly put their lives on the line at work. Maybe the researcher had an ulterior motive. At the time of the study, CareerCast was flush with more than 7,500 job postings for information security analysts, compared with roughly 1,000 openings for other positions.[4] Or, according to an argument hypothesized by at least one certified information systems security professional, perhaps CareerCast missed a critical attribute among the 11 tested: appreciation. As Jerod Brennen so eloquently opined via a LinkedIn blog:

> If you work in a back office or shared services role, it's likely that you produce something. HR? I'd argue that you produce jobs. You help people get hired. Finance? You produce budgets that pay for all the things. Payroll? You produce paychecks... IT? As unappreciated as you are, the fact remains that you produce systems and applications that end users rely on. But what do information security professionals produce? *Nothing.*[5]

S. Grobman and A. Cerra, *The Second Economy*, DOI 10.1007/978-1-4842-2229-4_6

And, it's this lack of production that leads Brennen to speculate that cybersecurity professionals are, in essence, the unsung heroes of their organizations—quietly toiling away at all hours of the day and night ensuring that *nothing* ever happens. For the majority of employees around them, this invisibility creates a lack of understanding, and appreciation, for the yeoman's work that is done inconspicuously in the background. In fact, the information security analyst is least appreciated when he is most seen—either due to a breach that critics will claim foresight could have prevented or when the latest software patch even slightly diminishes the productivity of an instant-gratification workforce. So, while the information security analyst may occupy the most enviable job according to CareerCast's study, he often garners the least appreciation from his coworkers. And, the "least stressful" job available can quickly turn the other way when *something* does happen, particularly when the thing one is securing was never built for protection in the first place.

Initial Battle Lines Are Drawn

At an otherwise garden-variety computer conference at the Washington Hilton hotel in October 1972, history was made. A team of researchers demonstrated a fledgling network in the making that would forever redefine communications. The era was mired by Cold War fears and the imminent threat of nuclear holocaust. At the time, expensive and highly controlled telephone networks were the modern-day convenience for communications. In the years preceding the conference, American engineer Paul Baran began contemplating a new network design that would withstand nuclear attack and allow a society to reinstitute communications to reconstitute itself. At the same time, and working independently, Welsh scientist Donald W. Davies envisioned a more efficient network design for data—one that would not tie up costly telephone lines in use by behemoth computers, particularly during long periods of silence between individual transmissions. The two visionaries ultimately landed in the same place: a network that transmitted packets of data, allowing several users to occupy the same telephone line, by efficiently distributing the slices of data across the wire. What would become the ARPANET, the forerunner to today's Internet that initially connected universities, was born. Its output was on display for the first time at that nondescript computer conference in 1972.

As anyone with experience in conducting live demonstrations of any sort at a major event will tell you, things don't always go as planned (as an interesting aside, event coordinators rank in the top ten of CareerCast's most stressful positions,[6] we suspect largely due to these unexpected occurrences). During a demonstration of the ARPANET's capabilities to a visiting delegation from one of the largest telephone companies at the time, the system abruptly crashed. The man behind the presentation, Robert Metcalfe, a Harvard University doctoral student who would later co-invent Ethernet technology and found networking juggernaut 3Com, was incensed when he noticed the "suits" from the telephone company snickering. He would later recall, "They were happy. They were chuckling. They didn't realize how threatening it was. … [The crash] seemed to confirm that it was a toy."[7]

The enmity between two sides of a technology battle—the "Bellheads," creators of highly reliable circuit-switched networks, and the "Netheads," aspirational visionaries of high bandwidth packet-switched networks—would fester as opposing views dictated radically different architectural principles. Of particular distinction between the two factions: where the intelligence resided in the network design. Bellheads built telephone networks with a highly intelligent core—the switches that dictated all functionality and terminated calls at dumb telephones on the customer's side of demarcation. Netheads had the opposite approach: their vision was predicated on a dumb core, with intelligence residing at the edges, or within the computers and terminals accessing the network. The dumb core allowed users easy access, albeit at the expense of security.

Netheads had little concern for security, given that the traffic in motion was hardly worth protecting. E-mail dominated the ARPANET and became the first "killer app." The initial sprouts of what would ultimately become today's Internet were little more than messages between academic institutions, hardly the bait to attract cybercriminals. And so, security became an afterthought to easy and ubiquitous access, leaving historian Janet Abbate to use an interesting metaphor for what we now have today:

> We've ended up at this place of security through individual
> vigilance. It's kind of like safe sex. It's sort of 'the Internet
> is this risky activity, and it's up to each person to protect
> themselves from what's out there.' ... There's this sense
> that the [Internet] provider's not going to protect you. The
> government's not going to protect you. It's kind of up to you to
> protect yourself.[8]

To be fair, the original visionaries of the Internet were nothing short of geniuses. They developed the blueprint for a network that would connect more people than the entire worldwide population at the time of their concept in the 1960s. It wasn't that they entirely dismissed security in their worldview. They just assumed that security would be limited to military strikes, not imagining that their invention could be undone by the very people it connected.

It's easy to forget that standing up a network capable of connecting billions of endpoints required a common protocol for doing so—a nontrivial undertaking in and of itself. That protocol, TCP/IP (Transmission Control Protocol/Internet Protocol), provides users with a common language through which to communicate over the Internet to this day. Initially, the Internet's founding fathers contemplated embedding encryption in the protocol directly. But, doing so would require extensive computing power, likely requiring new pieces of expensive hardware to properly work. This, coupled with uncertainty on how to effectively distribute encryption keys and the US Government's disdain of cryptography as a potential national security threat (which we covered in Chapter 1), led early creators to sideline security as a challenge simply too big to tackle. As Abbate so masterfully observes, security was of no consequence to architects believing they were building a classroom; in actuality, they were building a bank[9] at a time before "hacking" had even entered the common vernacular.

The Underestimated Troublemakers

Put another password in,

Bomb it out, then try again.

Try to get past logging in,

We're hacking, hacking, hacking.

Try his first wife's maiden name,

This is more than just a game.

It's real fun, but just the same

It's hacking, hacking, hacking.

—Hacker's anthem by "Cheshire Catalyst"[10]

They were described as the modern-day Robin Hoods of an information age. Young, male, wildly talented and obsessed with learning the deepest intricacies of computers that were increasingly becoming extensions of daily life. The underground hacker culture that emerged in the 1980s was glorified by the media and Hollywood alike, representing these computer geniuses as benign pranksters with nothing better to do with their time and talent than mess with a few computer systems and see what havoc they could wreak. Their inspiration was hardly the stuff of cybercrime harm. It was simply the achievement of doing something inconceivable and then sharing their feat with like-minded enthusiasts. Security was no hurdle for many of their ventures, with measures like strong password hygiene and basic firewall protections still lingering in the distant future. In actuality, adept hackers of the day longed to find the seemingly impenetrable target. Computer systems with tougher security borders offered more tempting bait with which to test their skills, as bragging rights are greatly diminished if the catch is too easy. Neal Patrick, a 17-year-old hacker at the time and member of an online gang of similarly interested teens who successfully penetrated more than 60 business and government computer systems across North America, put it like this:

> We were surprised just how easy it was. It was like climbing a mountain: you have the goal of reaching the top or accessing a computer, and once you reach the peak, you make a map of the way and give it to everybody else.[11]

Hackers were dismissed as harmless miscreants, incapable of doing any serious damage. Steve Wozniak, co-founder of Apple, commented at the time,

> There's this myth that kids can crack secure systems, and that's just not true. . . . I hope my kid grows up to be like them. It's the very best way to exercise your curiosity and intelligence—a nondestructive form of social deviancy.[12]

Being a hacker was hardly a career or crime; it was better defined as a hobby. The face of the hacker was clearly understood—young males dominated the trade. In fact, Wozniak estimated the life expectancy of one of these virtual nonconformists to be no more than 20 years of age. After that, the obligations of holding down a "real" job and becoming a "responsible" adult were simply too great to ignore and too much to jeopardize for possible imprisonment in the name of virtual bravado.[13]

Then, in 1988, the worldview changed. A Harvard graduate and son of one of the US Government's most respected computer security experts began experimenting with the notion of enslaving an army of drone computers, what would ultimately be referred to as a "botnet" in modern times. Motivated by curiosity, Robert Morris unleashed what would become the first widely insidious attack against the public Internet and the roughly 100,000 computers connected to it at the time.[14] His Morris Worm, as it would be called, was designed to replicate itself across the network, jumping from one machine to the next, spreading its contagion. To avoid infecting the same machine multiple times, which would slow the computer's performance and draw risky attention to Morris' creation, the hacker designed a mechanism in his code that would detect if the same machine was infected more than once. If so, a virtual coin of sorts was flipped, with the losing worm self-destructing. However, in what was later assumed to be an attempt to prevent a decoy worm from inserting itself in his code to destroy any existing worms, Morris created an exception to the suicide feature in every seven instances—when, instead of self-destruction, the redundant worm would make itself immortal. The move nullified Morris' original intention of infecting any machine only once.[15] Within days, the Internet was ravaged by a replicating worm with no signs of containment, sapping computers' resources with multiple spawns of its strain as users frantically attempted to find the antidote.

The media, completely oblivious to what this "Internet" thing was and how it could possibly become infected, vacillated between extreme panic (was this World War III in the making?) to complete ignorance (could this Morris Worm spread to human beings?). But, the roughly 100,000 early Internet adopters knew the implications with which they were dealing. The innocence of the Internet had been shattered. The unintentional by-product of a dumb core was virtual lawlessness. There was no government that could batten down the hatches; no white knight to save the day. At once, reality set in—the high jinks of an elite community of virtual rebels threatened the very existence of a globally connected community.

Ten years later, a group of seven hackers testified before US Congress to articulate what those early Internet users knew a decade before. In cautionary testimony provided by a leader of the hacking ring:

> If you're looking for computer security, then the Internet is not the place to be. . . . [It can be taken down] by any of the seven individuals seated before you [with 30 minutes of well-choreographed keystrokes].[16]

It was clear. If the prankster hackers of the 1980s had grown up to be the potentially dangerous online criminals of the 1990s, there had to be an answer. Unfortunately, jurisdictional boundaries are not so clean in a borderless reality, so law enforcement only goes so far. To fight fire with fire would require hackers on the good side of the battle. Every "black hat" attempt would require a "white hat" response. These white hats would share their adversaries' attraction for speaking a digital language few can understand. Their difference: using their talents to ward off, rather than launch, attacks. As an assistant professor of computer science in the 1980s presciently predicted, "If you can domesticate a hacker, you can get good work out of him."[17] Unfortunately, these domesticated good guys would find themselves in an unfair fight from the beginning.

The Domesticated Heroes

To understand today's white hat heroes—the cybersecurity professionals who use their hacking skills for their organization's good—requires an appreciation of their roots. Cybersecurity degrees are increasingly popular today—no surprise for a profession that currently enjoys a nearly 0 percent unemployment rate, earns attractive money, and (according to CareerCast) suffers the least stress of 200 possible occupations. But, it wasn't always this way. In the beginning, cybersecurity wasn't a degree available on college campuses. Aspirational white hat hackers found themselves deployed in traditional information technology (IT) environments with commensurate IT worldviews. And, these surroundings were hardly conducive to fighting an increasingly motivated adversary with intentions to do harm.

The IT profession has certainly seen its fair share of ebbs and flows. First, there was the boon of the computer era, which saw companies increase their percentage of capital budgets dedicated to information technology explode from less than 5 percent in 1965 to nearly 50 percent by the end of the millennium.[18] IT professionals were in hot demand as companies poured big money into building massive infrastructures to compete in an increasingly digital economy. Yet, as investment flowed, so too did increasing criticism of the profession. A 1987 *Harvard Business Review* article, aptly titled, "Make Information Services Pay Its Way," lamented the challenges of business leaders perplexed and underwhelmed by IT departments that were slow, inefficient, and unresponsive. The author provided a practical prescription for the growing refrain of corporate naysayers increasingly disillusioned by IT's seemingly empty promises:

> If IS [Information Services] is to achieve a strategic end, companies must manage it as a productive part of the organization. The best way to do this is to run IS as a business within a business, as a profit center with a flexible budget and a systematic way to price its services. In companies that have already turned their IS systems into profit centers, the results have been impressive: the top management complaints are greatly reduced, and the expected efficiencies have materialized. When organizational shackles are lifted, IS can and does serve a strategic purpose.[19]

As their field was booming, IT professionals found themselves both loved and loathed by the very organizations funding their efforts. By 2003, the cacophony of critics had reached deafening volumes, this time with a *Harvard Business Review* article simply titled "IT Doesn't Matter." In it, author Nicholas Carr prosecuted a cogent case encouraging organizations not simply to treat IT as a profit center but to ruthlessly restrict their investments in a function that could rarely yield sustainable competitive advantage. Carr's article provided compelling proof for his argument, offering several studies corroborating a negative correlation between IT investment and superior financial results. More important, Carr submitted an insightful view into the thinking behind a career that would first be lauded and later panned—specifically, that with the proliferation of technologies like data storage, data processing and data transport, leaders were wrongly inflating IT's value as a strategic asset to their firms. Quite the opposite of being a strategic resource, IT was more like a fungible commodity—as Carr contended that sustainable competitive advantage is only achieved through that which is *scarce* and difficult to duplicate, not *ubiquitous* and easily copied. He implored leaders of the day to treat IT as the commodity it truly was—and ruthlessly prune investment in it accordingly. He effectively escalated to a crescendo in his final arguments, punctuating his point with a bold assertion:

> IT management should, frankly, become boring. The key to success, for the vast majority of companies, is no longer to seek advantage aggressively but to manage costs and risks meticulously. If, like many executives, you've begun to take a more defensive posture toward IT in the last two years, spending more frugally and thinking more pragmatically, you're already on the right course. The challenge will be to maintain that discipline when the business cycle strengthens and the chorus of hype about IT's strategic value rises anew.[20]

Consider the dilemma for IT professionals as a whole, and, more specifically, for white hat hackers who were initially absorbed in this cohort from their early beginnings. They are under pressure to stand up defensible virtual infrastructures connecting their companies to a global marketplace. At the same time, they are misunderstood, if not outright unappreciated, by the business stakeholders they are paid to support. Oh, and by the way, those same business stakeholders not only increasingly wield the power on where IT investments are made but also persist in their demands for more frictionless experiences, bringing with them consumer-adopted attitudes about technology into a workplace where intellectual property must be guarded. To put one final nail in the proverbial coffin, the very thing they are paid to support and/or protect is more and more outside their control. By the turn of the millennium, technology spending outside IT was 20 percent of total technology investment; by 2020, it is expected to be almost 90 percent.[21]

This "shadow IT" conundrum is among the largest challenges for white hats. IT has been losing its grip as the owner and operator of its organization's technology for some time. With the proliferation of technologies increasingly acquired by organizations and employees residing outside IT, each additional component presents another entryway for hackers to penetrate. Even worse, when IT is not the purchaser of said technology, it is a bit difficult to expect these professionals to even know the extent of their organization's digital footprint. A 2015 Cisco study found the number of unauthorized cloud applications in an enterprise to be 15 times higher than predicted by the chief information officer (CIO).[22] As political finger-pointing between IT departments and business units grows with the opposing friction between these internal stakeholders, white hats are often left to pick up the pieces if and when a strike on their infrastructure occurs—whether they were aware of the digital estate in the first place or not. The challenge is only exacerbated with the "Internet of Things," where previously non-connected devices, such as sensors on factory floors, converge in a complex labyrinth that unites physical and virtual worlds. Each connected thing must now be secured, lest it provide an open door through which the adversary can enter to cripple infrastructures once quarantined from the virtual realm.

White hats must often endure in traditional IT environments with their own challenges, even without those of cybersecurity professionals thrown in the mix. While black hats enjoyed strength in numbers with like-minded allies, white hats were thrust into an environment of confusion, abiding by a set of IT principles that hardly makes sense against an adversary. Consider just a few of the more interesting conflicts for white hat heroes confined by traditional IT constraints:

- *In cybersecurity, black hats fuel the R&D agenda.* In traditional IT, the company or organization itself is responsible for research and development (R&D). The challenge is to optimize R&D against one's competition, ensuring the right level of investment to yield competitive advantage without wasting resources. While competitors seek to win in the marketplace, black hats have a different objective: to deliberately inflict organizational harm for profit, principle, or province. In this scenario, R&D advancements are initiated by black hats in the fight, as they are the first to launch a strike. White hats must be prepared to respond, not knowing the timing, origin, or nature of the next assault.

- *In cybersecurity, time is a white hat's enemy.* There's an old adage in software development: "In God we trust, the rest we test." Software developers in a traditional IT environment are expected to get it right; organizations cannot tolerate software releases that hinder productivity or otherwise create chaos. Understandably, these software engineers take measured steps in testing, and retesting, their creations. Test cycles are limited to off-peak hours so as not to disrupt the business-as-usual motion.

  While this instrumented process works well in an IT environment that can be tightly controlled, it increasingly loses relevance when that same environment is under attack by an adversary. White hat software developers must run testing scenarios without fully understanding what the next attack vector might entail. And, when such an attack is launched, there is hardly time to run, and rerun, meticulous testing scenarios during scheduled off-peak hours to inoculate the threat. While time is on the side of the traditional software developer, it is very much the enemy of a white hat coder.

- *Productivity trumps security.* When employees must choose between security and productivity, the latter nearly always wins. In a 2016 study among IT professionals conducted by Barkly, an endpoint security company, respondents lamented the biggest issues around implementing effective security measures in their companies. More than 40 percent cited the risk of effective cybersecurity tools slowing down internal systems, with nearly the same number expressing frustration with the frequency of software updates.[23] When cybersecurity (or even traditional IT processes, for that matter) are visible to employees, they are likely to be deemed ineffective. What employee wants to boot up her system each week with time-consuming software updates that protect her from an invisible villain she doesn't even know, or potentially care, exists? Worse yet, who wants to endure sluggish system performance to support multiple security programs in the environment? Many employees would likely take their chances with a potential attack, versus give up certain productivity, real or perceived.

- *Cybersecurity return on investment (ROI) is seen as fuzzy math.* Since at least that 1987 *Harvard Business Review* article, IT has been under pressure to show its companies the money. When one can test and prove the advantages of a new technological advancement that increases productivity or otherwise offers greater organizational effectiveness, ROI calculations readily follow. But, consider the plight of the white hat. How does one effectively prove the ROI of cybersecurity? As the LinkedIn blogger from our opening story so eloquently argued, cybersecurity professionals get credit when *nothing* happens. How does one go about proving that an attack was successfully diverted? Sure, there are plenty of indicators that these white hats use to show how many threats were thwarted from entering the environment. But, is there any real proof that the threats in question would have caused irreparable harm? And, how does one translate that value when considering the actual costs of cybersecurity deployment and the opportunity costs of real (or perceived) lost productivity associated with sluggish systems bogged down by software updates? Perhaps it comes as no surprise that 44 percent of cybersecurity professionals in a 2016 McAfee study indicated that the ROI of their efforts was ambiguous, at best.

- *Cybersecurity suffers the same back-office origin as traditional IT.* Thanks to advocates in Carr's camp, IT's strategic value has been questioned, if not outright undermined. To this day, CIOs are often not in strong standing in the executive suite. Another 2016 study found that, while 82 percent of board members were concerned about cybersecurity, only one in seven CIOs reported directly to the CEO and most were left completely off the board. Those sobering realities coexisted in a world where 74 percent of cybersecurity professionals believed a cyberattack would happen within the year.[24] With cybersecurity remaining a part of a historically back-office function, the opportunity to voice security concerns to a justifiably paranoid board of directors is filtered, if not muffled, when a white hat advocate isn't offered a seat at their table.

- *Traditional IT professionals need only understand the product, not the motivations of its developer.* When deploying a new technology, it is critical for IT professionals to understand how it will function in their environment. However, understanding what was in the mind of the developer when he designed the latest off-the-shelf commercial software package is hardly critical. For white hats, it's an entirely different matter. They must not only understand the nature of threats entering their perimeter but also give attention to the motivations of adversaries creating them in the first place. In fact, the best white hats have the ability to think like a black hat, all while understanding their organization's strategic imperatives. They intersect what is most valuable for the taking with how an enemy would potentially attack. From there, they attempt to anticipate and prepare for the most likely and dangerous threat vectors. This ongoing psychological computation is par for the course for white hats as they constantly calculate the motivations of their organizations, employees and adversaries—yet another distinction setting them apart from their traditional IT counterparts.

With these challenges and more, white hats often feel like aliens in their own world. They are not only unappreciated by business units that struggle to understand complex technology but also forced to play by a set of IT rules that never applied to them in the first place. Making matters worse, the black hats have no such rulebook, so the deck is stacked against the white hat heroes from the start. Cybersecurity professionals find themselves in a heavily regimented IT world, in which they play second fiddle to established principles that simply do not fit their reality. And, while white hats can and do identify with each other, they must also specialize in their skills and perspectives to surround their organization at all points of the threat life cycle, leading to occasional friction among players on the same team:

- Security architects are responsible for identifying necessary defenses, selecting the products and tools, and interconnecting them in a protective mosaic to secure their environment. These individuals must anticipate possible threat vectors to address the question: *How might the enemy infiltrate?*

- Security operators run the daily gauntlet of detecting and responding to threats in the organization. These professionals must answer: *How is the enemy infiltrating?*

- Incident responders have the task of executing a remediation plan when an attack does occur. These professionals are tasked with answering: *How do I respond now that the enemy has infiltrated?*

When tensions run high during a breach, natural organizational inertia drifts toward political infighting. Security operators may be quick to blame architects for failing to procure or integrate sufficient technology in the first place. Incident responders may blame operators for failing to detect the threat in a timelier manner. And, architects could blame both of their cohorts for failing to provide useful ongoing feedback to fortify an organization's defenses. The blame game knows no end. White hats must resist these political tendencies to undermine one another when a breach occurs, channeling their respective efforts to blame and take out the one truly at fault—their common enemy.

It should come as no surprise that this perfect storm of unfortunate circumstances leaves many cybersecurity professionals feeling downright unconfident in their ability to fight the good fight. One-third of cybersecurity professionals are not even aware of how many breaches their organization suffered in the past year.[25] The only way they receive credit for a job well done is when *nothing* happens. So, they focus their energies deploying ever-sophisticated cybersecurity technologies, hoping the next widget will be the silver bullet in their arsenal to ensure no damage by the enemy is done. Cybersecurity software vendors are often the proverbial arms dealers in the war, capitalizing on the anxiety of white hats to sell their wares. They have a willing customer, despite the seeming lack of ROI proof: More than half of IT executives state they "would still jump at the chance to purchase new, improved security software, and one in four say there is no limit to what they would pay for something more effective and reliable."[26]

A Second Thought

White hats and black hats have a lot in common, despite being on opposite sides of a virtual fight. They have an undeniable passion for technology. They possess a genius for making machines seemingly bow to their wills. And, they are misunderstood by "Everyday Joes" who will never fully grasp the depths of their talents. Yet, each day, they line up against one another—the black hats playing offense, the white hats on the defense, on a virtual battlefield the likes of which the vast majority of people will never comprehend.

Their difference in ideologies is obvious. So, too, is the point that bad guys don't play fair. They are not governed by organizational rules. They don't worry about falling out of favor in office politics or missing the next job promotion. They can remain laser-focused on their mission—taking out their target.

White hats also stand vigilant defending their turfs. They know their objective is to thwart the next attack. On this, both black hats and white hats have clear purpose, albeit on opposite sides of principle.

However, beyond the first-mover advantage and lack of rulebook enjoyed by black hats, they have one more leg up on their white hat counterparts: clarity of incentives. Whether for profit, principle, or province, black hats know their ultimate prize. They can fairly balance risk and reward when considering their opportunity. Most important, their incentive is linked to their ultimate goal, driving consistent behaviors among the black hat community.

In contrast, white hats don't simply suffer unclear incentives (due to the challenging IT environment in which they often reside), they are actually misled by wrong incentives altogether. If your ultimate goal is to keep *nothing* from happening, then you must prove your worth by doing *something*. As such, cybersecurity professionals continue plunking down money to install the next cybersecurity godsend, complete with attractive promises and marketing superlatives that all but guarantee successful aversion to their enemy's next attack. Boards of directors and CEOs would expect as much. If a white hat isn't deploying new technology, then he is clearly not shoring up defenses as effectively as he otherwise could. Of course, proving the value of these technologies is elusive at best, but what else is a good guy expected to do?

So, consider the scenario: You're a cybersecurity professional in an unfair fight. You have a limited budget to protect a network that was never purpose-built for security. You have a growing number of adversaries who seek to do your organization harm. And, you have employees who play as unwitting allies to your adversary in this virtual battle—aiding the enemy by taking increasingly seductive phishing bait or otherwise using poor security hygiene. In this unfortunate scenario, *activity* is perceived to be your friend. And, more than likely, your organization is directly or indirectly incentivizing you in this direction.

To put a finer point on organizational incentives, in general, consider that most reward structures have been found to be ineffective at driving the right employee behaviors. In the late 1980s, when incentive-based reward structures had enamored Corporate America, an industrious researcher investigated 28 previously published studies on the topic to determine if there was a conclusive link between financial incentives and performance. G. Douglas Jenkins, Jr. revealed that 57 percent of the studies indeed found a positive effect on performance. However, all of the performance measures were quantitative in nature, such as producing more of a widget or doing a particular job faster. Only five of the studies looked at the quality of performance. And, none of those studies found any conclusive benefits from incentives.[27]

Here is where the wheels simply fall off the track for well-intentioned cybersecurity professionals. The *quality* of their deployments is actually much more important than the *quantity* of what they attempt to ingest in their IT environments. Deploying one security widget after the next in a disintegrated fashion only serves to clutter the perspective through which these professionals must detect attacks. As we will see in the next chapter, the fragmented cybersecurity posture that often results leaves white hats overwhelmed by their own noise—with multiple cybersecurity products triggering alarms (some real, some false) with little to no automation or orchestration to remedy the threats.

Of course, this scenario presumes these white hats even successfully deploy multiple technologies in the first place. Thanks to tricky budget cycles, a common practice for companies is to buy software in a budget cycle, with money allocated to the next year for deployment and maintenance. Unfortunately, this strategy is often doomed to fail. In 2014, the average organization spent $115 per user on security-related software, with $33 of it (or 28 percent) underutilized or not used at all. This dreaded "shelfware," as it is derisively known by industry insiders, is often the result of overloaded cybersecurity professionals, who are simply too busy to implement it properly.[28]

And, in perhaps the most unfortunate case of an asymmetric advantage in an unfair fight, black hats need not worry about quality in their efforts. They only need one attack to land. If they can overwhelm their target with multiple assaults, the law of numbers begins to turn in their favor. Quality certainly helps their efforts, but it is not necessary. As many of the latest black-swan attacks in recent history show, even fairly crude attempts can yield big gains for the bad guys.

Understanding the plight of white hat heroes, who tirelessly and faithfully defend the borders of our organizations day and night, is one step forward in correcting the aberrations they unfairly face while doing so. Subjugating cybersecurity beneath parochial IT principles only handicaps their efforts further. In many ways, we submit cybersecurity is the most *anti-IT* of all the technology functions. It follows a radically different playbook given radically different circumstances. In the most dangerous of scenarios, flawed incentive structures (whether tangible or intangible) lead to devastating consequences, as white hats attempt to prove their value and thwart their enemy through lots of activity. Such behavior often leads to a disintegrated security environment that creates more work for its architects, in the worst of cases leaving scarce organizational resources to literally die on the vine as "shelfware."

Coming back to where we started in this chapter, it is very difficult to conceive how cybersecurity professionals enjoy the least stressful of 200 positions, given the set of circumstances they face each day. LinkedIn blogger Jerod Brennen finished his post with the words of the successful InfoSec professional's mantra: "Do you remember that awful, horrible, expensive incident that NEVER happened? You're welcome."[29]

To the white hats reading this, know that many of us greatly appreciate what you do. You often succeed in spite of scales that are tipped in your enemy's favor. Yet, balancing the scales goes beyond convincing your organizations that IT tenets are, more often than not, irrelevant in your daily work. It will also require you to take a second look at preconceived notions that have been indoctrinated in cybersecurity since its inception. Just as traditional IT provides a framework that is unsustainable, early and lasting cybersecurity principles also jeopardize the effectiveness of white hats who are already too limited in number and too overwhelmed by the battle, a topic we reserve for the next chapter. Leaving our heroes to play second fiddle to increasingly irrelevant paradigms only serves the enemy in *The Second Economy*.

A SECOND HELPING OF THE INTERNET'S DESIGN PRINCIPLES

In 1988, MIT scientist David D. Clark was presiding over a meeting of network engineers when news broke of a worm aggressively making its way across the Internet—the first widespread attack of its kind, leaving thousands of machines and their exasperated users crippled in its wake. What would ultimately become known as the Morris Worm exploited a vulnerability called "buffer overflow." Scientists in the 1960s knew buffer overflow was a problem. It occurs when a program, while writing data to a buffer, overruns the buffer's boundary and overwrites adjacent memory locations, leaving these areas exposed to malware infestation. In 1988, buffer overflow was still a problem. At Clark's meeting, an honest engineer working for a leading computer company, admitted to his fellow meeting attendees, "Damn, I thought I had fixed that bug."[30]

The Morris Worm exploited not only buffer overflow but also the most basic principles of the Internet's early design. In 1988, just a few months before Morris released his creation to the world, Clark authored a widely read whitepaper that documented the tenets of the Internet's architecture. These architectural characteristics were in support of the Internet's primary goal: to develop an effective technique for multiplexed utilization of existing interconnected networks. Specifically, the seven guiding principles of the Internet's initial design were:

1. Internet communication must continue despite loss of networks or gateways.

2. The Internet must support multiple types of communications service.

3. The Internet architecture must accommodate a variety of networks.

4. The Internet architecture must permit distributed management of its resources.

5. The Internet architecture must be cost effective.

6. The Internet architecture must permit host attachment with a low level of effort.

7. The resources used in the Internet architecture must be accountable.[31]

For those counting, the seven guiding principles consist of 75 words—not one of them being any derivative of *secure*. Morris' contagion would take advantage of the deliberately designed frictionless and highly accessible architecture of the Internet. Despite Morris acting out of curiosity and not malice, his effort resulted in millions of dollars in damage[32] and provided a harsh wake-up call to early netizens of the potential dark side to such open ubiquity.

More than a quarter of a century later, buffer overflow remains a perennial favorite vulnerability for hacker exploits. And, society is still struggling with a pervasive Internet design that was never calculated for security. Despite these mainstays, there was a change that occurred, at least partly thanks to the Morris Worm. Twenty years after his seminal 1988 paper, Clark published again—this time crafting a new set of priorities for a National Science Foundation project on building a better Internet. At the top of the list? One word: *Security.*[33]

Notes

1. William D. Marbach, Madelyn Resener, John Carey, Richard Sandza, et al., "Beware: Hackers at Play," *Newsweek*, September 5, 1983.

2. Kerri Anne Renzulli, "These Are the 10 Most Stressful Jobs You Can Have," *Time Money*, http://time.com/money/4167989/most-stressful-jobs/, January 7, 2016, accessed June 29, 2016.

3. Ibid.

4. Kieren McCarthy, "The least stressful job in the US? Information security analyst, duh," *The Register*, June 2, 2016, www.theregister.co.uk/2016/06/02/least_stressful_job_is_infosec_analyst/, accessed June 29, 2016.

5. Jerod Brennen, "The Curse of the Information Security Professional," LinkedIn, January 12, 2016, www.linkedin.com/pulse/curse-information-security-professional-jerod-brennen-cissp, accessed June 29, 2016 (emphasis added).

6. Renzulli, note 2 *supra*.

7. Craig Timberg, "A Flaw in the Design," *The Washington Post*, May 30, 2015a, www.washingtonpost.com/sf/business/2015/05/30/net-of-insecurity-part-1/, accessed June 29, 2016.

8. Ibid.

9. Ibid.

10. www.ocf.berkeley.edu/~mbarrien/jokes/hackanth.txt, accessed June 30, 2016.

11. Marbach et al., note 1 *supra*.

12. Ibid.

13. Ibid.

14. Timothy B. Lee, "How a grad student trying to build the first botnet brought the Internet to its knees," *The Washington Post*, November 1, 2013, www.washingtonpost.com/news/the-switch/wp/2013/11/01/how-a-grad-student-trying-to-build-the-first-botnet-brought-the-internet-to-its-knees/, accessed July 1, 2016.

15. Ibid.

16. Craig Timberg, "A Disaster Foretold – and Ignored," *The Washington Post*, June 22, 2015b, www.washingtonpost.com/sf/business/2015/06/22/net-of-insecurity-part-3/, accessed July 1, 2016.

17. Marbach et al., note 1 *supra*.

18. Nicholas G. Carr, "IT Doesn't Matter," *Harvard Business Review*, May 2003, https://hbr.org/2003/05/it-doesnt-matter, accessed July 1, 2016.

19. Brandt Allen, "Make IT Services Pay Its Way," *Harvard Business Review*, January 1987, https://hbr.org/1987/01/make-information-services-pay-its-way, accessed July 1, 2016.

20. Carr, note 18 *supra*.

21. "Gartner Says Every Budget is Becoming an IT Budget," *Gartner*, October 22, 2012, www.gartner.com/newsroom/id/2208015, accessed July 1, 2016.

22. Nick Earle, "Do You Know the Way to Ballylickey? Shadow IT and the CIO Dilemma," Cisco Blogs, August 6, 2015, http://blogs.cisco.com/cloud/shadow-it-and-the-cio-dilemma, accessed August 12, 2016.

23. Sarah K. White, "IT leaders pick productivity over security," *CIO*, May 2, 2016, www.cio.com/article/3063738/security/it-leaders-pick-productivity-over-security.html, accessed July 1, 2016.

24. Ibid.

25. Ibid.

26. Ibid.

27. Alfie Kohn, "Why Incentive Plans Cannot Work," *Harvard Business Review*, September-October 1993 Issue, `https://hbr.org/1993/09/why-incentive-plans-cannot-work`, accessed July 1, 2016.

28. Maria Korolov, "Twenty-eight percent of security spending wasted on shelfware," *CSO*, January 27, 2015, `www.csoonline.com/article/2876101/metrics-budgets/28-percent-of-security-spending-wasted-on-shelfware.html`, accessed July 1, 2016.

29. Brennen, note 5 *supra*.

30. Timberg, note 7 *supra*.

31. David D. Clark, "The Design Philosophy of the DARPA Internet Protocols," Massachusetts Institute of Technology, Laboratory for Computer Science, Cambridge, MA 02139, 1988, paper, `http://ccr.sigcomm.org/archive/1995/jan95/ccr-9501-clark.pdf`, accessed on July 1, 2016.

32. Timberg, note 7 *supra*.

33. Ibid.

CHAPTER 7

■ ■ ■

Take a Second Look

There is no castle so strong that it cannot be overthrown by money.

—Marcus Tullius Cicero

Google the worst monarchs of England, and King John is bound to appear more than once. Described as "nature's enemy,"[1] a "pillager of his own people,"[2] a raging madman who "emitted foam from his mouth,"[3] and a man with "too many bad qualities"[4] (this last point from someone who actually fought on the king's side), John was a ruler with few supporters and countless enemies. The contempt was hard-earned over several decades of a failed and corrupt regime—one so reprehensible, it inspired that of the villainous character portrayed in Robin Hood legend.

John's offenses are almost too numerous to count and too egregious to be believed, if not for historical record. Start with a base of treachery (John attempted to overthrow his own brother from the throne while the latter was away on crusade), mix in some lechery (he was notorious for sexually accosting the wives and daughters of nobles), sprinkle in unspeakable evil (he arranged the murder of his own nephew and chief rival to the throne and cruelly killed his enemies through starvation), and add a strong dose of military incompetence (he earned the disreputable moniker "Softsword" for his ineptitude and cowardice on the battlefield) and you have a recipe for a monarch who stands history's test as being among the worst.[5]

For these grievances and more, John soon found himself embroiled in a bitter civil war against nobles who would have rather risked their lives than see him continue his reign. By that time, his grip over the kingdom was already weakening. When John first took the throne in 1199, he enjoyed expansive territory rule, including not only England and large parts of Wales and Ireland but also the western half of France.[6] Within five years, due to political incompetence and military ineptness, he had lost almost all of his French dominion to Philip Augustus.[7] Determined to repair a bruised reputation, John levied punitive taxes on his nobles and countrymen to fund a significant war chest. But, true to form, King "Softsword" failed to recapture the lost territories, retreating from battle when challenged by French forces and ceding once again to Philip Augustus. When the battered monarch returned to England, void of both victory and treasure, a civil war was imminent. After months of fruitless negotiations between John and barons on mutually acceptable reform, it erupted.

© 2016 by Intel Corp.
S. Grobman and A. Cerra, *The Second Economy*, DOI 10.1007/978-1-4842-2229-4_7

In 1215, a rebel army took control of the capital city of London. Soon after, the cities of Lincoln, Northampton, and Exeter also fell. With John losing ground, he disingenuously signed the first version of what would become the historic Magna Carta, a document that established the basic human rights of his subjects. Seemingly unmoved by his empty commitment, the corrupt king was soon back to his old ways, arbitrarily seizing the land of his adversaries. The exacerbated rebellion was left with no other option than to ally with Prince Louis of France, not of English descent himself but a welcome alternative to a tyrannical ruler nonetheless.

Over the next several months, Louis gained momentum, conquering one city after the next, getting ever closer to seizing the throne. By the middle of 1216, there was one notable bastion still under John's rule that would determine the outcome of the war. Dover, also known as the "key of England," sat at the nearest sea crossing point to France, making it a strategic asset of military and political import. For Louis' star to rise, Dover had to fall. But, taking the fortress would require incomparable strategy, precision, and grit. In terms of defenses, Dover stood in a class all its own.

Dover was, in fact, a castle within a castle—the first of its kind in Western Europe. Laying siege to the "keep," the tower at the heart of the castle where the most valuable treasure and human lives were protected, required an enemy to pass a series of deadly obstacles. The keep itself was a formidable structure—an 83-foot-tall, 100-square-foot tower with walls up to 21 feet in thickness.[8]

Louis meticulously planned his assault, surveying the fortress for several days before charging. He would first have to restrict the castle's supply to outside reinforcements. That would require Louis to surround men on the ground and at sea as Dover was ensconced behind expansive land and an outer moat. Louis' army would then need to make their way past an exterior wall and fence of stakes, all the while avoiding archers deployed on the concentric rings of inner and outer walls—the former at a higher altitude than the latter—which allowed Dover to double up its aerial military strength. The geometry of the walls themselves presented another challenge for Louis' men. Most castles of the day had square towers, which introduced structural blind spots that left defending archers vulnerable. Dover had circular towers, in addition to square, offering its garrison maximum visibility and offensive coverage.

With Louis' army in place and Dover completely cut off from possible outside reinforcements, the siege was on. By all accounts, Louis put up an impressive fight— first attempting to take the castle with mangonels and perriers (military devices used to catapult stones and other weapons from considerable distances). When that failed, he went underground —literally—deploying miners to excavate their way under the structure's massive stone towers. Louis' army did damage to the behemoth, ultimately bringing down one of the towers but, after months of exhausting fighting, the French prince was unable to fully lay claim to Dover. On October 14, 1216, Louis opted for a truce, vanquishing hope for John to be dethroned by military force. Just a few days later, John was removed from his post by other means, via a deadly dysentery attack.[9] The throne was passed to John's untainted nine-year-old son Henry (King Henry III) and England remained under the rule of one of her own. Had Dover fallen or Louis' army withstood battle just a few more days until John's passing, history may very well have been rewritten.

The castle defenses popular in Dover's day existed to deter enemies. Moats were common, allowing defenders to shoot enemy encroachers attempting to swim or sail across. Ramparts provided steep walls that required expert scaling and physical strength to breach. Even taller towers and walls further fortified the most impressive fortresses, impenetrable by climbing and requiring weaponry (like mangonels and perriers) to take down by other means. Tunneling underneath a castle was possible, as Louis proved at Dover, but not for the faint of heart, as the defending army would burrow their way to meet their attackers underground to brutally fight in darkness and confinement. Even assuming an enemy was successful in making his way into the castle, murdering holes, openings in the ceiling just past the castle's front gate purposely designed to allow defenders to drench their adversary in boiling liquids, often served as an additional unfortunate surprise.

In short, as the refuges for their kingdoms' most precious assets, castles were built to withstand attacks at multiple levels. Defenses were designed to adapt to an adversary's countermeasure. This defense-in-depth strategy, as it would come to be known, became a highly effective military technique. The premise was simple: don't rely on any one defense for protection; instead, reinforce with multiple layers, each designed to anticipate the enemy's next move and mitigate risk of any single point of failure. If and when an attack does occur, each successive obstacle in the enemy's path buys the victim precious time to ready contingency plans.

When threats can be seen, such as a rabid army storming a castle, defense in depth has proven itself to be extremely effective. Further, when threats can be anticipated, such as said army tunneling underground or striking unscalable walls with weapons, defense in depth's layered approach successfully thwarts an enemy's advancement. Its success in military strikes can be chalked up to its rootedness in common sense. Why rely on only a single defense mechanism to protect lives and treasure? Indeed, when the enemy is visible and his countermeasures are known, defense in depth is smart practice. But, when adversaries form a new threat vector entirely, a strategy based on mistakenly flawed assumptions leaves victims unconsciously exposed, subject to an enemy's counterattack all the while trusting in their insufficient fortifications. As history would reveal, a victim believing his castle to be safe can be undone by his own defenses.

Taking the Keep

When Mohamed Atta checked in for his flight from Portland to Boston on September 11, 2001, his name was flagged in a computerized prescreening system known as CAPPS (Computer Assisted Passenger Prescreening System), indicating he should undergo additional airport security screening measures. CAPPS required any suspect's checked baggage be held until the subject was confirmed to have boarded the plane. No problem. Atta then proceeded through a standard metal detector, calibrated to detect the metal equivalent of a .22-caliber handgun. He passed. His bags were placed on an X-ray belt for potential weapons, like knives with more than a four-inch blade, or other restricted materials. All clear.

On that fateful morning, Atta and 18 other conspirators, more than half of whom were also flagged by CAPPS, boarded four different flights, each passing a series of airport security measures in doing so. They intended to hijack the planes and had successfully averted every airport screening defense designed to stop them. In metaphorical terms, they had made it past the outer wall of the castle. Next, they had to overcome security on the plane itself. Using the knives and box cutters they had successfully smuggled across airport security defenses, the terrorists forced airline crews into submission. The flight personnel likely easily surrendered, as their training instructed them to succumb to a hijacker's demands, focusing on landing the plane rather than fighting the enemy. Once the terrorists were in the cockpit, the inner wall of the castle was theirs.

Elsewhere, up to 50,000 office workers began their Tuesday at Manhattan's iconic World Trade Center (WTC). Some eight years prior, the site was attacked when a 1,500-pound bomb stashed in a rental van detonated in a parking garage beneath the building. The explosion claimed six casualties and more than 1,000 injuries and exposed serious vulnerabilities in the WTC's emergency preparedness plan. The bombing was likely a distant memory to those employed at the WTC that September morning in 2001. After all, following the 1993 attack, the WTC had fortified its defenses, spending $100 million on physical, structural, and technological improvements to the building and bolstering its evacuation plans.[10] In case of another bomb planted within the building, the WTC was presumably ready. Tragically, the WTC would not get the chance to test its defenses against a similarly placed bomb, as the imminent threat looming that morning would come from a completely different attack vector. At 8:46 AM on 9/11, it came in the form of a hijacked commercial airliner, crashing into the upper portion of the North Tower of the WTC, severing seven floors and killing hundreds instantly. At 9:03 AM, the South Tower was struck by one of the other four planes hijacked by terrorists. The "keep" was taken.

The flawed assumptions behind a failed defense-in-depth approach are difficult to ignore, if not unfair to criticize. The Federal Aviation Administration anticipated an explosive device would be left aboard a flight—not carried on by an attacker. It certainly did not envisage an outcome where a hijacked plane could be used as a guided missile any more than WTC security professionals fathomed their site to be the target. The crews aboard likely did not put up the same resistance they would have otherwise had they known no safe landing was possible once the hijackers seized the cockpit. One by one, 19 terrorists seeped through traditional, layered security defenses to execute a plot so unimaginable it would result in the deadliest terrorist attack on US soil. Defense in depth couldn't overcome the overlooking of one critical fact: the terrorist group behind the 9/11 attack, al Qaeda, desired death more than their victims desired life.[11]

But, to be fair, defense in depth was never designed to completely eliminate all possible threats. It was intended to thwart an enemy at each turn, buying the victim precious time to contemplate contingency plans. In this way, laying the 9/11 tragedy at the feet of a trampled defense-in-depth system seems grossly unfair. However, consider that this same system created distinct silos that actually impeded the ability of the United States to respond, and you now have a case where defense in depth failed in both protecting against and containing the threat.

Examine the distinct layered defenses involved in 9/11, each of which failed independently and none of which communicated with another to properly identify and remediate the threat. Several of the terrorists were on the CAPPS registry. Yet, airport security personnel were unaware of what intelligence had been collected on each subject to respond more earnestly to the alert. When the terrorists on the first hijacked flight to strike the WTC inadvertently broadcast this message intended for the plane's passengers to air traffic controllers instead, a known hijacking was in motion:

> Nobody move. Everything will be okay. If you try to make any moves, you'll endanger yourself and the airplane. Just stay quiet.[12]

Yet, no other flights were notified or grounded, even when it was later detected that the terrorists on the first flight had also exposed they had "some planes" in a transmitted message. After the first hit, occupants in the North Tower were instructed by 911 operators to remain in the building and stay calm. The deputy fire safety director in the South Tower told his counterpart in the North Tower that he would wait to hear from "the boss from the Fire Department or somebody," before ordering an evacuation.[13] No such directive came. Instead, like those in the North Tower, occupants in the South Tower were informed to remain where they were. Some in the process of evacuation were instructed to return to their desks. Less than 20 minutes later, the choice to evacuate was no longer an option for hundreds who instantly died upon contact with the second airliner. Had a message been relayed to WTC security and 911 phone operators that multiple planes had been hijacked, perhaps the order to evacuate would have followed, saving hundreds, if not thousands, of lives, including that of the South Tower deputy fire safety director himself.

The heroes who immediately sprang into action to rescue the trapped before both towers ultimately fell suffered from siloed conditions as well. Different radio frequencies in use by emergency responders delayed, if not confused, communications. As a result of this breakdown, many heroic first responders perished when the towers gave way.

To be clear, there's no telling how many other potential 9/11s were avoided prior to the actual tragedy thanks to the layered defenses deployed across the various US governmental agencies. Abandoning a commonsense defensive approach that mitigates against a single point of failure is equivalent to throwing the baby out with the bathwater. However, what is clear is that a defense-in-depth approach is only as effective as its architects are in anticipating new threats and identifying them when they emerge. Radically different or altogether ignored threats can readily penetrate a layered defensive system. And, in the asymmetrical battle against adversary and victim, the former only needs to succeed once while the latter must be right 100 percent of the time. When those points of failure are correctly calculated by adversaries, a disintegrated defense-in-depth approach cannot easily, let alone systematically, pass threat intelligence across its siloes to inoculate the attack. Victims are left confused, if not blinded, by the very layered security framework they employed—a point that becomes even clearer when the battle moves to the virtual realm.

Securing the Virtual Castle

The defense-in-depth approach for cybersecurity was initially recommended by none other than the National Security Agency (NSA). In an NSA whitepaper, the government agency advised defense in depth to be a practical strategy encompassing people, technology, and operations—one that considered adversarial motives associated with various threat actors (including nation-states, hacktivists, and cybercrime) across a holistic security paradigm of protecting, detecting, and reacting to attacks.[14] Similar to the castle strategy employed in medieval times, the cyber defense-in-depth approach advocated by the NSA examined various threat vectors with many layers of protection and detection to present adversaries with unique, multiple obstacles. For example:

- A passive attack could be first thwarted by link and network layer encryption to secure traffic flows; if adversaries made it past this first line of attack, they would be met with security enabled at the application layer as an additional line of defense.

- An active attack may be met with firewalls and intrusion detection systems; if those are bypassed, adversaries could face access controls on hosts and servers within the computing environment itself.

- Insider attacks must first overcome physical and personnel security measures; if successful, these adversaries would then be subjected to technical surveillance countermeasures.[15]

This layered approach to cyber defenses served to increase the risk of detection for the adversary, while reducing the chances of successful breach, if not to make it increasingly unaffordable for threat actors to continue their assault. The defense-in-depth approach became the veritable blueprint for cybersecurity strategy. Organizations rushed headlong into deploying multiple defenses to secure every aspect of their virtual castles. Antivirus software protected endpoints; firewalls and intrusion detection systems defended networks; encryption secured sensitive data; multiple factors of authentication provided authorized access; web application firewalls monitored traffic running to and from web applications and servers; and so on, and so on.

The most zealous organizations deployed redundancy in addition to defense in depth. Why rely on one antivirus solution that may not detect all possible malware when multiple installations from multiple providers could potentially catch even more threats? The same could be said for any other security countermeasure running in one's environment. In an arms race, suppliers typically win. And, cybersecurity professionals definitely faced no shortage of companies ready and willing to sell the next widget to further inoculate one's virtual castle against enterprising adversaries. In 2015 alone, private investors pumped a record $3.3 billion into 229 cybersecurity deals, with each budding company prepared to offer the latest weapon all but guaranteed to further solidify an organization's cybersecurity posture.[16] Cybersecurity professionals, eager to avoid being the next poster child of attack due to a lack of doing *something* responded in kind, deploying multiple technologies from multiple vendors.

If there was no shortage of cybersecurity products and technologies, sadly, the same could not be said for the pipeline of talent entering the cybersecurity labor force. With adversarial attacks showing no sign of abating, there simply aren't enough good guys in the fight to ward off the next threat. Consider just a few of the more startling statistics to prove the point:

- Only 26 percent of US organizations say they have capable personnel on staff to address cyber risks associated with implementation of new technologies[17];

- In 2014, there were nearly 50,000 postings for workers with a Certified Information Systems Security Professional (CISSP) standing, the primary credential in cybersecurity work, amounting to three-quarters of all individuals in the United States holding the certification, most of whom presumably already had jobs.[18]

- Security managers in North America and EMEA (Europe, the Middle East, and Africa) report significant obstacles in implementing desired security projects due to lack of staff expertise (34.5 percent) and inadequate staffing (26.4 percent). Because of this, less than one-quarter of enterprises have 24/7 monitoring in place using internal resources.[19]

- In 2014, there were 1,000 top-level cybersecurity experts in the United States, versus a need for at least 9,000 and up to 29,000 more.[20]

- In 2015, more than 209,000 cybersecurity positions in the United States went unfilled, with postings up nearly 75 percent over the past five years.[21]

- Demand for cybersecurity professionals is expected to rise to 6 million globally by 2019, with a projected shortfall of 1.5 million going unfilled by that time.[22]

Facing an unemployment rate hovering near 0 percent, cybersecurity professionals can literally write their ticket, forcing resource-constrained organizations into an escalating bidding war to recruit top talent. Those with the title "information security manager" represented the hottest job in information technology (IT) in 2016, boasting the biggest increase in average total compensation in the sector (up 6.4 percent from 2015 to 2016).[23] In the consummate seller's market, nearly 75 percent of cybersecurity professionals admitted to being approached by a hiring organization or headhunter.[24] And, the top-paying job in cybersecurity in 2015, that of a security software engineer, averaged $233,333 in annual salary, exceeding the $225,000 earned by the average chief security officer (CSO).[25]

True, some cybersecurity positions can be filled in short order—in as little as three months, on average, for entry-level positions. But, with an increasingly sophisticated adversary and ever-complex security tools and technologies, the more advanced cybersecurity positions take far longer to fill—more than one-fifth of jobs requiring ten or more years' experience sit vacant for at least a year.[26] Even when an organization can find the right talent for its cybersecurity concern, it will likely be forced to pay dearly to poach him away from the well-paying job he already enjoys.

Despite reaping the spoils from a hot job market, it's not all upside for cybersecurity professionals, many of whom are increasingly overwhelmed. Nearly two-thirds of them report being under pressure to take on new tasks or increase productivity, challenges that are not expected to subside anytime soon.[27] More than 60 percent expect their workload and responsibility to increase in the next 12 months.[28] These demands are the result of an innovative adversary market, always favored to make the first move in an attack, and the ever-expanding attack surface through which such advances can be made. No longer protecting a castle that is well understood and walled off from the outside world, enterprises are confounded by an increasingly mobile workforce spurred by limitless connectivity across all types of endpoints (computers, servers, mobile devices, wearables, and more) and public and private clouds. According to analyst Gartner, by 2018, 25 percent of corporate data traffic will bypass perimeter security and flow directly from mobile devices to the cloud.[29]

And, here is where the perfect storm of defense in depth run amok, an anemic cybersecurity labor market and an increasingly untethered workforce collide to drive the greatest of unintended outcomes. Cybersecurity professionals are working harder for the various tools deployed across an organization's environment to secure multiple domains. Approximately two-thirds of cybersecurity professionals cite "tool sprawl"—the unintended consequence of deploying multiple disintegrated security technologies across one's environment—as a significant concern[30] in impeding productivity of an already overtaxed labor pool. Disintegrated management and communications platforms are spiraling out of control for many cybersecurity first responders, making it more difficult to detect threats or creating sufficient confusion to overestimate risk at the other end of the spectrum. Both extremes offer disastrous consequences.

Erring on the Side of Caution

The Economic Development Administration (EDA) is an agency within the US government's Department of Commerce that promotes economic development in regions of the United States suffering from slow growth, high unemployment, and other unenviable economic conditions. The agency had suffered a weak security posture in its history, hardly deploying aggressive defense-in-depth principles. When a new chief information officer (CIO) took the helm of the agency in 2011, he quickly learned of his organization's unflattering history of cybersecurity missteps—ranging from incomplete security configurations to untimely patch updates to lacking security assessments and monitoring. Later that year, when the US Department of Homeland Security (DHS) issued a warning to the EDA and sister government agency the National Oceanic and Atmospheric Administration (NOAA) that it detected a malware infestation on its network, both organizations sprang into action. One, the NOAA, would completely remediate the threat within six weeks. The other, the EDA, would lose months of employee productivity and millions of taxpayer dollars chasing a threat that never even existed.[31]

Most of us likely remember the "telephone" game we played as children. A message was started on one end of a long daisy chain, moving from one person to the next in a whisper. By the end of the chain, the message hardly matched its original version, showing how a simple misinterpretation can reverberate out of control. No truer analogy can be found to explain the EDA debacle. On December 6, 2011, the US Computer Emergency Response Team (US-CERT), part of the DHS, passed a message to both the EDA and NOAA, indicating suspicious activity found on IT systems operating on the Herbert C. Hoover Building (HCHB) network.[32] As both agencies used this network, the warning came to ensure their respective systems were not compromised in any possible attack.

In requesting network logging information to further investigate, the incident handler for the Department of Commerce's Computer Incident Response Team (DOC CIRT) unknowingly requested the wrong data. The first responder's error resulted in what was believed to be 146 EDA components under risk within its network boundary[33]—a substantial malware infection of the organization's computer footprint.

The very next day, an HCHB network administrator informed the DOC CIRT incident handler that he had inadvertently pulled the wrong network logging information in his request (essentially retrieving all EDA components residing on the HCHB network). After a second, correct pull was extracted, only two components in the EDA's footprint were found to be suspicious. DOC CIRT sent a second e-mail notification to the EDA, attempting to clarify the mistake, but the e-mail was vague at best, leaving the EDA to continue in the inaccurate belief that 146 components were potentially at risk.[34]

Over the next five weeks, communications between DOC CIRT and the EDA continued, with each organization effectively talking past the other. The EDA was under the mistaken impression that most of its infrastructure had been potentially compromised thanks to DOC CIRT's original misinformation that was never properly clarified. DOC CIRT assumed the EDA had conducted its own audit finding a much more pervasive outbreak of up to 146 elements—even though the EDA hardly had the resources to complete such an investigation. As the newly appointed CIO of the EDA feared a nation-state attack and further blemish to his agency's already tainted cybersecurity record, tensions mounted and extreme measures were taken.

When DOC CIRT asked the EDA to invoke normal containment measures, as basic as reimaging the affected components, the EDA refused, citing too many incidents of compromise to contain the threat. Fearing the worst, the EDA asked to be quarantined off from the HCHB network on January 24, 2012.[35] Doing so would leave hundreds of EDA employees without access to e-mail or Internet servers and databases for months.[36] The EDA hired a cybersecurity contractor to actively investigate the threat, activity that commenced on January 30, 2012.[37] Based on a preliminary analysis, the contractor reported he had found indications of extremely persistent malware and suspicious activity on the EDA's components. Panic erupted into full-blown hysteria.

Two weeks later, the same cybersecurity contractor corrected his own version of events, reporting those incidents of compromise were nothing more than false positives—activity that appeared suspicious but was actually benign instead. To a CIO inheriting an agency with a sketchy cybersecurity record, the reassurance was hardly enough. He wanted a guarantee that all components were infection-free and no malware could persist—a bet any reasoned cybersecurity expert would be loath to make. By April 16, 2012, despite months of searching, EDA's cybersecurity contractor could find no other extremely persistent malware or incidents of compromise across the agency's system. The NSA and US-CERT confirmed the same.[38]

Convinced that any further forensics investigation would not lead to new results and compelled to clean up what it believed to be a widespread infestation, the EDA took drastic measures on May 15, 2012, and began physically destroying more than $170,000 worth of its IT components, including desktops, printers, TVs, cameras, and even computer mice and keyboards. If not for being refused for more money, the agency would have destroyed up to $3 million more of its infrastructure in an effort to contain an imaginary threat.[39]

All told, the EDA spent more than $2.7 million—over half of its annual IT budget— in an unfortunate overreaction to a threat that could easily have been remediated. More than $1.5 million of taxpayer dollars went to paying independent cybersecurity contractors and another $1 million went to standing up a temporary IT infrastructure after asking to be exiled from the HCHB network. And, of course, there was the $170,000 in destroyed equipment that could have soared much higher had cooler heads (and finite budgets) not prevailed.[40]

Beyond a folly of poor communication exacerbated by extreme paranoia, the agency's overreaction could be chalked up to a lack of skill and management tools in diagnosing the problem. Had the EDA simply verified for itself, it would have found that there was no risk of infection from its e-mail server, deployed with the latest version of antivirus software that was performing weekly scans and had found no incident of attack. In the end, there were only six components—a far cry from the wrongly assumed 146— with malware infections, each of which could have been easily remediated using typical containment measures, like reimaging, which would have had a negligible impact to operations and budget.[41]

In what would be heralded as an extreme case of overreaction, the EDA faced condemnation of a different sort. The seeming incompetence in wasting millions of dollars of taxpayer money chasing an imaginary adversary had critics excoriating the agency's ineptitude. Yet, had the danger been real and the agency not reacted, the public outcry would likely have been even greater. Rebecca Blank, appointed as acting commerce secretary in June 2012 and who ordered the investigation, put it simply:

> The EDA did not know what it was facing. Under those circumstances, given the cyber risks [to the government], one has to be cautious. In retrospect, it was not as serious as they originally thought. But it's a question of which side do you want to err on?[42]

Indeed, as another organization with no shortage of cybersecurity defenses would soon find, erring on the other side carries even greater consequences.

Ignoring One's Defenses

Unlike the EDA, retailer Target intended to be at the top of its class in employing cybersecurity professionals and equipping them with the latest technology. In the world of cybersecurity, retailers find themselves in the crosshairs of innovative adversaries often motivated by profit. Only 5 percent of retailers discover breaches through their own monitoring capabilities.[43] Target aspired to be different, building an information security staff numbering more than 300 by 2013, a tenfold increase in less than ten years.

That same summer, Target spent close to $2 million installing a malware detection tool using a new technology called sandboxing. Given the very nature of a zero-day threat means it has not yet been detected by other means and therefore can bypass other defenses, like antivirus capabilities that look for known malware attempts, sandboxing executes suspicious programs within a confined test environment, quarantined away from the rest of the corporate network. The malware, deceived into believing it is operating within the target's environment, begins executing. After unpacking its contents and finding the program to be malicious, the zero-day threat is thwarted by the sandbox, preventing it from entering the corporate network. Target had a team of security specialists in Bangalore to monitor its network around the clock. If anything suspicious was detected, Bangalore would immediately notify the company's security operations center in Minneapolis. The company intended to protect its castle against motivated criminals storming the gates.

Those raiders encroached in September 2013.[44] As mentioned in Chapter 1, cybercriminals performed basic online reconnaissance to locate approved vendors with remote access to Target's systems. No one knows how many targets were attempted before Fazio Mechanical Services, a heating, air conditioning, and refrigeration company based in Sharpsburg, Pennsylvania, fell prey to the thieves' phishing scheme. The phishing attempt would likely have been caught had Fazio deployed the latest available corporate antivirus solution. The company instead used free antivirus software intended for consumer use. The enemy was able to infiltrate the outer wall of Target's castle by stealing the credentials of a compromised vendor, one that would more than likely have had access to Target's external billing system. By November 12, the attackers had penetrated Target's inner wall, successfully breaching the company for the first time.[45] From there, adversaries ultimately snaked their way to Target's valuable point-of-sale (POS) infrastructure, testing their malware for close to two weeks.

On November 30, multiple alerts were sounded by Target's defensive software. The software deployed on the company's endpoints triggered suspicious activity alerts. Perhaps more important, the newly deployed sandboxing software triggered a severe alert the same day.[46] The alerts were passed from Bangalore to the company's security operations center, business as usual, all the while the adversary had fully installed the malware on the company's POS system. The "keep" was in the crosshairs.

On December 2, the attackers installed upgraded versions of their malware to exfiltrate data from Target's systems during the busiest times of day, apparently to obfuscate the traffic in the company's normal transactions.[47] Again, another sandboxing critical alert was triggered.[48] Again, Bangalore notified Minneapolis. Again, nothing happened.

It would take nearly another two weeks before Target would identify the threat and remove the malware. By then, more than 40 million credit and debit cards would be stolen along with the personally identifiable information of up to 70 million more customers. In all, the raiders had siphoned off 11 gigabytes of sensitive information from the company's "keep" in just two weeks. Not only did Target's defenses trigger alerts that would have more than stopped the invasion, had the company simply defaulted to having the malware automatically removed (an available option not taken when installing the new system), the missed alerts between Bangalore and Minneapolis would have been inconsequential.

Of course, hindsight is always 20/20 and one can easily play the "should have, could have, would have" game after an attack occurs. But, in Target's case, what is perhaps most interesting is the fact that the company was active in deploying the latest technology to secure its environment. It was also zealous in hiring cybersecurity experts to monitor its network. It had ostensibly taken the preventive measures to secure its castle and then summarily dismissed the very alerts provided by its own technology.

One may criticize the company for not automatically defaulting any alarm to a removal of the suspected malware. But, that would ignore the popularity of false positives in the industry (remember the independent contractor's initial assessment of the EDA's risk came with false positives diagnosed only after further investigation?). If companies like Target automatically responded to every suspected threat as a DEFCON 1 assault, they would risk interrupting operations and customer service when possibly no threat exists at all.

On the flip side, one could excoriate Target for not noticing the alarms detected by both its endpoint and sandboxing security defenses in its environment. A company with the infrastructure of Target's—more than 360,000 employees, roughly 2,000 stores, 37 distribution centers, and a heavily trafficked retail web site[49]—likely sees hundreds of thousands of alerts in any given day. Separating the signal from the noise for an already overtaxed cybersecurity team becomes par for the course in determining which of the threats are most severe and most worthy of further investigation and action.

And so it goes: even companies deploying the latest cybersecurity tools backed by hundreds of their own cybersecurity experts can find themselves tomorrow's headline, accused of rolling out the proverbial red carpet to marauders seeking their castle's most valuable keep.

A Second Thought

Defense in depth has proven itself a viable military tactic since medieval times, if not earlier. It's no wonder the NSA quickly endorsed a similar approach to defend one's information assets across people, process, and technology and throughout the threat defense life cycle (from protection to detection to reaction). When enemies are seen in a physical world, defense in depth makes perfect sense. But, increasingly, in a virtual world, it faces a new set of challenges:

- *Defense in depth works when all layers operate as one.* A siloed approach to a defense-in-depth system compromises a first responder's ability to react. Not unlike the multiple siloes in operation during the 9/11 attacks, easily transferring threat intelligence between disparate groups is challenging, at best. Automatically remediating a threat without the benefit of further diagnostics can result in a different form of losses (through either lost productivity or a negatively impacted customer experience) if the threat is actually a false positive in disguise. In either case, an organization requires a team of cybersecurity experts willing and able to separate valuable signals from cacophonous noise and armed with machine learning that quickly elevates the most insidious threats to the top of the list, while automatically remediating threats of lower importance.

- *Defense in depth assumes you have friendly insiders.* In the case of insider attacks or even in the more common occurrence of employees falling victim to phishing schemes, organizations must defend against attack vectors coming from within their own walls. Otherwise, multiple defensive layers are automatically bypassed when insiders are themselves the evildoers, if not the entryways for adversaries.

- *Defense in depth is increasingly challenging when the walls of the castle are no more.* In an increasingly cloud- and mobile-based world, the castle's keep is often on the outside of its perimeter. The only things separating an authorized user from his cloud-based application or file are an Internet connection and login credentials. Securing this keep requires more than the most well-intended defense-in-depth approach.

- *Defense in depth can add disastrous complexity.* With a cybersecurity talent pool that is insufficient at best, a defense-in-depth approach that selects best-in-breed technology from across the stack serves to create tool sprawl for first responders. Disintegrated security environments are accompanied by fragmented management systems. Already strapped cybersecurity professionals are now in the unenviable place of working harder for their tools, rather than the other way around. Imagine if castle defenders had to constantly learn how to employ each weapon— bows and arrows, catapults, trebuchets, and the like—each time attackers advanced. Now imagine that a castle lacked sufficient defenders to master the intricacy of each of these tools. Finally, visualize a case where the defenders are literally blinded by these same tools, perhaps by each tool being in the way of a clear line of sight to an encroaching army—and you have the metaphorical case facing so many cybersecurity first responders today.

- *Defense in depth can sometimes be more perception than reality.* As an example, consider the case where the same technology is deployed across multiple instances of one's security environment, such as a deterministic signature-based antivirus engine placed on e-mail gateways, e-mail servers, and endpoints. We may assume we have hardened our technology defenses with multiple layers. In actuality, one circumvention of the underlying antivirus engine causes all similarly lined defenses to fall. Bringing this back to our 9/11 analogy, the weapons detection techniques deployed at multiple security checkpoints and airports across the country failed at least 19 times, as the terrorists found a way to successfully evade exposure with effectively concealed box cutters.

- *Defense in depth works when all defenders are unified in purpose and collaboration.* Cybersecurity professionals find themselves on the same side of the battle with one another, but often with conflicting agendas. As we discussed in Chapter 6, cybersecurity finds its roots in IT, a highly structured discipline within the organization. IT professionals specialize across various aspects of the technology stack—for instance, some look specifically at device considerations, others care for network connectivity, some worry about servers and storage, and still others consider software applications. In many cases, these organizations function more like silos than an integrated operation, each behaving independently from the other, with unique budgets and objectives. Using the castle metaphor, it would be the equivalent of guards at the gate readying their defenses without concern for how guards in the tower were preparing the same. Even worse, since these organizations may not even consult one another on the tools being used to detect threats in their environment, it would be more similar to guards at the gate and tower not being able to communicate with each other when enemies stormed the castle.

Despite these challenges, defense in depth remains a popular strategy employed by many cybersecurity professionals. In a 2016 McAfee research study, nearly half of organizations admit they subscribe to a cybersecurity posture that employs best-in-breed technology across the stack; the other half favor an integrated view of cybersecurity across the threat defense life cycle. Presumably, one of these cohorts is less effective than the other. The question is, which one?

To answer the question, McAfee asked organizations to define their degree of integration based on the percentage of workloads consolidated with one vendor. In interpreting the data, those companies with at least 40 percent of their security workloads with one vendor were classified as having an integrated view to security—presumably advantaged with a common management toolset offset by any disadvantages associated with not having best-in-breed technology available from multiple competing vendors. The company then asked respondents to answer a series of questions related to their security posture.

In the study, those companies with an integrated view to security reported:

- Being better protected, with 78 percent suffering less than five attacks in the past year compared with 55 percent of those with a best-in-breed security approach;

- Having faster response times, with 80 percent discovering threats in less than eight hours compared with 54 percent; and

- Feeling more confident in their security posture, with 30 percent losing sleep more than once per week due to security concerns versus 57 percent.

These results would indicate greater effectiveness with a more comprehensive view to security, one that is not exacerbated by multiple technologies in the same domain, often offered by different vendors, that only serve to confuse, if not impede, cybersecurity professionals from being effective in their jobs. That said, who wants to consolidate most of their security workloads with one vendor? Doing so entails increasing long-term risk of putting all of one's eggs in a single provider's basket. If that provider fails to innovate faster than adversaries, a company's most integrated approach to security will do little to protect its customers from the next threat vector.

If defense in depth overcomplicates one's security environment and a less complex integrated view increases potential long-term risk, where does an organization go to secure its castle? We submit the answer lies not in identifying a better product but, rather, a better platform for long-term security sustainability. It's an approach not embraced by many cybersecurity professionals if, for no other reason, than misaligned incentive structures that are in direct opposition to a long game of security, a topic covered in Chapter 6. As we continue laying out the case for cybersecurity defense in an increasingly cloud and mobile world, one thing is increasingly clear: defense in depth is a sound approach when one's castle is bordered and one's enemy readily identifiable—two presumptions that are less relevant with each passing day in *The Second Economy*.

A SECOND HELPING OF 9/11

It's November 1996. A known al Qaeda member purchases a satellite phone from a store in a New York suburb. That phone is shipped to Osama bin Laden in Afghanistan. Soon after the al Qaeda leader begins making phone calls, the National Security Agency is on his tail. NSA operatives begin painstakingly listening to, translating and transcribing all of bin Laden's phone calls, particularly those to Yemen, thought to be a key base for al Qaeda efforts. They share the summary of their findings with their government colleagues at the Central Intelligence Agency, but the CIA wants more. Believing that the key to unlocking bin Laden's intentions rests in seeing the actual transcripts of the calls, the CIA asks for the raw output from the NSA's translations. As one CIA agent working the case at the time explains the rationale for the request:

> Over time, if you read enough of these conversations, you first get clued in to the fact that maybe "bottle of milk" doesn't mean "bottle of milk." And if you follow it long enough, you develop a sense of what they're really talking about. But it's not possible to do unless you have the verbatim transcript.[50]

Despite the justifiable need, the NSA flatly refuses to comply. Its policy since inception has been to never share raw data, not even with fellow government intelligence agencies. Exasperated, the CIA attempts to surveil bin Laden directly with its own ground station. But, its efforts can only go so far. Without a satellite, the CIA is limited to hearing just one side of his conversations. Still, the CIA captures the conversations and shares with its colleagues at the NSA, hoping to get the other half. Again, it is denied.[51]

In 2000, an emboldened al Qaeda launches an attack on the USS Cole, deployed off the coast of Yemen. The NSA, overwhelmed by lots of noise in the system and shrinking budgets due to escalating privacy concerns in the United States, misses the threat. There is no shortage of data, just an abject dearth of information. As one intelligence agent recounts:

> You may collect a lot of stuff, but you don't know what you've got. Really, the biggest technology challenge was how do you deal with volumes of information like that and find dots, connect dots and understand dots. That's the problem.[52]

Still, the NSA is able to find one important dot in the midst of all the noise. The agency intercepts a call to the house in Yemen, instructing two al Qaeda foot soldiers to fly to Kuala Lumpur, Malaysia, for what seems to be a terrorist summit. The two are none other than Khalid al-Mihdhar and Nawaf al-Hazmi, the first of the 9/11 terrorists to set up operation in the United States. The NSA passes along the terrorists' first names, but not their surnames, to agents within the FBI and CIA.

Despite only having a first name to go by, the CIA picks up al-Mihdhar's name in its database. They put security agents on alert, asking for a copy of his passport when he passes through a checkpoint in Dubai. To their shock, they find he has a valid US visa inside. Fearing the terrorists are on their way to the United States for a possible attack, the CIA agents insist on letting their FBI counterparts know. Again, no dice. As the exasperated CIA agent relives the moment:

> I said, "What's going on? You know, we've got to tell the Bureau about this. These guys clearly are bad. One of them, at least, has a multiple-entry visa to the US. We've got to tell the FBI."

> And then she said to me, "No, it's not the FBI's case, not the FBI's jurisdiction."[53]

Fearing for his personal freedom, the CIA agent stands down. Violating the order would break the law. Unfortunately, it may have also unintentionally helped the deadliest terrorist attack on US soil. Despite each unit surveilling the metaphorical castle for signs of threat and capturing actionable intelligence that could have helped its neighboring agency, the siloed approach to defense was readily dismantled by al Qaeda operatives unified in mission and coordination. Even with defense efforts employed by each, jurisdictional boundaries and organizational siloes prevented the US intelligence agencies from acting as one unit against a common enemy—a weakness their adversary readily exploited that fateful day in 2001.

Notes

1. Charlotte Hodgman, "In case you missed it . . . King John and the French invasion of England," *History Extra*, October 16, 2015, article first published in *BBC History Magazine* in 2011, www.historyextra.com/feature/king-john-and-french-invasion-england, accessed June 14, 2016.

2. Ibid.

3. Ibid.

4. Ibid.

5. Marc Morris, "King John: the most evil monarch in Britain's history," *The Telegraph*, June 13, 2015, www.telegraph.co.uk/culture/11671441/King-John-the-most-evil-monarch-in-Britains-history.html, accessed June 14, 2016.

6. Ibid.

7. Ibid.

8. Danelle Au, "Is Defense In Depth Dead?," RSA Conference, March 12, 2015, www.rsaconference.com/blogs/is-defense-in-depth-dead, accessed June 15, 2016.

9. Hodgman, note 1 *supra*.

10. The 9/11 Commission Report, http://govinfo.library.unt.edu/911/report/911Report.pdf, accessed June 15, 2016.

11. Ibid.

12. Ibid.

13. Ibid.

14. "Defense in Depth: A practical strategy for achieving Information Assurance in today's highly networked environments," National Security Agency, https://citadel-information.com/wp-content/uploads/2010/12/nsa-defense-in-depth.pdf, accessed June 17, 2016.

15. Ibid.

16. Reuters, "Cyber Security Startups Face Funding Drought," *Fortune*, February 24, 2016, http://fortune.com/2016/02/24/cyber-security-funding-drought/, accessed June 17, 2016.

17. PwC, "US cybersecurity: Progress stalled; Key findings from the 2015 US State of Cybercrime Survey," July 2015, www.pwc.com/us/en/increasing-it-effectiveness/publications/assets/2015-us-cybercrime-survey.pdf, accessed June 17, 2016.

18. Burning Glass Technologies, "Job Market Intelligence: Cybersecurity Jobs, 2015," 2015, `http://burning-glass.com/wp-content/uploads/Cybersecurity_Jobs_Report_2015.pdf`, accessed June 17, 2016.

19. Steve Morgan, "Cybersecurity job market to suffer severe workforce shortage," *CSO Online*, July 28, 2015, `www.csoonline.com/article/2953258/it-careers/cybersecurity-job-market-figures-2015-to-2019-indicate-severe-workforce-shortage.html`, accessed June 17, 2016.

20. Martin Libicki, David Senty, and Julia Pollak, "H4CKER5 WANTED: An Examination of the Cybersecurity Labor Market," Rand Corporation, 2014, `www.rand.org/content/dam/rand/pubs/research_reports/RR400/RR430/RAND_RR430.pdf`, accessed June 17, 2016.

21. Ariha Setalvad, "Demand to fill cybersecurity jobs booming," *Peninsula Press*, March 31, 2015, `http://peninsulapress.com/2015/03/31/cybersecurity-jobs-growth/`, accessed June 17, 2016.

22. Steve Morgan, "One Million Cybersecurity Job Openings In 2016," Forbes, January 2, 2016, `www.forbes.com/sites/stevemorgan/2016/01/02/one-million-cybersecurity-job-openings-in-2016/#57a37cc37d27`, accessed June 17, 2016.

23. Amy Bennett, "Survey: With all eyes on security, talent shortage sends salaries sky high," *CSO*, March 30, 2016, `www.csoonline.com/article/3049374/security/survey-with-all-eyes-on-security-talent-shortage-sends-salaries-sky-high.html#tk.cso_nsdr_intrcpt`, accessed June 17, 2016.

24. Ibid.

25. "May 2015: Top-Paying Tech Security Jobs," *Dice*, `http://media.dice.com/report/may-2015-top-paying-tech-security-jobs/`, accessed June 17, 2016.

26. Bennett, note 23 *supra*.

27. Ibid.

28. Ibid.

29. Gartner on Twitter, @Gartner_inc, June 24, 2014, #GartnerSEC, tweet pulled on June 17, 2016.

30. Michael Suby and Frank Dickson, "The 2015 (ISC)² Global Information Security Workforce Study," a Frost & Sullivan White Paper, April 26, 2015, `www.isc2cares.org/uploadedFiles/wwwisc2caresorg/Content/GISWS/FrostSullivan-(ISC)%C2%B2-Global-Information-Security-Workforce-Study-2015.pdf`, accessed June 17, 2016.

31. US Department of Commerce, Office of Inspector General, Office of Audit and Evaluation, "ECONOMIC DEVELOPMENT ADMINISTRATION Malware Infections on EDA's Systems Were Overstated and the Disruptionof IT Operations Was Unwarranted," FINAL REPORT NO. OIG-13-027-A, June 26, 2013, www.oig.doc.gov/OIGPublications/OIG-13-027-A.pdf, accessed June 17, 2016.

32. Ibid.

33. Ibid.

34. Ibid.

35. Ibid.

36. Lisa Rein, "At Commerce Dept., false alarm on cyberattack cost almost $3 million," *The Washington Post*, July 14, 2013, www.washingtonpost.com/politics/at-commerce-dept-false-alarm-on-cyberattack-cost-almost-3-million/2013/07/13/11b92690-ea41-11e2-aa9f-c03a72e2d342_story.html, accessed June 17, 2016.

37. US Department of Commerce, note 31 *supra*.

38. Ibid.

39. Ibid.

40. Ibid.

41. Ibid.

42. Rein, note 36 *supra*.

43. Michael Riley, Benjamin Elgin, Dune Lawrence, and Carol Matlack, "Missed Alarms and 40 Million Stolen Credit Card Numbers: How Target Blew It," *Bloomberg*, March 17, 2014, www.bloomberg.com/news/articles/2014-03-13/target-missed-warnings-in-epic-hack-of-credit-card-data, accessed June 17, 2016.

44. US Senate Committee on Commerce, Science and Transportation, "A 'Kill Chain' Analysis of the 2013 Target Data Breach," March 26, 2014.

45. Ibid.

46. Ibid.

47. Ibid.

48. Ibid.

49. "Did Target's Security Blow it or Just Get Blown Up with Noisy Alerts?," March 14, 2014, Damballa blog, www.damballa.com/did-targets-security-blow-it-or-just-get-blown-up-with-noisy-alerts/, accessed June 17, 2016.

50. *The Spy Factory: Examine the high-tech eavesdropping carried out by the National Security Agency.* Aired February 03, 2009 on PBS.

51. Ibid.

52. Ibid.

53. Ibid.

CHAPTER 8

■ ■ ■

When Seconds Matter

Now, here, you see, it takes all the running you can do, to keep in the same place.

—Lewis Carroll,
Through the Looking-Glass and What Alice Found There

Alice never could quite make out, in thinking it over afterwards, how it was that they began: all she remembers is, that they were running hand in hand, and the Queen went so fast that it was all she could do to keep up with her: and still the Queen kept crying "Faster! Faster!" but Alice felt she COULD NOT go faster, though she had not breath left to say so.

The most curious part of the thing was, that the trees and the other things round them never changed their places at all: however fast they went, they never seemed to pass anything. "I wonder if all the things move along with us?" thought poor puzzled Alice. And the Queen seemed to guess her thoughts, for she cried, "Faster! Don't try to talk!"

Not that Alice had any idea of doing THAT. She felt as if she would never be able to talk again, she was getting so much out of breath: and still the Queen cried "Faster! Faster!" and dragged her along. "Are we nearly there?" Alice managed to pant out at last.

"Nearly there!" the Queen repeated. "Why, we passed it ten minutes ago! Faster!" And they ran on for a time in silence, with the wind whistling in Alice's ears, and almost blowing her hair off her head, she fancied.

"Now! Now!" cried the Queen. "Faster! Faster!" And they went so fast that at last they seemed to skim through the air, hardly touching the ground with their feet, till suddenly, just as Alice was getting quite exhausted, they stopped, and she found herself sitting on the ground, breathless and giddy.

© 2016 by Intel Corp.
S. Grobman and A. Cerra, *The Second Economy*, DOI 10.1007/978-1-4842-2229-4_8

> The Queen propped her up against a tree, and said kindly, "You may rest a little now."
>
> Alice looked round her in great surprise. "Why, I do believe we've been under this tree the whole time! Everything's just as it was!"
>
> "Of course it is," said the Queen, "what would you have it?"
>
> "Well, in OUR country," said Alice, still panting a little, "you'd generally get to somewhere else—if you ran very fast for a long time, as we've been doing."
>
> "A slow sort of country!" said the Queen. "Now, HERE, you see, it takes all the running YOU can do, to keep in the same place. If you want to get somewhere else, you must run at least twice as fast as that!"[1]

When Lewis Carroll penned the above excerpt from his 1871 novel, *Through the Looking-Glass and What Alice Found There*, he hardly could have imagined his words would find staying power in today's lexicon. What is now referred to as the Red Queen Race (also known as the Red Queen Hypothesis or Red Queen Effect) is a useful metaphor for an evolutionary interspecies arms race of sorts, whereby predators and prey can and must selectively mutate in response to the other's capabilities to more successfully kill or survive. The notion of running as fast as one can to simply stay in the same place speaks to the accelerating challenges of survival (either as predator or prey) with each successive evolutionary mutation in its counterpart.

Take the most primitive of these species as an example: microbes. Staphylococcus aureus is one such pernicious variety, responsible for approximately 20,000 deaths in the United States annually.[2] Though it resides harmlessly within some 30 percent of the population via the nose or on the skin, Staphylococcus aureus is also known for insidiously penetrating its host via such pathways and infecting him with diseases ranging from treatable boils or abscesses to life-threatening pneumonia. In 1928, medicine fortuitously took a quantum leap forward when Alexander Fleming accidently discovered a colony of mold growing alongside the staph (as it is more commonly known) bacteria in a petri dish. Where the mold was forming, the staph microbes were noticeably absent. Fleming named the antibacterial compound penicillin, coining one of medicine's most notable discoveries in the process.

Penicillin's rise to fame started on a sluggish climb before reaching meteoric momentum. It took ten years following Fleming's discovery before Oxford researchers conducted the drug's first clinical trial. Though the patient in question, a policeman suffering from a severe staph infection, ultimately died, his improvement within five days of receiving the drug (before supplies ran dry) was nothing short of remarkable. The medical community had its poster child for vanquishing infectious bacterial diseases. Penicillin was heralded as a miracle drug and supplies increased exponentially to treat Allied soldiers fighting in World War II.

As the general public gained access to the antidote in 1944, giddy with the prospect of eradicating menacing diseases, Fleming himself foretold a more sobering future. When accepting the Nobel Prize for his work in 1945, Fleming cautioned,

It is not difficult to make microbes resistant to penicillin in the laboratory by exposing them to concentrations not sufficient to kill them, and the same thing has occasionally happened in the body.[3]

Indeed, less than five years following Fleming's warning, antibiotic resistance promised a future where diseases were determined to survive. In one English hospital alone, the proportion of resistant staph infections quadrupled from 14 percent in 1946 to 59 percent just two years later.[4] What was happening to cause the once proclaimed miracle drug to fall so quickly from the utopian hype of disease eradication? Fleming had anticipated correctly that by stroke of evolutionary luck, some bacteria would be naturally resistant to even a wonder drug like penicillin due to one mutation in their genetic code. With enough bacteria to battle, the law of numbers would dictate that penicillin's effects would ultimately reach strains that were genetically blessed for resistance, as it were. But, even Fleming had no idea just how powerful bacteria are to survive against a new threat in their environment.

As it turns out, bacteria have an added advantage against medical warfare. Bacteria can actually *transfer* their antibiotic resistance to one another. These microbes have the intelligence to exchange small pieces of DNA, called plasmids, the carriers for resistance to antibiotics, not only between parent and offspring but also from neighbor to neighbor. It's this sharing behavior that is the single largest contributor to bacteria becoming drug resistant.

With the benefit of hindsight and an acute understanding of how microbes mutate, it should come as no surprise that penicillin's effectiveness as a cure-all was limited from the start. Nature had already preprogrammed certain bacterial species, such as E. coli, impervious to penicillin's effects from the very beginning. It was only a matter of time before these strains of bacteria passed their genetic advantage on to their neighbors, such as those malignant staph infections that fell early to penicillin's might, giving their disadvantaged counterparts new genetic weaponry in the fight. And, the more antibiotics grew in popularity—from doses in livestock feed (given antibiotics have also been found to enhance body weight) to prescriptions that may be unnecessary (such as using antibiotics to treat infections for which the cause is unknown) to patients failing to complete their entire dosage (which actually serves to make surviving microbes resilient)—the more resistant previously "curable" diseases became.

The Red Queen Race was on. Researchers scrambled to find new chemical compounds capable of fighting ever-evolving microbes. In a ten-year period, new antibiotics entered the scene—streptomycin, chloramphenicol, tetracycline, and erythromycin—each designed to take out a specific bacterial strain previously immune to defeat.[5] As scientists tinkered in their labs, they began adding synthetic improvements to nature's raw materials, delivering a blow to infectious diseases that had acquired genetic mutations via the natural course of evolution. Methicillin, immune to enzymes that could destroy penicillin, debuted in 1960. Since enzymes were powerless against it, Staphylococcus aureus simply found another way—it acquired a mutant protein from a neighboring staph species, which rendered methicillin ineffective. Within two years following methicillin's introduction, methicillin-resistant S. aureus (more commonly known as MRSA) became the latest dreaded bacterial infection invulnerable to antibiotic effect—manmade or otherwise.

On and on the race went—and still goes—with microbes mutating faster than scientists are able to respond. As additional varieties of antibiotics have entered the scene in more recent decades, innovation has slowed. Chemical adaptations could extend the life of former drugs, but not by more than a few years. At the same time, antibiotics became prolific and cheap, creating more difficult incentives for drug companies to invest in curing the seemingly incurable. And, finding new compounds capable of wiping out a bacterial strain, without doing the same to the host, is a crapshoot at best. Determining where a compound may fail is an unsolvable problem. Trial-and-error experimentation is costly, time-consuming, and uncertain. The money pit that results in building an arsenal for an escalating biological arms race is all too real—it takes approximately ten years and a billion dollars to bring one new drug to market.[6] And that figure doesn't include the expense associated with fighting existing antibiotic-resistant infections, such as MRSA, which costs the US health care system up to $10 billion *per year* on its own.[7]

All the while, deadly contagions have reached pandemic proportions, with MRSA-related staph infections infiltrating 60 percent of American hospitals in 2002 and killing more Americans than HIV (human immunodeficiency virus) and tuberculosis combined by 2005.[8] Indeed, the human race is running faster just to stay in the same place. And, the adversary continues to change its approach, literally down to its DNA, to overcome ever-sophisticated countermeasures—a familiar allegory to the cybersecurity race accelerating at this very moment.

Losing the Race

March 6 is an otherwise ordinary date without much fanfare. Don't get us wrong—there are definitely historic events worth celebrating on that date, but their popularity appeals to niche audiences at best. Baseball fans, particularly fans of the New York Yankees, may drink a celebratory toast to late hero Babe Ruth for extending his contract with the franchise on that date in 1922. Londoners can thank the date for marking the introduction of minicabs in 1961. On that day in 1964, one Cassius Clay shed his name to become the great Muhammad Ali. Sure, these are momentous occasions in their own right, but otherwise hardly worthy of a major global phenomenon. Yet, in the weeks and days leading up to March 6, 1992, the world would learn the date meant something special to an anonymous hacker determined to have it live on in cybersecurity infamy.

As it turns out, March 6 is also the date of Michelangelo's birthday. To commemorate the occasion, a hacker created a virus of the Renaissance man's namesake, transferred via floppy disk and programmed to lay dormant until March 6, at which point in time unsuspecting victims would boot up their computers to unleash its curse and have it erase their hard drives. Thanks to some organizations realizing the virus was resident on their computers, the world had an early tip that Michelangelo was scheduled to detonate on that fateful day. Consumers and companies scrambled to disinfect potentially compromised computers and protect themselves from further infestation via the latest antivirus software, courtesy of burgeoning cybersecurity software vendors. As a major newspaper advised just three days before doomsday:

> In other words, run, don't walk, to your software store if
> you have recently "booted" your computer from a 5.25-inch
> floppy in the A drive. Buy a full-purpose antiviral program
> that does more than just snag the Michelangelo virus. . . . Such
> programs also scan new disks and programs to prevent future
> infections.[9]

Hundreds of thousands of people dutifully obeyed, bracing themselves for an epic meltdown expected to crash up to a million computers. March 6, 1992, arrived with much anticipation and anxiety. The date so many feared would come with a bang left barely a whimper. In the end, no more than a few thousand computers were infested. Journalists turned their ire to those greedy cybersecurity software companies for hyperbolizing the potential effects and duping so many consumers into buying their wares.

As is customary after a major hype cycle, critics admonished the hysteria and attempted to bring the conversation back to reality: viruses like Michelangelo were automatically contained by locality. Unlike viruses of the biological variety that can spread freely, computer viruses in a pre-Internet age were confined by passage from one computer to the next, usually via floppy disk. As long as one didn't receive an infected disk from a neighbor, the chances of being victimized by said virus' plague were virtually nil. While some extremists estimated that up to 50 percent of an organization's computers could be at risk for eventual infection, empirical data suggested the actual probability was far below 1 percent.[10] The widespread panic for Michelangelo and its ilk was quickly extinguished, convincing Joe Q. Public that a nasty superbug of the technical kind was still the imagination of science fiction zealots.

Even as the risk of infestation increased with the dawning of an Internet age, antivirus software packages seemed to largely address the threat. Once a form of malware was released and detected, the equivalent of its fingerprint was also captured. These antivirus software solutions were programmed to recognize the fingerprint—referred to as a signature in industry parlance—of known malware to prevent further infestation. It seemed that, for all intents and purposes, computer viruses were no more harmful than the common cold in many respects—affordably treated and somewhat inoculated.

The days of ignorant bliss were short-lived. Much like their biological counterparts, these viruses, courtesy of their creators, simply mutated to avoid demise. Polymorphic viruses, capable of changing their signature on a regular basis to conceal their identity and intention, entered the scene, rendering existing antivirus software powerless against their evasion tactics. Within 20 years of the Michelangelo fizzle, those same antivirus software companies were again taking heat from critics—this time for developing a mousetrap that had purportedly far outlived its usefulness. With the number of new strains of malware increasing from one million in 2000 to nearly 50 million just ten years later, traditional antivirus capabilities struggled to keep pace, even as consumers and businesses spent billions per year attempting to protect an increasingly digital asset heap.[11] Criticizers pointed to studies showing initial detection rates of these software packages failing to identify up to 95 percent of malware and the days, weeks, months, or even years required to spot a new threat.[12] For such identification to occur, the malware in question would first need to strike at least one victim in order for its signature to be obtained. And, with more customized and targeted attacks on the rise, preventing one's organization from being that dreaded Patient Zero required white hats to run faster still. In short, the black hats were winning the Red Queen Race.

The More Things Change . . .

Early scientific research on microbes was a precarious trade. In determining the qualities of a particular culture, researchers were confounded in how to study the microbe in a controlled environment, where it could behave normally, without simultaneously contaminating themselves in the process. In 1887, German microbiologist Julius Richard Petri invented a way for scientists to observe the behavioral properties of unknown microbes, safely and effectively. The petri dish, as it would fittingly be called, revolutionized microbiology and allowed researchers to examine not only the characteristics of potentially unsafe organisms but also the possible antidotes that could render them harmless.

Fast forward more than a century following Petri's invention. Cybersecurity professionals, perplexed by zero-day attacks that seeped through porous antivirus software packages, were hard-pressed to identify these unknown threats before they had an opportunity to do widespread harm. Taking a page from Petri, what promised to be a more advanced approach to cybersecurity was launched as the latest weapon in the white hats' arsenal—sandbox technology. Sandboxing was nothing new for the traditional information technology (IT) guard, who knew of the benefits of containing a new software release in a test environment, where all bugs could be identified and removed before deployment. Sandboxing in cybersecurity took a similar approach, though this time the software in question would be comparable to those unknown microbes in Petri's day—potential malware attempting to circumvent traditional antivirus defenses to find its Patient Zero. At a very basic level, sandboxes were virtual petri dishes, allowing organizations to send any suspicious file or program into a contained environment, where it would operate normally and could be observed to determine if it was friend or foe. If the former, it was cleared for passage. If the latter, the sandbox would also act as the virtual bouncer, denying it entry.

Much like antivirus software before it, the early growth of sandbox technology was explosive. White hats rushed to purveyors of the latest silver bullet, designed to finally thwart against the feared zero-day exploit. The sexiness of the new technology could hardly be ignored as industry analysts goaded overwhelmed cybersecurity professionals to adopt in droves, lest they face ridicule. In the words of one expert dispensing advice to these white hats:

> Very soon, if you are not running these technologies
> and you're a security professional, your colleagues and
> counterparts will start to look at you funny.[13]

Again, similar to antivirus software, the world felt a little safer thanks to the latest cybersecurity remedy. And, at least in the beginning, adversaries were foiled in their attempts. However, it wouldn't take long for threat actors to find new ways to dupe their intended targets, developing ever more sophisticated evasion techniques to consign sandboxing to the latest innovation with diminishing returns. Just two of the more common countermeasure techniques show how creative and intelligent adversaries can be in mutating their behavior.

The first can be loosely explained as playing dead. Borrowing from this instinctive animal behavior, malware authors program their creation to remain asleep while the anti-malware analysis of the sandbox runs its computation. Understanding sandboxes are limited in the amount of time that can be spent observing a program for malevolent behavior (usually less than a few minutes); adversaries simply wait out these defensive appliances with an extended sleep function in their creation. Of course, any reasonable sandbox would quickly identify a program that did nothing, so black hats outsmart their counterparts by concealing their malware behind useless computation that gives the illusion of activity—all while the malevolent aspect of their code lies in wait. As long as the malware remains asleep while in the sandbox, it will likely be incorrectly assessed as benign, free to pass through the perimeter where it ultimately will awaken to inflict damage.

The second involves a technical judo of sorts that allows malware to readily identify a sandbox, based on its operating conditions, before it can do the same to the specimen in question. In particular, a sandbox is a machine, easily recognized as such by malware programmed to detect non-human cues. For instance, early sandboxes didn't use mouse clicks. After all, there is no need for a machine to click a mouse when running its computation. Malware authors seized this vulnerability, programming their affliction to recognize a mouse click as a virtual cue that it was no longer operating in a potential sandbox and was now safe to wreak its havoc in the wild. Sandbox companies responded in kind by mimicking mouse clicks in later generations of their invention, but adversaries persist in mutating once more (such as waiting for a certain number of mouse clicks before detonating or measuring the average speed of page scrolls as an indicator of human behavior). In the end, it's increasingly difficult to program human tendencies into a sandbox that is anything but.

Once again disillusioned by how quickly their lead in the Red Queen Race had vanished, white hats realized that sandbox technology was just the latest in a string of point solutions, effective for a brief period of time before adversaries adapted their countermeasures. The sandbox was just the latest cybersecurity defense mechanism to enter the scene. It had followed various firewall technologies, network detection innovations, and, of course, antivirus software capabilities before it. Each eventually was relegated to diminishing returns once black hats mutated their response.

Realizing that any defense mechanism would ultimately be rendered fallible, cybersecurity professionals struggled to find a new way forward. While the technologies in question relied on identifying malware to prevent it from doing harm (a form of virtual blacklisting), another approach involved first identifying sanctioned programs and files and only allowing their use within the organization (virtual whitelisting). While whitelisting can certainly prove useful in some instances, even it is not sustainable as the cure-all to the problem. With cloud and mobility all but obliterating the perimeter of the organization, whitelisting becomes unwieldy at best, leaving strained cybersecurity professionals as the last line of defense in authorizing applications and web sites from a seemingly infinite market and for an increasingly intolerant workforce. Whitelisting as the *only* means of cybersecurity is the equivalent of discovering a promising compound that not only eradicates disease but does the same to the host itself, though it certainly has its place as one additional weapon in an ever-growing arsenal. Once again, cybersecurity professionals are forced to run twice as fast simply to remain in the same spot—but it can at least be helpful to understand how the race favors the Red Queen from the onset.

The Red Queen's Head Start

One key question is, Why do we see this pattern where a new cybersecurity threat defense technology, like antivirus or sandboxing solutions, works well at first, but later falls apart or re-baselines to a new equilibrium of effectiveness? The answer, like so much else in this book, is driven by incentives. In this case, the confluence of the incentives for black hat attackers and white hat defenders, along with the forces of time and delay, create a cyclical pattern of efficacy.

- *Before the starting pistol is fired*: Part 1 of this book focused on the black hat perspective and the asymmetric ability for adversaries to continuously innovate on how they will construct new attacks and expand the scope of their targets. In essence, this innovation phase commences before white hats even enter the race. Threat actors establish the problem statement. They dictate the rules of the race initially. The security industry must then respond with tools and technology that equip cybersecurity operations teams for the run. Typically, it is not until new techniques are used in the wild or published at security research venues that a refined problem statement is exposed and white hats are aware a new race has begun.

- *Getting out of the starting blocks*: part of the challenge in understanding the problem statement from the security industry's perspective is to identify what threat vectors will matriculate into issues of enough impact and volume that enable a profitable defensive market. If a cybersecurity technology company predicts that a threat will be a major issue in the future and develops defensive technology and the threat does not materialize, the misstep will result in lost profits and create an opportunity cost that could have been invested in more viable areas. As we noted earlier, ransomware was seen in its embryonic forms in the late 1980s; however, it did not cause major pandemic until the 2010s. If a zealous cybersecurity company had invested in defensive ransomware technology back in the 1980s, it would have been due for a long wait of 30 years before the market realized a need. There are many potential areas that could represent the next wave of threat vector be they attacking firmware to causing permanent destruction in future ransomware environments to moving into adjacent areas such as smart and connected devices and vehicles. The challenge in predicting "what's next" causes many cybersecurity technology companies to take a more responsive approach and invest in defeating the latest high-impact threat techniques that have recently become real and damaging to potential customers who are willing to pay for a defense.

When a cybersecurity vendor initially builds a new defensive technology, incentive structures are the metaphorical wind at their back in the race. Specifically, this is where cybersecurity software purveyors cause black hats to pick up their pace. The earlier a cybersecurity technology is in its market maturity, the less customers will have deployed it as a countermeasure to the latest threat vector. If you are a black hat creating said threat vector, you must now accelerate the speed of propagating your scourge before white hats begin deploying the latest technology designed with countermeasures against it. As the market begins adopting the latest defense mechanism, black hats run into complexity—their pace is affected in the race. Therefore, there are incentives on both sides to move fast—black hats must ship their wares quickly and white hats must step up their defenses. For example, initial viruses could be mass-produced and distributed as identical copies as there was no concept of antivirus signature detection to detect and remove them. Similarly, early malware could initially assume it had reached its target victim. There was no need for it to identify if it was, in fact, running in a forensic analysis sandbox. The implication of this phenomenon is that the first generation of a new defensive technology is typically very effective against the "in the wild" threat that it is targeting. Ironically, it takes time associated with market maturity of a particular defensive technology until the black hats are sufficiently incentivized to create countermeasures of their own.

- *The early pace of the race*: there is an inherent lag between the development of a new defensive technology and its pervasive existence as a component of the cybersecurity defense landscape. In the early phase of the technology's existence, it will have strong technical appeal due to its marked improvement in efficacy as compared to existing technologies. This benefit often leads to rapid acquisition and deployment; however, there are counterforces that slow adoption. Procurement processes, quality assurance cycles, and certification can add significant lag to operationalizing a new defensive technology. As examples, IT needs to ensure that new capabilities don't create incremental false positives or network or functional bottlenecks—both of which impede the productivity of the organization and slow the adoption curve.

The deployment ramp of a new defense technology will directly impact when and how aggressively threat actors must develop countermeasures, which directly affects their return on investment from their "products." Rather than using their time and resource to distribute and operationalize their malware, adversaries are instead forced to convert their investment into researching and developing new countermeasures. A good way to think of this is with the following equation:

$$ICM = E * DV$$

Where ICM (incentive to develop countermeasures and evasion tactics) is directly driven by the combination of how effective the new defensive technology is (E) and how pervasively deployed it is within the environments that are being targeted (DV). ICM starts very low when a technology is released, even if the efficacy is remarkably high (this is because there is nascent deployed volume). The ICM value will typically be exponential as almost all organizations will be prevented from an immediate deployment due to internal processes associated with procurement and installation lead times, as stated above, but timelines quickly hasten as adoption starts. For example, once the quality and negative impact hurdles have been overcome by one Fortune 50 company, this tacit endorsement clears the way for the technology to be adopted as "proven" by others. This effect creates a snowball of customer references that exponentially builds upon itself in spurring adoption of the latest technology by white hats.

- *Changing the lead runner*: when ICM hits a threshold that indicates that the new defensive technology is preventing maximized value to the adversary without offensive countermeasures, a tipping point is reached where the threat actor must develop an "upgrade" focused on circumventing and evading the new defense. Much like the first cycle of defense development favors early white hat deployment, this initial cycle of offensive countermeasure innovation is very much in favor of the black hat. Similar to a first generation of malicious technology being relatively simple to defeat with a new approach, adversaries developing their initial countermeasures are offered the maximum number of options to evade newly deployed defenses. Additionally, given that the defensive technology is typically sold as a commercial offering, it is possible for threat actors to procure (or steal) the technology to analyze exactly what they need to evade. Here again, the race shifts in favor of the black hat, who can painstakingly tweak every version of a malicious exploit. In contrast, cybersecurity professionals require stability of commercial offerings to be acceptable to IT operating environments. Whether polymorphism to defeat antivirus, sandbox fingerprinting (the technique for a piece of malware to determine if it is running in a sandbox) or delay tactics, the first set of countermeasures can redefine a defense technology from being a silver bullet to yet another element in the complex arsenal of defense.

- *The Red Queen advantage*: the first cycles in development, deployment, and countermeasure creation are amplified by time incentives. At the end of the initial countermeasure development, most technologies will move into an equilibrium cycle where there will be both improvements in the core technology and evasion tactics. Yet, even during this equilibrium portion of the race, the advantage goes to the black hat, who enjoys virtually no restraints in one-upping his opponent. As sandbox fingerprinting alone illustrates, the difficulty in programming a sandbox to realistically mimic human behavior is a defensive complexity that can be readily exploited by adversarial countermeasures.

It's grossly unfair. White hats are forced to run a race they neither started nor can win, as their opponent consistently gains an advantage in playing by a different set of rules. There will be some who read this chapter and inherently understand they are running a race they cannot complete, let alone win. Yet, at the same time, they won't be able resist fantasizing about the next great technology promising to turn the race finally in their favor.

For example, at the time of this writing, the industry is abuzz with the potential of machine learning, artificial intelligence, and big data analytics. Before being seduced by the next "it" technology, it is critical to first contemplate the full life cycle of its defensive capabilities and project how countermeasures and evasion tactics will impact both its near-term efficacy and long-term effectiveness when it reaches an equilibrium point.

With regard to our forward-looking example, we need to understand all the tools that black hats will use to confuse and poison our models. We need to imagine how excessive noise and false-positive bombardment will be used by the adversary to muddy the waters—because they will. Cybersecurity professionals, already inundated with too much noise in the system, will adjust their latest machine-learning savior to compensate for the false-positive deluge. In the process, they will unwillingly open the door for their adversary to strike with a highly targeted and devastating threat through which to circumvent even the smartest analytics. It is not to say that these capabilities and technologies are not important in our forward-looking architectures, but, rather, we should not base their long-term value solely on the results we measure at initial launch and inception.

As hard as it is to accept, very often a deployed technology will have little to no incremental effectiveness within a corporate infrastructure. So why would anyone have deployed it? Technologies are implemented when they have either initial or equilibrium value that justifies the operational costs. In cases in which the equilibrium efficacy value is less than the ongoing costs, those defensive technologies should be removed from the environment to make way for others with higher impact.

Running the race in the same way—deploying one point product after another in a disintegrated fashion, convoluting one's cybersecurity operations environment in the process—yields the advantage to the adversary every time. To flip the script on the Red Queen requires white hats to think differently about their approach to cybersecurity—one that places speed on their side.

A Second Thought

There is no such thing as a super antibiotic, capable of killing all potential bacterial microbes, any more than there is an equivalent comparison in cybersecurity. As previously discussed, there are multiple ways through which predators can encroach upon a virtual castle's "keep." In an effort to protect their organization's expanding digital footprint, cybersecurity professionals have rushed headlong into purchasing the latest cybersecurity technology, creating several problems:

- *The latest cybersecurity technology's effectiveness reaches diminishing returns the more it is deployed in market.* Here is another interesting observation where cybersecurity departs from traditional IT notions: In cybersecurity, it usually doesn't pay to be a late adopter. While traditional IT favors followers who adopt technologies once others have had an opportunity to work out the bugs and bring down the price point (after all, who wants to be the market guinea pig?), cybersecurity follows the exact opposite pattern. Similar to microbes that build up a resistance as antibiotics are more widely distributed, cybercriminals quickly learn how to mutate their creations to circumvent cybersecurity technology that stands in their way. First movers of cybersecurity technology, such as early adopters of those antivirus or sandbox technology solutions, saw immediate benefit from their investments. But, the more the market begins adopting the latest cyber wonder product, the more incentive adversaries have to develop countermeasures. Being first often pays in cybersecurity.

- *Deploying the latest cybersecurity technologies creates other challenges for white hats.* As discussed in Chapter 7, there simply aren't enough white hats in the race. Oftentimes, the best laid intentions of implementing the latest innovation literally collect dust on the shelf as cybersecurity professionals struggle to install the new wares in their environment. This dichotomy of needing to move quickly despite not having sufficient resources to operationalize and maintain the market's latest widget creates enormous pressure for white hats to run faster still.

- *Maximizing cybersecurity return on investment (ROI) becomes a race against time itself.* If there is no such thing as a particular product capable of eradicating all threats permanently, then the existing race is not a fair match. Black hats will always win if white hats run the race set in their adversaries' favor. Instead of pursuing the elusive better product, cybersecurity professionals are better served striving for a superior platform—one that allows for swift onboarding of new technologies over an architecture backed by common tools and workflows, along with automation and orchestration capabilities to lessen the burden on an already strained workforce. As cybersecurity software companies continue to evolve any given brainchild deployed in this environment, the technology in question moves toward a sustaining steady state of innovation. This level of innovation does not exceed that of the initial technology breakthrough but rather progressively responds to each successive mutation by threat actors, thereby extending the life of the product in question (much the same way pharmaceutical adaptations can prolong the effectiveness of drugs, if only by a few years).

In short, new cybersecurity technologies generally follow the threat effectiveness curve shown in Figure 8-1.

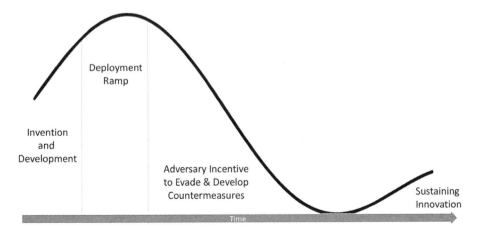

Figure 8-1. *Grobman's Curve of Threat Defense Effectiveness*

The goal for cybersecurity professionals becomes deploying new technologies as quickly as possible with the lowest level of effort to capitalize on the threat effectiveness associated with early adoption. In turn, the goal for cybersecurity software vendors is to minimize the slope of descending threat effectiveness by anticipating future offensive countermeasures and building resiliency into their creations with these evasion tactics in mind to prolong product utility. The result is an approach that maximizes speed and ROI of cybersecurity investments, with cybersecurity operations represented by shifting the bull's eye as far left to the curve as possible with the lowest level of effort and the software vendor community focused on decreasing the slope of descent by delivering greater product resiliency (Figure 8-2).

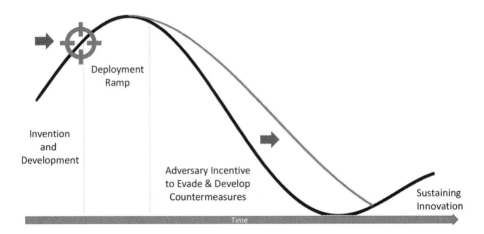

Figure 8-2. *Grobman's Curve of Maximizing Defense Effectiveness*

Grobman's Curve, named after the book's lead author, provides a different perspective through which to examine an organization's cybersecurity posture. New cybersecurity technologies will come and go. It's the nature of an industry where human beings on the good and bad side of the fight are incentivized to continue mutating their approach. In this escalating race, cybersecurity professionals are outmatched given the reality of Grobman's curve, which suggests that, just as many are deploying the latest cybersecurity defense mechanism, its effectiveness is due to significantly deteriorate as adversaries have sufficient time to develop successful evasion techniques. White hats are always disadvantaged in this race if they do not reexamine their approach. An integrated platform that enables swift adoption of the latest widget allows these professionals to maximize ROI, elongate the effectiveness of their deployed products, and establish a framework through which running faster results in going farther.

It's important not to think of the curve as a single oscillation but, rather, a sequence of volleyed innovation by the black and white hats working to counter each other's tactics. At each cycle, the amount of effort increases as low-hanging fruit dries up. The result is that defensive technologies will find an equilibrium for their general effectiveness driven by the continuous innovation and evasion investments made by the technologists on both sides of the equation. Although the general pattern is common for all technologies, the exact shaping of the curve and speed to equilibrium will vary for every technology. One way to represent this mathematically would be with the approach shown in Figure 8-3.

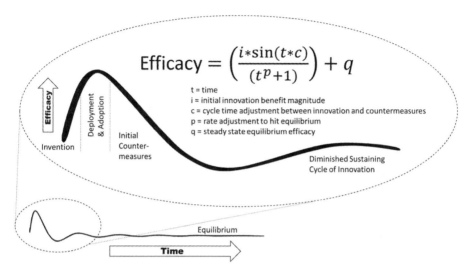

$$\text{Efficacy} = \left(\frac{i * \sin(t * c)}{(t^p + 1)} \right) + q$$

t = time
i = initial innovation benefit magnitude
c = cycle time adjustment between innovation and countermeasures
p = rate adjustment to hit equilibrium
q = steady state equilibrium efficacy

Figure 8-3. *Finding an equilibrium*

By grasping this phenomenon, key questions can help guide the selection and adoption of technologies by understanding the efficacy pattern and examining it along with the cost and complexity of deploying a solution.

When a technology has an equilibrium efficacy value that is greater than its operational costs in the long run, it will generally make sense to adopt, regardless of the point in time on the curve. A good example of this is deterministic signature based anti-malware. This mature technology is key to reducing the volume of threats that need to be analyzed with more sophisticated approaches and has reasonable return on the cost structure required to operate the capability. One could think of this scenario looking like the curve in Figure 8-4.

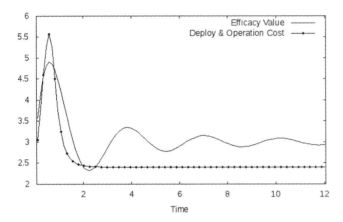

Figure 8-4. *Long term positive ROI*

There are clearly benefits of deploying early, but given that the equilibrium efficacy value is greater than operational equilibrium, the technology makes sense in the long run regardless of when it is deployed. Contrast this with an example where benefits are strong at first but the long-term efficacy collapses below the operational management costs (Figure 8-5).

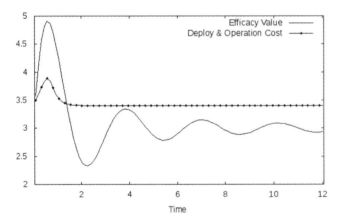

Figure 8-5. *Short-term benefit, version A*

In this case, the long-term value cannot be realized, and likely, the opportunity cost of maintaining the capability in the long run would be better suited elsewhere. The caveat is that if it was possible to do a rapid deployment right when technology is launched but then remove it from the environment, the same curve would look like Figure 8-6.

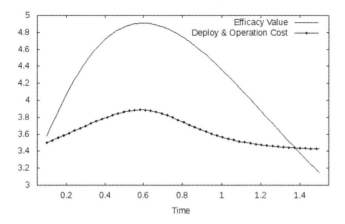

Figure 8-6. *Short-term benefit, version B*

Although this is theoretically possible, many of the point products and technologies that exhibit this type of curve will have significant deployment challenges in their initial offering, decreasing the viability of a comprehensive deployment in the initial amplified oscillation of efficacy.

The question then becomes: is there a way to use the curve to the white hat's advantage? Using a platform approach (Figure 8-7) where a pipeline of technologies is able to flow through a framework managing deployment and messaging, along with supplier business models that allow access to technologies without requiring a full procurement cycle, is the solution. This will allow a pipeline of leading-edge efficacy defensive measures to be practically deployed into an environment. For each technology in the pipeline, it can efficiently be managed to support either a long-term sustaining role in the configuration or a short-term benefit if countermeasures are identified that defeat its ROI.

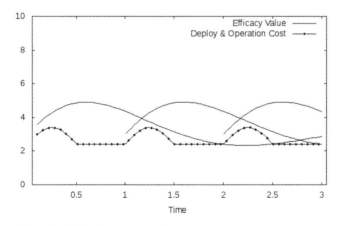

Figure 8-7. *Platform approach*

Thankfully, a different approach may also be the answer in the biological race that started this chapter. Scientists have discovered a new antibiotic, teixobactin, which attacks microbes in a very distinct way. Rather than hitting one defined target, such as an important protein in a particular cell, teixobactin hits two targets, both of which are polymers that build the bacterial cell wall.[14] Unlike a cell's protein, which is comprised of DNA that can be mutated through genetic evolution and the sharing between microbial neighbors, these polymers are made of enzymes, not genes. In short, there is nothing to mutate. In shifting the antibiotic approach, researchers may just have discovered how to avert an impending superbug crisis—a good thing, since the first superbug resistant to all antibiotics of last resort entered the United States in 2016. While the Red Queen Race accelerates, choosing to run it a different way actually results in getting somewhere in *The Second Economy*.

A SECOND HELPING OF THE RED QUEEN RACE IN THE WILD

A fear of snakes consistently ranks among the top phobias for people. As it turns out, a phobia of rattlesnakes, in particular, may be exaggerated, as their venom is very rarely deadly to humans. The same, however, cannot be said for the rattlesnake's prey, typically small rodents, like mice, rats, and squirrels. These slithering predators often lie in wait for their prey before inflicting a deadly, venomous bite. Yet, snakes and squirrels are engaged in their own evolutionary arms race to make this venom more or less effective in rendering death.

Scientists have discovered very different constitutions of rattlesnake venom in various parts of California. At the same time, squirrels have developed varying degrees of resistance factors that prevent the venom from taking effect. It is interesting to note that not all rattlesnake venom is equally deadly against squirrels, with the composition of venom varying significantly in areas as close as 20 miles apart. But, what is perhaps more intriguing is that rattlesnakes appear to be winning their version of the Red Queen Race. The researchers found that the snake venom is up to three times more effective when pitted against a squirrel living in the same habitat.[15] While squirrels are evolving, their enemy is evolving faster still. What explains the evolutionary advantage still has researchers confounded, but the outlook for California squirrels is bleak, as their Red Queen Race may result in their untimely demise.

Notes

1. Lewis Carroll, "2: The Garden of Live Flowers," in Martin Gardner (ed.), *Through the Looking-Glass and What Alice Found There* (The Annotated Alice ed.) (New York: The New American Library, 1998 [1871]), p. 46. https://ebooks. adelaide.edu.au/c/carroll/lewis/looking/chapter2.html. Accessed July 24, 2016.

2. E. Klein E, D. L. Smith, and R. Laxminarayan, Hospitalizations and deaths caused by methicillin-resistant Staphylococcus aureus, United States, 1999–2005. *Emergent Infectious Disease*, December 2007, wwwnc.cdc.gov/eid/article/13/12/07-0629, accessed July 24, 2016.

3. Alexander Fleming, Penicillin, Nobel Lecture, December 11, 1945, www.nobelprize.org/nobel_prizes/medicine/ laureates/1945/fleming-lecture.pdf, accessed July 25, 2016.

4. Katherine Xue, "Superbug: An Epidemic Begins," *Harvard Magazine*, May-June 2014, http://harvardmagazine. com/2014/05/superbug, accessed July 26, 2016.

5. Ibid.

6. Ibid.

7. Klein et al., note 2 *supra*.

8. Xue, note 4 *supra*.

9. Peter H. Lewis, "Personal Computers: Safety in Virus Season," *The New York Times*, March 3, 1992, www.nytimes. com/1992/03/03/science/personal-computers-safety-in- virus-season.html, accessed July 27, 2016.

10. John Markoff, "Technology; Computer Viruses: Just Uncommon Colds After All?," *The New York Times*, November 1, 1992, www.nytimes.com/1992/11/01/business/ technology-computer-viruses-just-uncommon-colds- after-all.html, accessed July 27, 2016.

11. Nicole Perlroth, "Outmaneuvered at Their Own Game, Antivirus Makers Struggle to Adapt," *The New York Times*, December 31, 2012, www.nytimes.com/2013/01/01/ technology/antivirus-makers-work-on-software-to- catch-malware-more-effectively.html?_r=0, accessed July 28, 2016.

12. Ibid.

13. Ibid.

14. Cari Romm, "A New Drug in the Age of Antibiotic Resistance," *The Atlantic*, January 7, 2015, www.theatlantic.com/health/archive/2015/01/a-new-drug-in-the-age-of-antibiotic-resistance/384291/, accessed July 29, 2016.

15. Matthew L. Holding, James E. Biardi, and H. Lisle Gibbs, "Coevolution of venom function and venom resistance in a rattlesnake predator and its squirrel prey," *Proceedings of the Royal Society B*, April 27, 2016, http://rspb.royalsocietypublishing.org/content/283/1829/20152841.full, accessed July 29, 2016.

CHAPTER 9

■ ■ ■

Second to None

If you want to be incrementally better: Be competitive. If you want to be exponentially better: Be cooperative.

—Unknown

In most car crashes, there are actually two collisions. The first occurs when the automobile strikes another object. The next is a split second later within the cabin of the car itself. It happens as the driver and accompanying passengers smash into the dashboard, windshield, steering wheel, and other protrusions of the car's interior when the vehicle abruptly decelerates upon contact. Given the inherent risk more than a billion people worldwide take when getting behind the wheel of their car every day, safety is a selling point in the car-buying process. Just try to ignore the plethora of advanced safety features promoted in today's more innovative automobiles —from blind spot warning indicators to forward collision alerts to driver-assisted capabilities. Some of the latest models even compensate for poor performance on the part of their driver, sensing when he may be drowsy or otherwise inattentive and sounding a warning, if not automatically correcting for lane drifting, to reduce accidents.

While ubiquitous in marketing messages today, there was a time when automobile safety was placed in the metaphorical back seat of feature priorities. In the 1950s, a post-World War II boon saw American auto manufacturing plants, at one time responsible for one-fifth of the country's entire military production,[1] reconfigured into doing what they did best—building cars. Flush with available manufacturing capacity, auto makers pumped some 58 million cars into the US economy during the 1950s—nearly one vehicle produced and sold for every three Americans living at the time.[2] During the heyday of this decade, consumers benefited from technological advancements that made their automobile easier to drive (with automatic transmission), faster (featuring more powerful V8 engines), and more comfortable (including suspension improvements and air conditioning).

As consumers raced to their local dealership and took to the roads, accidents increased. By the 1960s, with an annual death toll topping 55,000 due to car accidents in the United States alone,[3] the automobile industry found itself embroiled in a contentious battle against advocates who demanded car safety be given priority. Auto manufacturers resisted, unable to make the economics work, citing a consumer market less interested in safety and more interested in performance, comfort, and price. In 1964, at an automobile conference in New York led by safety proponents, including the American Automobile Association, a national director of the industry group excoriated auto manufacturers for turning a blind eye toward safety recommendations:

> The auto makers scoff at suggestions for improvement,
> even when offered by organizations that have designed
> safer vehicles. [They look at the automobile as] glamour
> merchandise, not as a mechanism that should be made as
> safe as possible.[4]

By 1967, mounting pressures from advocacy groups and government regulators began taking their toll on reluctant car manufacturers and the dealers within their ecosystem. According to 85 percent of auto dealers at the time, new safety features, including collapsible steering wheels, were ineffective at stimulating sales, all the while manufacturers offered sobering predictions of substantially higher prices for 1968 models to accommodate the enhancements. Annual sales were expected to take a 6 percent drop.[5] Pointing to necessary changes in the manufacturing process, higher wages demanded by union employees, longer warranties to assuage lingering consumer doubts, and escalating advertising budgets to drown out the chorus of auto safety critics, one auto dealer of the time laid the ultimate burden at the feet of the buyer, who would inevitably be forced to pay higher prices for features he didn't necessarily want. Of course, the dealer was quick to dismiss any potential suggestion that his cohort saw rising prices as anything but a vicious circle:

> Don't think for one moment that higher car prices mean
> better profits for us. We are the guys who get the squeeze. The
> long warranties lead Mr. Car Buyer to believe that we do his
> entire maintenance for free, and to keep a customer we will do
> servicing that's not in the fine print of the warranty.[6]

By 1968, the US Government, compelled to take action in light of the industry stalemate that had ensued, imposed a number of mandated, not optional, safety features in the year's models. Among them: those collapsible steering wheels that auto dealers claimed were inconsequential in generating more sales, dual-braking systems, safer tires and rims, stronger door locks, and laminated windshields.[7] As auto manufacturers raised prices, allegedly to cover the increased costs imposed by safety requirements, critics claimed that auto safety was getting a bad rap by being the scapegoat for price hikes. One newly mandated safety feature, in particular, drew the attention of criticizers for what appeared to be a blatant markup on the part of auto makers suspected of corporate greed. The three-point safety harness, intended to replace the customary lap belt in the two front seats, was estimated to cost anywhere from $23 to $32, according to car manufacturers.[8] In contrast, US senators close to the matter suggested the harness cost no more than $1.25 to $1.50, accusing auto manufacturers of attempting to bilk consumers out of $100 million in profit from one safety device alone.[9] As tensions mounted, US auto companies squabbled with safety advocates and regulators alike for being forced to capitulate to onerous requirements at escalating costs—following a very different playbook than the one written by a Swedish auto manufacturer less than ten years prior.

Doing the Unthinkable

When Volvo Chief Executive Officer (CEO) Gunnar Engelau lost a relative in an automobile accident, he set out on a mission to make the automobile a safer method of transport. In 1958, he hired Nils Bohlin and appointed him as the newly created chief safety engineer for the company. Bohlin's first pursuit was to find a way to protect drivers and passengers from the dreaded second crash upon collision. Two-point lap belts were standard at the time but often did more harm than good by causing serious internal damage to the vehicle's occupants upon an accident's impact, particularly at high speeds. Before joining Volvo, Bohlin's impressive resume included designing ejector seats for Saab fighter airplanes. As such, he was intimately familiar with the four-point elaborate harnesses fighter pilots used and the safety advantages of the more sophisticated contraptions over their more rudimentary lap-belt alternatives. Yet, with consumer usage of lap belts hovering well below 30 percent,[10] Bohlin knew that drivers and passengers would reject anything that otherwise compromised comfort, no matter the potential safety benefits. Though a three-point belt had been patented by two Americans, Roger Griswold and Hugh de Haven in 1951, the inventors had left the buckle in the middle, with anchoring points positioned such that the occupant could move on impact, leaving vulnerable organs across the midsection yet again exposed.[11] As Bohlin would later recount, "It was just a matter of finding a solution that was simple, effective and could be put on conveniently with one hand."[12]

In August 1959, Bohlin filed a patent[13] for the three-point safety harness, with the buckle to one side, which is now standard operating equipment in every automobile. Engelau was sitting on a veritable gold mine. Bohlin's invention was estimated to reduce the risk of fatality or serious injury due to car accident by more than 50 percent.[14] And, the contraption couldn't be easier or quicker to use—allaying concerns of an impetuous driver motivated by convenience. At a time when auto dealers were scrutinizing every possible option for additional profit—either as add-ons to base models or as included features in higher-priced alternatives—Volvo literally stood to make a potential killing off Bohlin's innovation. And then, the auto manufacturer with a reputation rooted in safety did the unthinkable: *it gave its most valuable patent away.*

There was no selling of the design. No fee for using the patent. No exclusive manufacturing rights by Volvo to drive competitive advantage. No optional feature for an incremental price to consumers or any attempt to upsell higher-end models with the three-point belt as standard. Believing that Bohlin's invention could materially save lives, the company struggled to put a price on this greater societal good—and so it didn't. Volvo not only included it as a baseline feature in its models, it literally handed its competition the design—complete with a lecture tour across the United States put on by Bohlin himself espousing the benefits of his contraption[15]—all gratis.

To put the magnitude of this gesture in perspective, consider that the BBC estimates that Bohlin's invention has saved over a million lives worldwide since its introduction. It has been heralded by German patent registrars as one of only eight patents to have the greatest significance for humanity during the 100 years from 1885 to 1985, putting Bohlin's innovation in good company with the likes of Benz, Edison, and Diesel.[16] It is the single most important safety device in the history of the automobile to date[17]—and it was given as a gift from one auto manufacturer to its competitors and to humankind at large. For an auto manufacturer committed to attaining competitive differentiation from its reputation as a safety leader, the act was tantamount to surrendering its most prized asset to the market. Imagine what the world of cybersecurity could learn from such magnanimity.

Protecting One's Advantage

Competitive advantage is defined as a condition or circumstance that puts a company in a favorable or superior business position. It can be derived from a better cost position, from a highly differentiated product or service, or through advanced segmentation strategies that allow companies to exploit underserved market niches. For a competitive advantage to be sustainable, it must prove extraordinarily difficult for opponents to copy or otherwise imitate. In Volvo's case, the patent on the three-point safety belt would have offered years of protection against competitors claiming the same. If a patent isn't available, competitive advantage may be obtained through prohibitive barriers to entry (think of the first-mover advantage broadband providers enjoyed as architects of capital-intensive fiber-optic networks). Alternatively, one's installed base can be a source of major advantage (consider the power of Facebook's enormous social network), if not one's extensive information (like Google's ability to mine billions of searches per day to inform more targeted hits).

In a category cluttered by more than 1,400 software security vendors globally with no signs of imminent abatement,[18] these competitors find a market landscape overwhelmed by noise and confusion. With nearly one new cybersecurity startup funded by private investors each business day in 2015 alone,[19] incumbents face a deluge of competitive entrants seeking their piece of the market. Newer entrants are advantaged by carving a particular technology niche in the marketplace, attempting to sell their wares to eager cybersecurity professionals yearning for the silver bullet in their arsenal. The established guard have a very different advantage: that of their incumbency, which, in some cases, affords them visibility to hundreds of thousands of threats per day. In a world where adversaries continue to step up their game, the ability to aggregate threat intelligence across an extensive installed base and offer such insights to potential and existing customers provides real competitive value, at a minimum. For example, one security vendor's threat intelligence found 97 percent of 2015's malware seen on only a single endpoint in its network, reflecting the highly targeted nature of evolved threats.[20] Harnessing such information and making it available to all of its customers simultaneously allows others to avoid falling victim to the same while enhancing the competitive value of the firm in question. Large incumbents are incentivized to keep such learnings to themselves and their customers—offering it to their competitors is tantamount to giving away the family silver. Even better, selling this threat intelligence to help overwhelmed cybersecurity professionals identify looming attacks in their networks is equivalent to the treasure trove that Volvo was sitting on before it offered its three-point belt to the market at no charge. As many white hats know, the cybersecurity industry has not been quite as charitable, with historical incumbents prizing the competitive value of threat intelligence above larger societal benefits, leaving strapped cybersecurity professionals to stitch together their own disparate view of the threat landscape with questionable benefits.

Celebrating a Hollow Victory

In September 2012, six US banks, including Bank of America, JPMorgan Chase, and Wells Fargo, found their web sites suddenly deluged with unprecedented traffic in a coordinated distributed denial of service (DDoS) attack. Though the DDoS launch was fairly innocuous compared with the more insidious threat typically facing these financial institutions (no sensitive customer information was exfiltrated in the campaign), the companies were caught flat-footed by their adversary nonetheless. For days, customers were frustrated by crashed web sites, cut off from their online banking accounts.

The DDoS campaign was highly sophisticated in its execution. Rather than enslaving personal home or business computers to execute strikes against the targeted web sites, attackers used compromised web servers—each capable of flooding sites with 100 megabits of data per second, about a 100-fold increase over personal computers.[21] In addition to using the metaphorical equivalent of a cannon (vs. many rifles) in doing their bidding, the enemy also varied the scope of its weaponry to keep its victims on their back heels. By targeting three different layers (or parts of the network that can congest due to high volumes), adversaries were able to vary their techniques, flooding one area of the network with junk traffic and then shifting their focus quickly to the next. Banks that were unsuccessful at addressing all three possible congestion points found themselves incapable of responding quickly enough to overcome the successive waves of attack.

The result? The victim banks were barraged with a torrent of data anywhere from 15 to 60 times greater than that seen from more garden-variety DDoS attacks.[22] The targeted web sites were down more than 5 percent during the initial campaign launch.[23] A Middle East-based hacktivist group, Izz ad-Din al-Qassam Cyber Fighters, took credit for the attack, leaving some to speculate the hacktivists may be fronting for a more insidious nation-state actor, Iran. The hacktivists threatened to increasingly turn up the heat on their targets if the United States did not remove a controversial anti-Muslim video from YouTube.[24] With more banks threatened in the seemingly unending spate of attacks, the victims banded together to share what they could about the enemy encroaching upon their mutual gates, taking advantage of a government decision made several years before.

The Financial Services Information Sharing and Analysis Center (FS-ISAC) was established in 1999, shortly after a US Government order was enacted to encourage sharing between the public and private sectors regarding cyberthreats and vulnerabilities. By the time of the DDoS campaign of 2012, member institutions of the FS-ISAC had been working together for some time and saw the attack as an unfortunate opportunity through which to test the mettle of their comradery. Among some of the more valuable intelligence shared in the community: the command and control server instructions used by the DDoS botnet in the initial attacks. By the time the hacktivists geared up for their next wave of attacks, their victims were ready. In January 2013, even with a slightly modified version of its botnet attack, the adversary was successful in interrupting its victims' web sites with only 3 percent downtime[25]—a measurable improvement in the banks' countermeasures and a result of successful threat intelligence sharing within the community. Following the hacktivists' launch of the third tranche of their campaign in March 2013, the victims' response had improved even more, suffering just a two percent downtime (admittedly nearly double the "normal" downtime experienced a year before when the banks were not under siege but significantly better than the more than 5 percent interruption of service suffered when the DDoS attacks first commenced).[26]

Victory was declared for threat intelligence sharing as traditional competitors shared success against a common threat by pooling their resources and cooperating with one another. Yet, the success story of the FS-ISAC did little to change old behaviors in other industries. A 2015 study found that only 37 percent of North American companies share threat intelligence with their peers regularly. Nearly 20 percent reported no sharing of intelligence, with only 10 percent of this cohort having any plans to do so within the next 12-24 months.[27] With a real-world case study proving the value of threat intelligence sharing, the question of why the practice had not caught fire within three years of the FS-ISAC DDoS incident demands answering. Doing so requires dusting off a time-tested model comprised of equal parts human behavior and economics.

Facing the Dilemma

Imagine you and your partner-in-crime are caught and imprisoned, each of you placed in solitary confinement with no means of communicating with each other. The prosecution has you red-handed on a smaller charge but lacks sufficient evidence to convict you on a much more egregious offense, so they offer you and your accomplice the opportunity to turn state's witness. If one of you confesses while the other remains silent, the one who does the talking gets off free, while his partner is imprisoned for three years. If both of you confess, you will each serve two years in prison. Finally, if you both remain silent, you'll each serve one year in prison for the lesser crime.

If the two of you could cooperate in advance, you would seek to optimize your combined outcome—the obvious choice would be to remain silent. You would each receive the least amount of time in prison by keeping your mouths shut—that is, if you *both* remain silent. But, putting yourself in this scenario with no means of communicating with your partner results in a very different behavioral outcome. One can quickly compute that, if someone caves under pressure, the one who does the confessing fares better than the one who remains silent. And, since one has no control over what his partner will do, he is better off betraying his partner and minimizing his risk of serving the longest possible sentence. As such, behavioral tendencies are to revert to an outcome that is less desirable for all parties involved. This is the classic prisoner's dilemma game—part behavioral psychology, part economic probability—that helps explain why threat intelligence sharing has failed to capture the masses of cybersecurity professionals.

To explain how threat intelligence sharing fits the prisoner's dilemma paradigm, one must consider the analogous concern for cybersecurity professionals. While prison sentences are hardly on the line, what is at stake is exposing one's own cybersecurity weaknesses, potentially making oneself vulnerable to predators with similar intentions if not critics quick to play the blame game toward an organization admitting a potential incident of compromise or attack. Instead of confessing one's own weaknesses, it is in an organization's greater interests to free-ride on the efforts of others. By capitalizing on others sharing their threat intelligence, free riders benefit from the information without having to expose their own dirty laundry. The challenge is that all organizations are in the same boat when it comes to the free-rider dilemma. The incentive structure accompanying most threat intelligence sharing programs, government-mandated or otherwise, compels organizations to keep their secrets to themselves and hope that others will share first. Like the classic prisoner's dilemma, though all organizations benefit the most from sharing their threat intelligence, the behavioral tendency is to revert to an outcome that is suboptimized for all parties involved, particularly since one has no control over her competitor's tendency to cooperate.

The basic prisoner's dilemma problem was initially framed by two scientists at the Rand Corporation in 1950. However, it wasn't until 1978 that a Dr. Axelrod evolved the model by using computer simulations to conduct experiments on how individuals would behave as the game continued. This iterated prisoner's dilemma, one that allowed subjects to respond to how one another reacted, led to a different finding, coined "tit-for-tat."

A tit-for-tat approach calls for one to mirror his opponent's response. If the opponent cooperates, you cooperate. If the opponent betrays, you betray. Dr. Axelrod found that tit-for-tat always performed better than strategies that always betrayed, betrayed at random, or otherwise used sophisticated computer algorithms to determine the next move. Tit-for-tat trumped all other strategies due to its simplicity—retaliatory enough to prevent one from being duped and forgiving enough to encourage cooperation.[28] When individuals played the prisoner's dilemma game multiple times and employed a tit-for-tat strategy, the tendency toward a mutual cooperation outcome benefiting all parties prevailed.

It would stand to reason that tit-for-tat would also dominate in the field of cybersecurity threat intelligence sharing. After all, there are multiple opportunities for companies to share threat intelligence and iterate upon the classic prisoner's dilemma game. However, the challenge remains that the inherent incentive structure underlying threat intelligence sharing does not favor a tit-for-tat strategy. Unless free riders are punished, the tendency to feed off the contributions of others will remain. To change behavior, one must first change incentives.

Punishing the Free Rider

The year is 1999. With e-mail as its killer application and 56k modems as its primary onramp, the Internet has yet to earn its place as an entertainment mainstay. The world of music is powered by cumbersome CDs, with fans readily shelling out $15 to buy a full album from an artist—even when only a couple of songs are often wanted. Shawn Fanning, a shy teenager hanging out on the messaging service Internet Relay Chat (IRC) and going by the handle "Napster" (a derogatory nickname he earned from an opponent on the basketball court), begins engaging with like-minded hackers about an idea he has for making it easier to share music online.[29] Napster, an online peer-to-peer sharing service that revolutionizes the way music is consumed and pits the recording industry against online file sharers in a contentious legal battle, is born. It allows music enthusiasts to seamlessly locate one another via an online directory that captures the music catalogue of those within its network. Once located, users can arrange to swap music from one another, by directly connecting their computers together in a distributed peer-to-peer network configuration, rather than relying on a traditional centralized client-server architecture for the same.

Other peer-to-peer networks quickly ensue. However, they are all afflicted by the same Achilles heel that jeopardizes their very existence: the free-rider problem. Free riders threaten to undo the systems off of which they leech, by consuming resources in the network without contributing their own. In 2000, 70 percent of users on a popular peer-to-peer network provided no files for download, while 37 percent of files available were offered by the top 1 percent of sharers. By 2005, the situation had grown worse, with 85 percent of users on the same network free-riding and contributing no files of their own.[30]

While easy to criticize these free riders, it isn't difficult to understand their motivations. With each peer on the network acting as a self-interested agent, one need only consider the prisoner's dilemma to explain their behavior. Downloading and uploading files from the network represent two ends of the extreme—with the former providing positive utility in the way of free media and the latter imposing negative utility in the way of bandwidth consumption and prosecutorial risk. At the time, free riders were not punished or sanctioned by these peer-to-peer networks—that is, until a new file sharing service called BitTorrent made its mark.

Borrowing from the learnings of the iterative prisoner's dilemma model, the BitTorrent service used a rate-based tit-for-tat incentive mechanism to reciprocate services among peers. Without getting into the weeds of the technical details, BitTorrent's algorithm essentially mirrored cooperative or retaliatory behaviors between members in its network. Peers "unchoked" other peers who provided files for download by uploading to them. Conversely, when a peer did not receive an adequate level of service from another, or found the other peer to defect altogether, he retaliated by "choking" him and restricting further uploads to him. Randomly, the peer optimistically unchoked one peer at a time, in an effort to solicit mutually cooperative behavior and enable discovery of peers with better and faster connectivity options in the network.[31] Though several academics have brought forth evidence suggesting its tit-for-tat algorithm could be optimized further, one could hardly argue the effectiveness of BitTorrent's incentive scheme—by 2004, the exchange accounted for more than half of all peer-to-peer traffic.[32]

If successful in file-sharing networks, could the same tit-for-tat approach be used for threat intelligence sharing purposes? In 2014, researchers at the University of Texas at San Antonio and Kennesaw State University put forth their own simulated experiment to model the effects of such behavior on the FS-ISAC itself. To maintain its operations, the FS-ISAC subsists on membership fees. The authors modeled three different fee structures in their analysis: (1) a free membership for small firms with a limited amount of information; (2) a hierarchical membership fee structure where the fee is commensurate with the member firm's total assets; and (3) a hierarchical structure that is proportional to the amount of information requested by the member firm.[33] In any case, the authors point to several problems with these various membership fee scenarios.

1. A membership firm's objective is to protect its organization from suffering a security attack and attempt to minimize associated costs (whether the attack was successful or not). In the case of a free membership, firms are incentivized to free-ride, as the costs associated with revealing a breach (both in the way of attracting potential hackers or criticism from its stakeholders) more than offset the benefits of sharing (particularly since each firm is acting in its own interests). Therefore, free-riding behavior prevails with a free membership.[34]

2. In the case of a membership fee made proportional to a firm's asset value, free-riding again is expected as the norm. While firms with more assets will benefit from sharing, as a potential breach imposes greater risk of damage, these firms are also entitled to more information under the proportional fee structure, thereby offsetting their incentive to share.[35]

3. Finally, though rational at face value, a membership fee commensurate to the amount of information requested by a member firm carries with it its own challenges. Given that firms have limited cybersecurity resources, they must divide those they do have between building their cybersecurity defenses and paying the proportional FS-ISAC membership fee. While security technologies can mitigate the risk of attack on their own, the same cannot be said for information collected from the FS-ISAC. Information without commensurate action hardly thwarts adversaries. And, the persistent downside of sharing threat intelligence with one's competitors remains. Therefore, in this case, the optimal strategy entails the firm investing only in security technologies and not exchanging threat intelligence.[36]

The crux of the free-riding problem remains the difficulty in measuring how much security-related information a firm possesses vs. that which it consumes. Unlike an easily monitored peer-to-peer network that can be programmed to "choke" non-sharers, how do member firms in an ISAC really ever know how much information each is withholding from the others? However, all is not lost for ISACs seeking to overcome seemingly unstoppable behavioral inertia or to answer this impossible question. The researchers modeled one additional fee structure for consideration: one where the membership fee is replaced with an insurance premium equal to the average expected breach losses across all firms in the network, with losses capped by the total premiums collected. In this scenario, rather than operating within its own self-interest, a firm is better served looking out for the broader societal good of all participating members. To further protect smaller firms from being penalized under such a structure, the ideal model forces larger firms to pay an extra fee to equalize risk.[37]

The insurance model not only optimizes the extent of threat intelligence sharing across the network and obviates the free-rider problem, it also addresses a challenge inherent in the cybersecurity insurance space. Though an interesting concept given the popularity of breaches, cybersecurity insurance has yet to reach full market potential, with just one-third of US and 2 percent of UK companies having a policy.[38] Companies question the value of existing insurance policies with limits often set below buyer expectations.[39] The inherent challenge of the cybersecurity insurance model rests in the asymmetry between policy holders and insurance companies, with the former having far more information than the latter. The result has been a cautious play on the part of insurance companies loath to find themselves on the hook for just one major cybersecurity breach that could bring with it cataclysmic damages. By tying threat intelligence sharing to a collective insurance policy with member organizations bearing a premium associated with the average cost of a breach, the authors simulated a successful theoretical model where incentives align with desired behaviors. Critics may rightfully argue that theoretical models are only as viable as one's simulator-based assumptions. However, the researchers provide a cogent case deserving debate, if not practical exploration, among ISACs today to drive the right threat intelligence sharing behaviors while providing additional market opportunity for cybersecurity insurance as a tangential benefit.

Assuming real-world outcomes matched the researchers' simulated assumptions, the industry would be a step closer toward effective threat intelligence sharing. Yet, it would still face other obstacles that an aligned incentive structure alone fails to address. Among them are the following:

1. *A common goal requires common understanding.* Thanks in no small part to zealous cybersecurity marketers attempting to plant their software vendor's flag firmly in the newly discovered land of "threat intelligence," the market is hopelessly confused over what the term even means. As one example, while 90 percent of UK cybersecurity professionals are familiar with the term, 77 percent conflate it specifically with security information and event management (SIEM), a category within cybersecurity that offers management tools for monitoring one's own cybersecurity environment, not sharing intelligence with other organizations.[40] In fact, little more than one-third even understand that threat intelligence is shared information provided within the security community.[41] And, slightly more than one in ten see the value of intelligence beyond data collection, finding real value in correlating behavioral analysis with threat data feeds.[42] All of this combines to create a marketplace of confusion, where white hats fail to align on a consistent definition of threat intelligence, making it impossible to attain a common goal.

2. *Being intelligent and actionable are often not one and the same.* In a 2015 study, more than two-thirds of cybersecurity professionals who were in some way dissatisfied with their firm's threat intelligence approach cited that the information was not timely.[43] More sobering, less than one-third reported that the information they received was accurate, yet alone actionable.[44] Congesting the already tenuous signal-to-noise ratio among resource-constrained white hats with volumes of data that are difficult to interpret (let alone activate) retards progress for the threat intelligence cause.

3. *Charity starts at home.* While indiscriminate attacks still dominate, adversaries are becoming more sophisticated in targeting particular companies or organizations. By doing reconnaissance on a company, inclusive of what commonly deployed programs with known vulnerabilities are operating within its environment or what suppliers may be in its network with weaknesses of their own, threat actors are upping the stakes through targeted campaigns. Thus, when a firm has limited resources to invest in its cybersecurity posture, its highest outcome will be served by first examining its own intelligence.

4. *Context, not content, is king.* In the big data conundrum plaguing so many cybersecurity first responders, there is little time or resource to effectively marry internal and external data signals to identify context. With adversaries evolving tactics, it is context that becomes the most salient intelligence attribute going forward. For instance, say that someone in the organization is an approved user of an internal sales force automation tool. The user accesses the program with no issues in validating her credentials. This may appear to be a normal activity. However, one's interpretation may change after learning that the access originated from a country through which the user rarely travels and from which a recent spate of targeted hackings against the organization's industry are suspected. Considering that nearly two-thirds of UK firms in one study admitted to not marrying external threat intelligence with internal data feeds, the journey toward contextually based analysis has hardly begun.[45]

5. *Nobody is minding the shop.* Little more than one in three organizations has a dedicated team managing its threat intelligence agenda. The vast majority have left the mission to information technology (IT), or worse yet, to lines of businesses.[46] And, the most popular way that threat intelligence is shared with others is through informal peer-to-peer exchanges; less than half use a vendor threat exchange service and only one-third participate in an industry group.[47] White hats are failing at instrumenting a threat intelligence program that can be leveraged beyond informal tips through a buddy network.

If misery does in fact love company, white hats may be pleased to know their black hat counterparts face the same set of challenges. Behavioral and economic motivations that exist in the prisoner's dilemma problem of free riders reign supreme whether one is working on the good or the bad side of the fight. Black hats must find a way to share their intelligence without compromising their own market opportunity. For example, if I make my latest malware exploit available to my peers who, in turn, begin launching similar campaigns, I risk tipping off white hats who can more readily identify the attacks and develop countermeasures to thwart them. Thus, where white hats must walk the line of how much information to share while minimizing risk, black hats must balance how much to leverage their collective talents to unlock additional market opportunity while maximizing the take for each unique individual. All the while, black hats must not only concern themselves with free riders but with law enforcement spies in disguise. For this reason, black hat forums where such intelligence is traded for free or at a price often rely on trusted personal referrals through which to grow their membership.

That said, white hats again seem to be disadvantaged in the fight. In 2015, when the US Government reported the takedown of Darkode, an underground site with up to 300 dangerous hackers responsible for some of the most infamous exploits (including the ring responsible for the 2014 Christmas attacks on the Sony PlayStation Network), the FBI estimated at least 800 other underground forums like Darkode in existence.[48] Compared with the less than two dozen ISACs in operation, the numbers are once again on the bad guys' side, meaning the good guys must attempt to narrow the gap with superlative threat intelligence capabilities, despite being challenged with regulatory and legal constraints that affect how much sensitive customer information can even be shared. Yet, even when confidential information is a moot point, threat intelligence among white hats is still not being shared pervasively. In an environment where malware details should be among the easiest and most obvious elements to share with one another, a full 25 percent of organizations are not willing to pass on this basic information.[49] With the industry having a long way to go in both the number of functioning ISACs and the quality of threat intelligence shared, cooperative efforts are necessary but insufficient in attaining the goal. The industry is desperate for its Volvo to turn the category of threat intelligence on its ear.

Raising the Elevation

In 2014, four security software vendors banded together with a united mission of sharing threat intelligence. The Cyber Threat Alliance (CTA) included founding members Fortinet, Palo Alto Networks, Symantec, and McAfee with an objective of moving threat intelligence from rudimentary malware exchanges to actionable threat intelligence on zero-day vulnerabilities. Beyond unifying some of the biggest names in the software security space, the CTA was meaningfully different from ISACs in three notable ways.

- *It sought to eliminate the free-rider problem.* Each member was expected to contribute threat intelligence, equal in quality and quantity, to other participating members. As the CTA grew in membership, it intended to put greater focus on the quality of threat intelligence over the quantity of information shared.

- *It sought to bolster the product effectiveness of all members.* Once a member shared a critical piece of evidence, such as a malware sample, all participating members included such intelligence to improve their product lines.

- *It sought to eliminate the customer as a middleman.* ISACs rely on customers to take aggregated intelligence and adopt the findings in their security environments. The CTA was founded to put the onus back on the software security vendors themselves, requiring each member to adapt its products with ever-evolving releases to address the latest threat, and make those patches available to customers with little to no customer intervention.

Beyond these unique characteristics, the CTA also established a more evolved approach to threat intelligence sharing. Realizing that context is king, the organization set its sights at evaluating threats from a higher altitude. Rather than simply exchanging malware samples with one another (an original premise of the alliance), the CTA understood the asymmetric battle in which it fought. Adversaries release approximately one million unique pieces of malware each day.[50] Even with noble intentions of sharing at least 1,000 new malware samples among their members on a daily basis, the CTA's results would be negligible.

Instead of being outmatched in a case of death by millions of paper cuts, the CTA altered its perspective. It wouldn't set its target at the individual malware sample level; rather, it would share entire playbooks of specific campaigns launched by adversaries. These campaigns number anywhere from 5,000 to 25,000 (depending on which expert you ask) in the world *at any given time*—a far more manageable number to tackle than the million pieces of malware generated *each day*. This is not the number of attacks but the number of coordinated assaults, each with its own playbook, launched by adversaries against multiple victims. The membership would share everything they knew about a campaign at every juncture of its life cycle, allowing it to develop a playbook of its own — one of countermeasures that could be deployed across all potentially targeted companies.

In 2015, the CTA put its methodology to the test and released its findings on one of the most insidious ransomware campaigns to date, known as CryptoWall 3. Its report exposed an estimated $325 million in damages from tens of thousands of victims worldwide (a conservative estimate, based on what the consortium could quantifiably measure), 4,046 malware samples, and 839 command-and-control URLs (uniform resource locators), among other identifiable markers, associated with CryptoWall 3.[51] Most important, due to the high degree of specialization across the cybersecurity market in general and among the CTA members in particular, no one member of the alliance knew every aspect of the adversary's campaign—they each brought unique intelligence to the table to benefit the greater good.

Lauded for their efforts, the CTA's 58-page report on one ransomware campaign in 2015 signaled a new frontier in threat intelligence sharing in the industry. The celebration was short-lived as, within days of the report's release, adversaries had already unloaded the next threat upon their victims, appropriately dubbed CryptoWall 4.

A Second Thought

Threat intelligence sharing has suffered its fair share of ups and downs. If it isn't heralded as the veritable panacea against a scourge inflicted by adversaries, it is criticized for its woeful limitations in doing any meaningful good. Both sides of the extreme are wrong. Threat intelligence has a definite place within cybersecurity, though it has yet to find permanent residence with a solid, scalable foundation through which to grow.

At their core, government-induced programs and industry consortiums suffer from free-rider problems. With no way to measure how much an organization is truthfully surrendering in the way of its own threat intelligence, regulators and memberships can do little to fundamentally overcome this behavioral inertia, unless the underlying incentive structure is changed. Despite the free-rider conundrum, these initiatives are a step in the right direction toward stronger cooperation, albeit a modest step in many cases.

The CTA puts more of the onus on software security vendors themselves. By examining attacks at a campaign level, it also sits at the right elevation to effectively combat adversaries advantaged by greater numbers. Additionally, by removing the customer as middleman from the equation, it overcomes the big data problem white hats suffer in making threat intelligence actionable. For these reasons, the CTA sits at the right perch in the industry through which to make significant strides. But, even it is not enough.

As Volvo proved with the three-point seat belt, the change occurs not when a few founding members of a Cyber Threat Alliance pool their collective resources but when *every* software security firm exposes its raw materials to all others for ongoing improvement across the industry's collective cyberwarfare arsenal. Threat intelligence can no longer be seen as the prized competitive advantage for any one firm. As Volvo demonstrated, there is too much at stake to be relegated to profit or differentiation.

Even if this radical shift in the vendor community were to occur, threat intelligence sharing has practical limitations. The very premise entails some form of attack being identified in the wild. By that definition, threat intelligence sharing does *nothing* to eradicate the zero-day attack or even early onset campaigns. That said, what it does do is force the adversary to redirect more of his resources from operationalizing attacks to developing them. This shift from operations to research and development requires adversaries to continue innovating and curtails their return on investment for any campaign that is prematurely thwarted when good guys effectively share what they know. And, even if threat intelligence sharing does not solve for the zero-day attack, its benefit in stopping existing attacks is worth the cause. Just as the seat belt does not save every life in every accident, it has saved more than a million. The opportunity for threat intelligence sharing to save companies from a common threat is a worthwhile effort, even if it must ride on the backs of others who initially fall prey.

When the vendor community supporting the good guys in the fight cooperates by sharing threat intelligence captured across the entire threatscape, all customers benefit. Just as consumers were afforded a safer automobile that continues to save lives, organizations stand to suffer fewer attacks when threat intelligence is aggregated and activated to make the mousetraps in their cybersecurity infrastructure smarter. And, when cybersecurity software companies evolve from vendors to partners by sharing such intelligence with their customers, they allow the latter to free up valuable talent resources in attempting to cobble together such intelligence within their own communities of interest.

The obvious obstacle to such a bright future resides in the motivation of software security vendors to keep their intelligence sacred. They are beleaguered by the prisoner's dilemma themselves as the first to offer its prized jewels to competitors risks ceding its marketplace advantage. Of course, even with every software security vendor opening its kimono to the industry on what it knows of the bad guys, there still exists meaningful areas of competitive differentiation in this complex landscape. As we have discussed, intelligence involves context, and, increasingly, attacks are targeted to a particular company or organization. Vendors that allow organizations to interpret context in addition to content stand to meet adversaries where they are most insidious—on day zero of their attack—a place that no successful threat intelligence sharing will ever be. And, those software security leaders that willingly offer their threat intelligence as a metaphorical safety belt to the industry not only benefit their competitors but, more important, their customers in *The Second Economy*.

A SECOND HELPING OF THREAT INTELLIGENCE SHARING 1.0

In 2014, Nevada's gaming industry was the largest in the state—collecting more than $2 billion in taxes and fees and representing 45 percent of the state's total revenues. In its early beginnings, gaming was threatened by insidious actors looking to cheat casinos and delegitimize the budding industry in the process. Seeing the threat, Nevada established the Nevada Gaming Commission in the late 1950s, a group of regulators who, among other activities, released what would become famously known as the Black Book. In it were the descriptions and photographs of known cheaters and wrongdoers outlawed from casinos for their criminal acts.

The first release of Nevada's Black Book contained the names of just 11 men, some of whom had already earned their place in history as notorious villains. Not only were casinos expected to eject the criminals from their establishments, the Nevada Gaming Commission required it. Among the more high-profile individuals punished for failing to comply was famed singer Frank Sinatra, who had his gambling license revoked after allowing one of the Black Book members hospitality in his hotel and casino.[52]

Today, Nevada still uses its Black Book (in more acceptable terms, it is referred to as the "Excluded Person List"). At the time of this writing, there are 32 men and women[53] featured on the Nevada Gaming Commission's web site, each banned from casinos for which they are suspected of intending harm. If any enters a casino and is caught, he or she faces up to a year in prison. And, those looking to remove themselves from the Book's prestigious membership have one and only option: death itself. Even then, a death certificate is required to prove to the state regulators that the member has, in fact, truly departed. When an industry that literally powers an entire state's economy is at stake, fierce competitors have found common ground in containing an existential threat to all—and only a hearse will suffice in proving the threat has been removed.

Notes

1. *Encyclopedia Britannica,* www.britannica.com/topic/automotive-industry, accessed July 5, 2016.

2. Wikipedia, https://en.wikipedia.org/wiki/American_automobile_industry_in_the_1950s, accessed July 5, 2016.

3. "What Future for Auto Safety?," *The New York Times,* February 8, 1969, p. 30, http://timesmachine.nytimes.com/timesmachine/1969/02/08/79946884.html?pageNumber=30, accessed July 5, 2016.

4. Joseph C. Ingraham, "Car Makers Prefer Glamour to Safety, Auto Club Charges," *The New York Times,* March 3, 1964, p. 37, http://timesmachine.nytimes.com/timesmachine/1964/03/03/106942688.html?pageNumber=37, accessed July 5, 2016.

5. Paul Hofmann, "Car Dealers Predict Price Rise As Safety Features Are Added," *The New York Times,* January 30, 1967, p. 19, http://timesmachine.nytimes.com/timesmachine/1967/01/30/83016462.html?pageNumber=19, accessed July 5, 2016.

6.   Ibid.

7.   "The Price of Auto Safety," *The New York Times*, January 10, 1968, p. 42, `http://timesmachine.nytimes.com/timesmachine/1968/01/10/88920155.html?pageNumber=42`, accessed July 5, 2016.

8.   Ibid.

9.   Ibid.

10.   "U.S. Seeks to Spur Use of Car Seat Belts," *The New York Times*, September 17, 1972, p. 330, `http://timesmachine.nytimes.com/timesmachine/1972/09/17/91346640.html?pageNumber=330`, accessed July 5, 2016.

11.   "The man who saved a million lives: Nils Bohlin—inventor of the seatbelt," *Independent*, August 18, 2009, `www.independent.co.uk/life-style/motoring/features/the-man-who-saved-a-million-lives-nils-bohlin-inventor-of-the-seatbelt-1773844.html`, accessed July 5, 2016.

12.   "Nils Bohlin, 82, Inventor of a Better Seat Belt," *The New York Times*, September 26, 2002, `www.nytimes.com/2002/09/26/business/nils-bohlin-82-inventor-of-a-better-seat-belt.html`, accessed July 5, 2016.

13.   Safety belt patent US 3043625 A, originally filed August 17, 1959 by N. I. Bohlin, `www.google.com/patents/US3043625`, accessedaccessed July 5, 2016.

14.   Tony Borroz, "Strapping Success: The 3-Point Seatbelt Turns 50," *Wired*, August 13, 2009, `www.wired.com/2009/08/strapping-success-the-3-point-seatbelt-turns-50/`, accessed July 5, 2016.

15.   Volvo press release, "A million lives saved since Volvo invented the three-point safety belt," August 11, 2009, `www.media.volvocars.com/uk/en-gb/media/pressreleases/20505`, accessed July 5, 2016.

16.   Borroz, note 14 *supra*.

17.   Ibid.

18.   Richard Stiennon, "The IT security industry is not consolidating," *CSO*, March 16, 2016, `www.csoonline.com/article/3043997/techology-business/the-it-security-industry-is-not-consolidating.html`, accessed July 5, 2016.

19.   Reuters, "Cyber Security Startups Face Funding Drought," *Fortune*, February 24, 2016, `http://fortune.com/2016/02/24/cyber-security-funding-drought/`, accessed July 5, 2016.

20. "The Webroot 2016 Threat Brief: Next-Generation Threats Exposed," www.wecloud.se/uploads/Webroot-2016-Threat-Brief.pdf, accessed July 5, 2016.

21. Dan Goodin, "DDoS attacks on major US banks are no Stuxnet—here's why," *Ars Technica*, October 3, 2012, http://arstechnica.com/security/2012/10/ddos-attacks-against-major-us-banks-no-stuxnet/, accessed July 11, 2016.

22. Ibid.

23. "eCrime Trends Report: Fourth Quarter 2012," *JJD*, http://internetidentity.com/wp-content/uploads/2014/02/Q4_2012_IID_ecrime_report_020613.pdf, accessed July 11, 2016.

24. David Goldman, "Major banks hit with biggest cyberattacks in history," *CNN Money*, September 28, 2012, http://money.cnn.com/2012/09/27/technology/bank-cyberattacks/, accessed July 11, 2016.

25. "eCrime Trends Report: Fourth Quarter 2012," note 23 *supra*.

26. Mathew J. Schwartz, "Banks Hit Downtime Milestone In DDoS Attacks," *Dark Reading*, April 4, 2013, www.darkreading.com/attacks-and-breaches/banks-hit-downtime-milestone-in-ddos-attacks/d/d-id/1109390?, accessed July 11, 2016.

27. Kelly Jackson Higgins, "A Threat Intelligence-Sharing Reality-Check," *Dark Reading*, May 26, 2015, www.darkreading.com/cloud/a-threat-intelligence-sharing-reality-check/d/d-id/1320560?ngAction=register, accessed July 17, 2016.

28. James Gleick, "Prisoner's Dilemma Has Unexpected Applications," *The New York Times*, June 17, 1986, www.nytimes.com/1986/06/17/science/prisoner-s-dilemma-has-unexpected-applications.html?pagewanted=all, accessed July 17, 2016.

29. Richard Nieva, "Ashes to ashes, peer to peer: An oral history of Napster," *Fortune*, September 5, 2013, http://fortune.com/2013/09/05/ashes-to-ashes-peer-to-peer-an-oral-history-of-napster/, accessed July 18, 2016.

30. Peter Selby and Jonathan MacDougall, "Achieving Fairness in BitTorrent," April 22, 2009, www.cs.ubc.ca/~kevinlb/teaching/cs532l%20-%202008-9/projects/Peter-Jonathan-bittorrent_fairness.pdf, accessed July 17, 2016.

31. M. Zghaibeh and F. C. Harmantzis, Peer-to-Peer NetwOrking and ApplIcations, 1, 162-173 (2008), http://link.springer.com/article/10.1007%2Fs12083-008-0013-7, accessed July 17, 2016.

32. Ibid.

33. Charles Zhechao Liu, Humayun Zafar, and Yoris A. Au, "Rethinking FS-ISAC: An IT Security Information Sharing Network Model for the Financial Services Sector," *Communications of the Association for Information Systems*, 34, Article 2 (2014), http://aisel.aisnet.org/cais/vol34/iss1/2, accessed July 17, 2016.

34. Ibid.

35. Ibid.

36. Ibid.

37. Ibid.

38. Matthew Heller, "Cyber Insurance Market to Triple by 2020," *CFO*, September 14, 2015, http://ww2.cfo.com/risk-management/2015/09/cyber-insurance-market-triple-2020/, accessed July 19, 2016.

39. Ibid.

40. Duncan Brown, "Towards Threat Wisdom: Combining Data, Context and Expertise to Optimise Threat Intelligence," *IDC*, November 2015, www.secdata.com/resource/idc-threat-intelligence-whitepaper, accessed July 18, 2016.

41. Ibid.

42. Ibid.

43. Ponemon Institute Research Report, "Second Annual Study on Exchanging Cyber Threat Intelligence: There Has to Be a Better Way," November 2015, http://content.internetidentity.com/acton/attachment/8504/f-00a6/1/-/-/-/-/Ponemon%20Study%202015.pdf, accessed July 18, 2016.

44. Ibid.

45. Brown, note 40 *supra*.

46. Ponemon Institute Research Report, note 43 *supra*.

47. Ibid.

48. Alastair Stevenson, "All the details about the FBI's Darknode takedown in 6 easy facts," *Business Insider*, July 16, 2015, www.businessinsider.com/darkode-fbi-shuts-down-the-worlds-most-dangerous-hacking-forum-arrest-70-2015-7, accessed July 18, 2016.

49. Vincent Weafer, "When It Comes To Cyberthreat Intelligence, Sharing Is Caring," *Dark Reading*, March 31, 2016, www. darkreading.com/partner-perspectives/intel/when-it-comes-to-cyberthreat-intelligence-sharing-is-caring/ a/d-id/1324936, accessed July 18, 2016.

50. Virginia Harrison and Jose Pagliery, "Nearly 1 million new malware threats released every day," *CNN Money*, April 14, 2015, http://money.cnn.com/2015/04/14/technology/ security/cyber-attack-hacks-security/, accessed July 19, 2016.

51. Cyber Threat Alliance, "Lucrative Ransomware Attacks: Analysis of the CryptoWall Version 3 Threat," October 2015, http://cyberthreatalliance.org/cryptowall-report.pdf, accessed July 19, 2016.

52. Michael Zennie, "The most exclusive club in Las Vegas? Black Book of 11 banned mobsters, cheats and crooks tells sleazy history of Sin City," *Daily Mail*, December 3, 2011, www. dailymail.co.uk/news/article-2069709/The-exclusive-club-Las-Vegas-Black-Book-11-mobsters-cheats-crooks-banned-casinos-sells-auction-5-250.html, accessed July 19, 2016.

53. http://gaming.nv.gov/index.aspx?page=72, accessed July 19, 2016.

CHAPTER 10

■ ■ ■

Cybersecurity's Second Wind

Not everything that can be counted counts, and not everything that counts can be counted.

—Albert Einstein

When New York City Mayor Rudolph Giuliani sought reelection of his post in 1997, he ran on a compelling record of accomplishments—particularly in making his citizens much safer. Facts were on the mayor's side. Crime rate in the city had reached its lowest level in more than 30 years. With a reputation for tough policing across the crime spectrum from minor offenses (such as noise ordinance violations, public drinking, and vandalism) to violent felonies, Giuliani had successfully cleaned up a city once notoriously a cesspool of criminal activity. During his term, the number of murders, rapes, and armed robberies dropped a staggering 61 percent, 13 percent, and 47 percent, respectively.[1] While critics were quick to point to macroeconomic conditions, such as changing demographics and a healthier national economy, as tailwinds in his favor, few could discount Giuliani's remarkable achievements in restoring order to the city. And, as it turned out, few of his citizens did discount him: Giuliani handily won reelection in a veritable landslide, ousting his opponent by a 59-41 margin, becoming the first Republican to win a second term in the heavily Democratic city in more than 50 years.[2]

Upon entering office for his first term, Giuliani warned New Yorkers against measuring his performance based solely on statistics. Within his first six months in his newly elected post, he remarked about the continuing decrease in crime rates that commenced midway through his predecessor's regime:

> I have never been one who strongly relies on statistics as a way of measuring what we're doing. Obviously, you prefer the trend in the direction of declining crime, but I don't want the department to be overly focused on statistics.[3]

By the time of his second term, Giuliani was a bit more willing to let statistics tell his story, and for good reason. Statistics had become his friend in not only allowing him to tout his accomplishments but helping him make them in the first place. Upon

© 2016 by Intel Corp.
S. Grobman and A. Cerra, *The Second Economy*, DOI 10.1007/978-1-4842-2229-4_10

taking office, he suspected his force was focused on the wrong measurements. At the time, law enforcement had historically measured its success based on responsiveness to emergency 911 calls and number of arrests made in a given day. Giuliani recognized that these lagging indicators could hardly help him identify where crime was most likely to occur. Instead, he began measuring the nature of crimes, including their frequency, locality, and timing, to determine patterns and allocate resources more effectively.

His approach worked. Focusing on the noise of small crimes actually diminished the occurrence of violent felonies. Asking the right questions to derive the correct metrics provided insights on where to deploy officers, rather than relying on reports that merely recorded previous activities. Giuliani successfully challenged conventional notions of big-city crime tactics and had won in the court of public opinion with a second term. By virtually every account, New York City was the safest it had been in several decades. And then, far under the radar of Giuliani's meticulous management and reporting, the deadliest terrorist attack on American soil struck one of the nation's most crime-vigilant cities on September 11, 2001, revealing communications fissures across its first responder units and proving that even the most-well-intended focus on metrics can be blinding.

Of course, it would be patently unfair to criticize Giuliani for the 9/11 attack. As previously discussed, the lack of intelligence shared across various governmental units, including with the mayor himself, created a smokescreen for the impending threat. Giuliani's dashboard of metrics was confined to those immediate and imminent threats for which he and his team had visibility. From that perspective, it is fairer to laud the former mayor for putting in place a system that precipitously reduced city crime through a relentless focus on metrics (such as petty crime incidents) previously thought to be too noisy and insignificant by prior regimes. Yet, despite making the city safer, Giuliani's activities were insufficient to prepare for the black-swan attack looming beyond his preparedness for even the worst imaginable felony. Giuliani could have no reasonable way of predicting that his nation was at impending war with al Qaeda or that his city would take center stage as the target. Certainly, understanding that his city was soon to be Ground Zero for the most perilous strike on US soil would have likely changed the outcome, or would it?

Raising the Noise

Tension in the Middle East has been simmering for at least the past 100 years. A persistent fight for territory divides the region across various factions with a complex history and even more complicated relationships. In 1967, the simmer reached a boiling point during the Six-Day War, during which Israel, fearing imminent invasion by Egypt, launched a preemptive attack to capture the Gaza Strip, the Sinai Peninsula, the West Bank of the Jordan River, and the Golan Heights—some of which were former territories of Egypt and Syria. Realizing their opponents would not take the loss lightly, Israel began securing its position along the Suez Canal, spending $500 million in fortifications along the designated ceasefire line. Israel couldn't have been more right in predicting the motives of its adversaries—just six years later, the region would once again find itself at war.

When Egyptian President Anwar Sadat succeeded his predecessor in 1970, he was determined to restore pride to his country by reclaiming what was lost in the Six-Day War. Inheriting an economy in desperate need of reform, Sadat was convinced that his people would only tolerate such change if their territories were returned. He found an ally in Hafiz al-Assad, the head of Syria, who saw the retaking of the Golan Heights his country had lost years prior as a strictly military option. The imminence of war was hardly a secret—Egypt publicly announced as much in 1972 when Sadat stated his willingness to "sacrifice one million Egyptian soldiers"[4] in his fight against Israel.

The intelligence arm of the Israel Defense Forces, known as Aman, was responsible for estimating the probability of war. In examining their situation, Aman had determined that war was predicated upon two factors. The first involved Egypt and Syria joining forces as it was (correctly) assumed that Syria would not go to war against Israel solo. Second, it had acquired intelligence from a confidential Egyptian source that Egypt would not engage unless first supplied defenses by the Soviets, specifically fighter-bombers to neutralize Israel's aerial forces and Scud missiles to be used against Israeli infrastructure in deterring a comparable attack against Egypt. By late August 1973, the necessary Scud missiles had only just arrived in Egypt. No fighter jets had yet been supplied. And, it would take Egyptian forces at least four months of training to prepare themselves for battle, according to Aman's estimates. For these reasons, Aman came to the conclusion that war was not imminent.

At the same time, Egypt did its part to reinforce this thinking in its enemy. The country had expelled almost all of the 20,000 Soviet advisors residing within it the year before, after believing the Soviets were undermining its military efforts by leaking secrets. Aman believed Egypt was in a weakened military state as a result of the Soviet exodus. Egypt furthered the misconception by planting false information of maintenance problems, lack of spare parts, and a shortage of personnel to operate the most advanced equipment. All the while, Sadat blustered war threats at his opponent, seemingly numbing them into believing he was neither serious nor prepared.

Israel had already invested $10 million responding to what it believed to be impending attacks by the Egyptians along the Suez Canal in recent months. As it turned out, the "threats" were nothing more than training exercises by Israel's opponent. In the week leading up to Yom Kippur, the Egyptians once again staged a week-long training exercise adjacent to the Suez Canal. The Israelis, determined not to make the same mistake a third time, dismissed the effort. They also disregarded movements of Syrian forces along the border, given they believed Syria would not attack without Egypt and Egypt would not attack until the Soviet fighter-bombers had arrived.

In fact, the war had arrived, right under the Israelis' noses. On the Jewish holiday of Yom Kippur of 1973, Egyptian and Syrian forces crossed the ceasefire lines in the Sinai and Golan Heights. The choice of raiding on Yom Kippur was no accident, as it rendered Israel ill-prepared on a day where the country comes to a virtual standstill in holy observance. Over the next roughly three weeks, Israel fought back, incurring considerable loss of blood and treasure, until an Egyptian-Israeli ceasefire was secured by the United Nations on October 25.

The aftermath of a war the Israelis should have seen coming was significant. While Israel readily defeated Syria once the ceasefire with Egypt was negotiated, taking more land in the Golan Heights as a result, Israeli Prime Minister Golda Meir stepped down just six months later. And, although Egypt technically suffered another military defeat at the hand of Israel, Sadat's early military successes with his surprise attack on Yom Kippur enhanced the leader's prestige and paved the way for the economic reforms he sought in his country. In the end, Egypt successfully deadened its opponents' senses in detecting the imminence of strike, even though Israel was "measuring" its enemy's activities leading up to the very day of attack.

The examples of Giuliani's New York City crime rate in the years leading up to 9/11 and the Israelis' oversight of impending attack on Yom Kippur are, in a strange way, opposite sides of the same coin. On one hand, Giuliani was fanatical about measuring

177

leading indicators, down to the most microscopic of petty crimes, as harbingers of pending violent offenses against his citizens. His techniques worked in creating an absolute free fall in violent crime metrics during his tenure. Yet, despite his emphasis in creating a safer environment for New Yorkers, his radar was not tuned to a much more severe national threat and his forces were unprepared for anything on the scale of 9/11.

On the other hand, Israel was all too familiar with the stakes of war. It had multiple warnings from its enemies stating as such. Israel witnessed Egyptian and Syrian forces coalescing along the border. It had erroneously responded to what were nothing more than false alarms by Egyptian forces conducting training exercises and was determined not to be duped again. It even had intelligence from friendly allies in the region, aware of the Egyptian-Syrian plan and unwilling to join the fight, that war was on the immediate horizon. All the real signs to indicate an attack was under way were ignored as noise. If Giuliani's radar was not tuned to a national threat, Israel was caught flat-footed by not heeding the warning signals clearly visible on its own. Both examples reflect the challenges inherent in anticipating a major event as unpredictable as war.

Obeying the Law

Cybersecurity is rich with metrics. Security operations first responders often receive hundreds, if not thousands, of alarms each day to inform where threats may be entering the perimeter. CISOs (chief information security officers) have no shortage of metrics available, though determining which are most important in how to position people, tools, and processes for success is another matter. Executives are perplexed with understanding how cybersecurity fits within a company's broader growth or innovation agenda, if at all, leaving many to virtually ignore it entirely until their company becomes the next poster child for a breach. Case in point: despite cybersecurity breaches capturing more headlines, only a little more than one-third of corporate boards review their cybersecurity posture on a quarterly basis.[5] Vendors confuse matters more by touting the latest in big data analytics, promising to point the company's compass to the desired North Star of business-oriented outcomes, including the elusive return on investment of cybersecurity plans. Yet, many cybersecurity professionals remain overwhelmed, not helped, by the deluge of data multiplying each day. And, it's disconcerting to think that even the best laid plans of measuring the right outputs may fail to reliably predict when or where the next adversarial campaign may strike.

That's because cybersecurity follows a distinct pattern, also seen by nations struggling to anticipate major wars while addressing smaller, though more frequent, acts of violence. While major attacks like 9/11 or the Yom Kippur War are difficult, if not impossible, to predict, mathematicians have proven that the occurrence of war can in fact be modeled.

In statistics, a power law describes the relationship between two quantities, whereby a change in one results in a proportional relative change in the other. Graphically, what results is a principle of the vital few and trivial many. You've undoubtedly seen this before in daily observation. The Pareto Principle, or 80-20 rule, is one example of a power law, where 80 percent of the outcomes are generated by 20 percent of the inputs. As it turns out, a power law can also be seen in the occurrences of terrorist attacks, such as 9/11, or more conventional conflicts, such as the Yom Kippur War.

Researchers Aaron Clauset and Maxwell Young applied statistics to analyze the set of terrorist attacks worldwide between 1968 and 2004. While terrorist attacks had been believed by some to be outliers in any statistical sense, Clauset and Young instead found that the nature and frequency of events followed a power law distribution with mathematical precision. Further, the researchers found that the slope of the power law curve varied across industrialized and non-industrialized nations. Specifically, while terrorist events occurred much less frequently in industrialized nations, the severity of those attacks (as measured in the number of deaths and injuries) was significantly greater than those in non-industrialized countries.[6]

Lewis Fry Richardson found conventional wars followed the same power law distribution. In studying virtually every war from 1815 to 1945, Richardson found a higher frequency of small fights, in which only a few people die, and a lower frequency of major wars that kill many. The power law has been found to apply to the frequency of the most common words in any language, the number of web hits dominated by a relatively few sites, the citations earned by the most popular scientific papers, and, yes, even the nature of cybersecurity attacks.

Researchers Deepak Chandarana and Richard Overill analyzed the degree of financial losses associated with publicly reported cybercrimes from 1997 to 2006. Their analysis revealed a double power curve pertaining to different organizational cohorts. Specifically, crimes targeted at larger organizations with stronger defense mechanisms succeeded less frequently, but with significant financial impact when they did prevail. Attacks carried out against organizations with weaker defenses succeeded with greater frequency, although they yielded smaller financial returns to the adversary.[7]

Finally, in examining the nature of cybersecurity incidents for a large organization over six years and across 60,000 events, researchers Kuypers, Maillart, and Pate-Cornell found the power law alive and well in the data set. Specifically, a single rare event accounted for nearly 30 percent of the total hours allocated by the security operation center over a six-month time frame. Over time, the researchers found the number of extreme incidents to be tapering off, hypothesized to be as a result of better detection and remediation of the organization in addressing attacks.[8]

In graphical terms, a typical power law distribution describing the effect of cybersecurity incidents might resemble that shown in Figure 10-1.

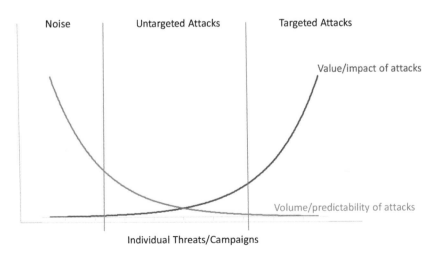

Figure 10-1. *Power law of threat volume and value in cybersecurity*

The left side of the chart is replete with nuisance attacks that trigger volumes of alarms for resource-constrained cybersecurity professionals. Garden-variety viruses and worms fall into this category. While they can cause damage, they are not targeted to any particular organization and therefore carry less financial impact. Once identified, industry providers record the malware's signature in protection products to prevent further infestation. The challenge with these viruses and worms, particularly the enhanced polymorphic varieties that change their signatures to evade detection, is the sheer number of them that cybersecurity professionals must address on a daily basis. For adversaries, the take on these crimes may not be as significant as more targeted attempts, though the opportunity to launch these attacks indiscriminately and with relatively little effort provides sufficient aggregate incentive to congest the market with scores of generic malware. Included in this category would be the Blaster worm, which infected more than ten million computers in less than a year, causing its victims to suffer repeated crashes. Annoying to disinfect? Yes. Irrevocable damage to any one victim? Not exactly.

The middle portion of the chart represents threats that are less common, although more severe. While the threats are not necessarily targeted at a potential organization, they carry more damaging consequences. In this bucket are generic phishing schemes that may also include a ransomware component. Predicting these attacks is a bit more problematic than in the first category, as unsuspecting employees are typically the weakest line of defense in any cybersecurity posture, and they can also fall victim to a generic phishing scheme if not paying careful attention. This category would contain the CryptoWall ransomware malware covered in our last chapter—which singlehandedly bilked its victims out of $325 million worldwide. Certainly, victims felt the impact in their pocketbook, but with tens of thousands of them worldwide, CryptoWall also did not bring any one organization to its knees.

The right end of the chart illustrates the most dangerous, targeted attacks to a particular organization. These black-swan attempts are intended solely for their victim and are not generally repeatable. Adversaries may spend months, seasons, or even years plotting how to infiltrate the organization to inflict the greatest harm. In April 2015, federal authorities detected an ongoing remote attack targeting the US Office of Personnel Management (OPM), the human resources department for the civilian agencies of the federal government. Over the weeks and months that followed, it would be revealed that infiltrators absconded with the private records (including social security numbers, birth dates, and fingerprints) of more than 22 million government employees, recruits, and their families,[9] bypassing the organization's newly minted $218 million upgrade to its cybersecurity defenses in the process. The director of the unit resigned under pressures from Congress three months later. The highly targeted OPM breach cost the organization $140 million in the year it occurred with ongoing annual costs estimated at $100 million *per year* for the next ten years—all to provide victims with identity theft insurance and restoration services.[10] Attacks in this realm are highly personalized and significantly devastating when they strike unsuspecting targets.

Cybersecurity professionals must address the breadth and depth of attacks across the range of threats represented by a statistical power law. Distinguishing the signal from the noise is one challenge when dealing with such volumes. The other, and perhaps more insidious, concern pertains to executives and board officers. It entails properly aligning cybersecurity incentives with intended outcomes. Organizations are overwhelmed by both imperatives, giving adversaries one more advantage in this lopsided battle.

Running the Gauntlet

The 1960s have been coined by some as marking the true beginning of computer security. In 1965, one of the first major conferences on the topic convened experts across the industry. Computers were expensive and slow. Engineers had architected a new means of maximizing scarce processing resources—allow multiple users to share access to the same mainframe via communications links. The idea greatly maximized the efficiency and benefits of mainframes while it simultaneously introduced security concerns associated with its sharing principle. An employee for one of the sponsors of that 1965 conference, a government contractor, was able to demonstrate the vulnerability of his employer's time-sharing computer system by undermining several of its system safeguards. Conference attendees demanded more studies be conducted along the same lines of breaking into time-sharing systems to expose weaknesses. It would be one of the first formal requests to initiate and formalize this sort of war-game testing in the computer industry.

Shortly thereafter, the use of tiger teams emerged in the industry. These teams were employed white hat hackers incentivized to find the vulnerabilities within their organization's own defenses. Soon, the process was heralded as a best practice in cybersecurity, with organizations pitting cybersecurity team against team—one to launch adversarial attacks and the other to detect and respond. By 2015, 80 percent of organizations reported a process to test their security controls at least annually.[11] The problem? The vast majority (50 percent[12]) report annual testing intervals—far too infrequently for the velocity of attacks and increasing dwell times among adversaries. The figure is even more startling given more than half of organizations were also not confident in their security team's ability to remediate complex threats, if any at all.[13]

Even among those who do deploy some form of penetration or red-team testing, as it is commonly known in industry parlance, within their organizations, there are common pitfalls limiting its effectiveness.

- *Failing to measure what is truly important.* When an organization designs a penetration test, it does so by pitting a team mimicking an adversary (the red team) against a team of cybersecurity defenders (the blue team). To be successful, the red team must first understand what is most important to the organization, as adversaries launching targeted attacks will have already done their homework on the matter. While an executive may be quick to mention theft as the most critical outcome to avoid, this may not be true in all cases. For example, a large automobile manufacturer would likely find theft of customer records to compromise its integrity in the market; however, an infrastructure attack that shuts down a large fraction of its manufacturing capacity would probably have far more devastating impact. Knowing where to point the red team to attempt the most damage is essential.

- *Shooting the messenger.* The most effective red teams *always* succeed. You read that right. An organization actually wants to hire the best possible red-team hackers and incentivize them extremely well to relentlessly pursue any vulnerability lurking in their environment. When red teams bring such weaknesses to the table, they may be admonished by the very leader who hired them in the first place. After all, when that indictment is directed at the same leader who established the organization's cybersecurity framework, the pill can be hard to swallow. Yet, if red teams are not celebrated for finding vulnerabilities, it is only a matter of time before a far more persistent enemy does so instead.

- *Punishing the innocent.* Likewise, organizations must realize that the best red teams *always* win. Punishing overwhelmed blue teams for failing to secure every defense will lead to a demoralized cybersecurity team. Rather than punish the innocent, use the exercise to productively shore up weaknesses. And, executives should be careful not to indirectly create a climate of low morale among blue-team members, those who are responsible for protecting the perimeter of the organization daily, as this will only be another bullet in your enemy's gun.

- *Inflating success.* Red-teaming should be an ongoing, persistent exercise. Relegating the effort to an annual event neglects the velocity of change occurring as adversaries continue innovating. Worse still, some organizations inform blue-team members, if not employees, that such an exercise is under way. This activity is tantamount to an adversary notifying an organization in advance it's coming for them. While some forewarning can and does exist (such as among hacktivists who are attempting to invoke change on the part of their targets), the far more common tendency is for adversaries to strike like proverbial thieves in the night. Inflating one's success during a notified penetration test simply creates a false sense of security that is readily welcomed by the predator.

- *Focusing only on cybersecurity professionals.* Of course, cybersecurity first responders should be involved in penetration testing. After all, the object of the test is an organization's cybersecurity posture. But, that posture extends far beyond the technical staff standing watch over a company's digital assets day and night. It also includes the communications team of the company, which must spring into action the moment a breach is detected. Having a robust communications disaster readiness plan is essential in preparing for the unexpected. Knowing a company's policy for communicating to key stakeholders—both internal and external—for varying degrees of threat (from web defacement to e-mail exposure to a breach of customer information) is essential for the communications engine to respond in a timely fashion. At the moment of an exploit, the last thing an organization needs is for its management to have a vigorous debate around the table on what should and should not be communicated. Here again, time will not be on the side of the victim, so any exemplary red-teaming exercise will include the communications function in its assessment.

The more organizations begin thinking and behaving like their adversary, the more prepared they will be if and when one of those disastrous and highly unpredictable targeted attacks occurs.

A Second Thought

Cybersecurity is too important to be left to the corridors of information technology (IT). Nearly 80 percent of company board members indicate they are concerned with the topic.[14] This strong majority is good news for white hats in the fight. However, the unfortunate reality is that caring about a topic and aligning the correct incentives toward its acceptable outcome are often not one and the same. Too often, organizations are chasing meaningless alerts in a tsunami of data that overwhelms their ability to properly diagnose an impending serious threat. Worse yet, some organizations are being lulled to sleep by their own metrics, which may indicate cybersecurity "success," all the while concealing an incapacity to respond to a disastrous black-swan attack. At the same time, cybersecurity professionals are indirectly encouraged to practice behaviors contrary to that which will improve a company's security posture. Among the more immediate opportunities for cybersecurity professionals and board members concerned with their efforts are the following:

- *Kill invisible incentives misaligned to effective cybersecurity outcomes.* It's the cross that so many white hats bear everyday— they toil in virtual anonymity to ensure that *nothing* happens against their organization. CISOs, loath to be the next day's headline for seemingly resting on their laurels, often indirectly encourage the adoption of the latest cybersecurity widget designed to cure what ails them. Fast adoption is a good thing, as discussed in Chapter 8. However, tool sprawl is not. Current cybersecurity environments are woefully lacking an integrated cybersecurity platform through which fast implementation of the latest technologies is possible without simultaneously multiplying operational complexity for already overburdened fast responders. As has been the common theme in this book, time is not on the side of CISOs, who have an average tenure of just 17 months.[15] Consider the point: is it sexier to adopt a point release of an already installed technology that may result in a single-digit improvement in current security defenses or go for broke to install the latest wonder product before the music stops and your chair is once again up for grabs? Many CISOs have become poster children for the latter case, introducing more complexity in their environment as a result, even though an organization's best interests are likely fulfilled by the former.

- *Reward failure.* We've already discussed this in the context of red-team exercise best practices, but the same holds true for senior leaders within cybersecurity. As discussed in Chapter 8, a cybersecurity defense mechanism will greatly lose effectiveness once it has been widely adopted in market. The reason is that adversaries have more incentives to develop countermeasures against a particular technology as it is used by more targets in their addressable market. By necessity, this means that products previously deployed in an organization's environment will outlive their usefulness. In some cases, the fall from grace can be fast. Imagine the difficulty of being the CISO who adopted said technology, using the company's scarce resources to do so, and must now inform her board that the technology has passed its prime. Rather than excoriate her for coming to the conclusion, she should be respected for challenging the status quo and forcing her company to innovate at the pace of her adversaries. There is no question that investments in cybersecurity create challenges for organizations with significant opportunity costs. At the same time, leaving dated technology in one's cybersecurity environment only serves to muddy the waters with unnecessary complexity, if not impede adoption of newer technology poised to address more sophisticated threats—as long as doing so uses an integrated security approach that unifies workflows and simplifies back-office operations.

- *Change the scorecard.* Billy Beane's legendary success in taking the Oakland Athletics, a mediocre baseball team at the time, to 20 consecutive wins in 2002 has been immortalized in the popular movie and book of the same name, *Moneyball.* Baseball, like cybersecurity, is dominated by numbers. At the time, the most popular statistics used to measure a player's worth included stolen bases, runs batted in, and batting average. Beane, dealing with the loss of three of his most valuable players and a payroll that could not compete against much larger franchises, reevaluated the scorecard. Rigorous statistical analysis revealed that on-base percentage (a measure of how often a batter reaches base) and slugging percentage (a strong measure of the power of a hitter) were better leading indicators of offensive success. Since the data were widely available but not used by competing teams, Beane was able to recruit underestimated players and build a winning franchise—all at a fraction of the cost of teams with much deeper pockets.

  Beane didn't take advantage of any metrics that weren't readily available to his competitors. He simply looked differently at the data. Right now, there are countless organizations with cybersecurity scorecards that measure the number of incidents captured and responded to in any given period of time. More often than not, these scorecards are measuring the left-hand side of the power curve discussed earlier—large volumes of alerts that are largely untargeted in their nature. Instead, organizations can and should reevaluate the nature of threats to determine the probabilistic nature of any as part of a highly targeted campaign. By reorienting the perspective of correlating threats to suspected campaigns (as we discussed the industry should also do with threat intelligence sharing), organizations can begin to stack-rank the severity of threats based on campaign association. By relying on existing products to handle the routine threats common on the left-hand side of the power curve, more time can be spent understanding potential threats on the right. Don't trust your existing products to handle the routine nature of voluminous threats? That's where red-teaming comes in to cover the gap—perceived or real.

- *Realize that imperfect data may be a threat signal in and of itself.* Ask any well-intentioned cybersecurity professional one of his greatest fears, and if you don't first get the answer "false negatives" (disregarding a real threat), you'll likely hear about "false positives" (false alarms that are hardly threats at all). The former is an obvious concern. The latter is more insidious in its nature, since a high degree of false positives can impede a first responder's ability to find the real threats in his environment by consuming his precious time.

At least, that's what conventional wisdom would have you believe. In fact, the reality is far more complex. While false positives certainly can and do eat away at a first responder's attention and time, dismissing them out of hand can be even more dangerous. Consider the Yom Kippur War and Israel's dismissal of threats that appeared to be false alarms in their nature but were in fact signals of their enemy's impending attack. Adversaries will intentionally bombard their targets with false alarms to raise the noise level and numb their victims' senses in connecting the pattern of false positives to a very real and highly targeted looming threat. Capturing false positives in isolation, apart from examining their correlation to campaigns, not only deadens an organization's responsiveness but relegates some of its most valuable intelligence to the trash bin.

As with any function, a misguided incentive structure can weaken a company's cybersecurity posture and produce unintended consequences that favor its adversaries. Reporting without red-team exercising limits an organization's field of view to only those threats it can immediately see, not potential ones looming in the future, as Giuliani learned when his city, hardened against crime, fell to an enemy of a much deadlier stripe. At the same time, ignoring what are perceived to be meaningless alarms may in fact play into the hands of an enemy bent on deadening its victim's responses, as Egypt so skillfully did against Israel in the Yom Kippur War. Unfortunately, there is no easy answer, as is often the case when discussing a topic as complex and important as cybersecurity. Yet, there are practices organizations can employ to upend and challenge conventional wisdom and put the value back into cybersecurity metrics and objectives. Organizations that capably distinguish their response plans across high-volume and high-value attacks, rigorously test their own capabilities to expose vulnerabilities, and reward "failure" along the way increase their chances of developing a team of white hats properly refined and motivated for the task and enemy at hand. In so doing, they stand to change the game of cybersecurity in their favor in *The Second Economy*.

A SECOND HELPING OF STATISTIC'S POWER LAW

Language is extraordinarily complex. There are roughly 6,500 spoken languages in the world today, 700 of which are used by at least 100,000 people each. According to the Global Language Monitor, on June 10, 2009, one of the world's most popular languages, English, passed the million-word threshold, when linguists officially recognized "Web 2.0" as bona fide. For the English language alone, there is a new word created every 98 minutes. With such an extraordinary number of possible words through which to convey meaning between intelligent beings, one would expect language to be one domain inexplicable by mathematical models. To the contrary, however sophisticated we may like to believe we are in communicating with one another, a fairly simple, if not mysterious, mathematical reality proves we are actually quite structured in our patterns.

In 1949, linguist George Zipf made a fascinating discovery. He found that a small number of words were used all the time, while the vast majority were used only rarely. This seems quite obvious at face value but, what was extraordinary about Zipf's finding was the precise mathematical equation that predicted just how often a particular word was used. Zipf found the most popular word to be used twice as often as the second most popular, three times as often as the third most popular, and so on and so on. What would ultimately be coined "Zipf's Law" is a completely enigmatic phenomenon that holds true, no matter the language or obscurity of the word.

To illustrate the point, the most common word in the English language is "the," representing about 6 percent of everything we say, read, and write. Wordcount.org ranks words as found in the British National Corpus, a 100-million-word collection of samples of written and spoken language designed to represent the popularity of words in the English language. According to Wordcount, the word "sauce" is the 5,555th most popular word. Using Zipf's Law, we would expect to find the frequency of the word "sauce" to be approximately (1/5,555) that of the word "the." In examining the frequency of both words across Wikipedia and the Gutenberg registry of tens of thousands of books to determine how many times each appears, "the" occurs about 181 million times. The word "sauce"? Nearly 30,000 times—or about (1/5,555 x 181 million).[16]

While no one has yet to crack the code on why Zipf's Law is so pervasive and universally true in language, the discoverer himself offered a reason. Zipf hypothesized that the rank-frequency phenomenon was explainable by human behavior. He believed that humans tended toward a path of least resistance and suggested that speakers throughout history preferred to use as few words as possible to communicate their thoughts. Accordingly, the most frequent words became more popularized and utilized for each civilization and its language. However, there is a long tail of language (as evidenced by the more than one million words in the English language alone). The explanation, according to Zipf, is due to listeners, who preferred larger vocabularies with more specificity, so that they had to do less work. The result? A power curve that applies to every language spoken.

The power curve phenomenon of Zipf's Law is literally universal—every language, every book of repute (from *Moby Dick* to the *Holy Bible*)—follows the pattern. It is pervasive, if not curious. To illustrate the point, the most popular word in this chapter follows that of the English language, "the." It appears some 445 times. According to Zipf's Law, the second most popular word should appear roughly half as much. It does. The second most popular word in this chapter, "of," appears 213 times. For two authors who didn't even know Zipf's Law existed before writing this book, it is a bit eerie to realize that conformance to some laws is simply unavoidable. In much the same way, cybersecurity professionals are governed by the power law present in their daily struggle. While this law may be a bit better understood in this context (fewer threats cause the biggest impact and vice versa), some follow antithetical approaches in measuring their cybersecurity effectiveness nonetheless. Perhaps a deeper examination of the "conventional" wisdom influencing an organization's cybersecurity agenda may lead to different outcomes, even if governed by the same law.

Notes

1. David Kocieniewski, "The 1997 Elections: Crime; Mayor Gets Credit for Safer City, but Wider Trends Play a Role," *The New York Times*, October 28, 1997, www.nytimes.com/1997/10/28/nyregion/1997-elections-crime-mayor-gets-credit-for-safer-city-but-wider-trends-play-role.html, accessed July 30, 2016.

2. Justin Oppmann, "Giuliani Wins With Ease," CNN, November 4, 1997, www.cnn.com/ALLPOLITICS/1997/11/04/mayor/, accessed July 30, 2016.

3. Kocieniewski, note 1 *supra*.

4. "Yom Kippur War," *New World Encyclopedia*, www.newworldencyclopedia.org/entry/Yom_Kippur_War, accessed July 30, 2016.

5. PwC, "Turnaround and transformation in cybersecurity; Key findings from The Global State of Information Security® Survey 2016," www.pwc.com/gsiss, accessed July 30, 2016.

6. Aaron Clauset and Maxwell Young, "Scale Invariance in Global Terrorism," Department of Computer Science, University of New Mexico, February 2, 2008, http://arxiv.org/pdf/physics/0502014.pdf, accessed July 30, 2016.

7. Deepak Chandarana and Richard Overill, "A Power Law for Cybercrime," Department of Computer Science, King's College London, http://i.cs.hku.hk/cisc/news/9Aug2007/PowerLawforCyberCrime(slides).pdf, accessed July 30, 2016.

8. Marshall A. Kuypers, Thomas Maillart, and Elisabeth Pate-Cornell, "An Empirical Analysis of Cyber Security Incidents at a Large Organization," Department of Management Science and Engineering, Stanford University, School of Information, UC Berkeley, http://fsi.stanford.edu/sites/default/files/kuypersweis_v7.pdf, accessed July 30, 2016.

9. Brian Naylor, "OPM: 21.5 Million Social Security Numbers Stolen From Government Computers," NPR, July 9, 2015, www.npr.org/sections/thetwo-way/2015/07/09/421502905/opm-21-5-million-social-security-numbers-stolen-from-government-computers, accessed July 30, 2016.

10. "OPM Breaches Still Resonating," *Fedweek*, March 16, 2016, www.fedweek.com/fedweek/opm-breaches-still-resonating/, accessed July 30, 2016.

11. "State of Cybersecurity: Implications for 2015 An ISACA and RSA Conference Survey," www.isaca.org/cyber/Documents/State-of-Cybersecurity_Res_Eng_0415.pdf, accessed July 31, 2016.

12. Ibid.

13. Ibid.

14. Ibid.

15. Scott Hollis, "The Average CISO Tenure is 17 Months—Don't be a Statistic!," *CIO*, September 17, 2015, www.cio.com/article/2984607/security/the-average-ciso-tenure-is-17-months-don-t-be-a-statistic.html, accessed July 31, 2016.

16. "The Zipf Mystery," www.youtube.com/watch?v=fCn8zs9120E, accessed July 29, 2016.

Epilogue

"You'll find this game worth playing . . . Your brain against mine . . . And the stake is not without much value, eh?"

—Richard Connell, *The Most Dangerous Game*

Richard Connell was a prolific writer, penning more than 300 short stories over his relatively short 30-year career, perhaps none more popular than his 1924 masterpiece *The Most Dangerous Game*. The story challenged basic principles of morality as it terrified readers with a gruesome plot. In it, the protagonist, an avid big game hunter, finds himself thrown overboard while in transit to his next hunting excursion. He discovers refuge on an island where he meets a fellow ardent hunter, the island's only civilized inhabitant, who gives him a chilling ultimatum: survive a three-day deadly match pitting human against human as hunter versus hunted or suffer a grizzly death by torture as an alternative.

The story grips the reader with the horrifying thought of turning from hunter to hunted. While the protagonist and antagonist are equally matched in skill, the antagonist has the upper hand the entire story: he sets the parameters of the game, he determines when the match starts and ends, he is familiar with the geographical territory in which the hunt ensues, and so on. For the antagonist, hunting animals had long outlived its challenge—only a "new" animal capable of reasoning would test his skills. As Connell so disturbingly conceived, human versus human is the ultimate most dangerous game.

Of course, cybersecurity professionals live out this story every day. While they may not be fighting for their own lives in the middle of a remote jungle, the challenge in matching wits against adversaries seeking to do their organizations harm is a dangerous game in and of itself. With nation-state actors threatening critical infrastructures, the notion of saving lives, both their own and those around them, is less dramatic and more imminent for these veritable heroes as more dangerous hunters enter the game.

Like the hero and villain in the short story, skills are comparably matched between white and black hats. Also, similar to Connell's fictional tale, black hats set the parameters of the "game," playing by and often changing their own set of rules. And, as the protagonist discovers, winning the game would simultaneously entail a reliance on his basic skills and an upending of conventional notions. And, though not a typical character, the element of time is a main actor in the story—the hero must survive the perilous plight for three frightening days while the villain seeks to end his opponent's life before expiry.

© 2016 by Intel Corp.
S. Grobman and A. Cerra, *The Second Economy*, DOI 10.1007/978-1-4842-2229-4

Consider the "rules" of the cybersecurity game white hats are up against.

1. *Black hats initiate.* White hats are doomed to play defense against threat actors who launch the assault. Understanding where the next threat vector may emerge and how the organization could be vulnerable, including through unwitting employees, become the ongoing challenges for white hats.

2. *Black hats need not play fair.* Cybersecurity professionals are governed by a standard of ethics and business compliance. Many in the industry are reluctant to share threat intelligence with their peers, lest they be excoriated in the court of public opinion or unintentionally violate privacy information entrusted by customers. Black hats are not confined by ethics, standards, or office politics. They can freely share with one another (for a price or otherwise) without fear of repercussions. Of course, this isn't to say hackers aren't concerned with verifying the identity of what appears to be a virtual like-minded kindred spirit—after all, that wolf in sheep's clothing may be a law enforcement official in disguise. Yet, despite this rub, black hats can and do play dirty. White hats are held to a standard.

3. *Black hats can, and do, frequently change the parameters of the game.* While cybersecurity professionals are confined by information technology (IT) environments predicated upon stability and testing, black hats can iterate on their creations as many times as they choose, based on their own tolerance for personal investment. This means hackers can frequently change the nature of the game to suit them, from polymorphic viruses that obfuscate signature collection to iterations in more advanced countermeasures (such as sandbox evasion techniques) to keep white hats on their heels.

4. *Black hats can easily gain access to the white hat's secret sauce.* Cybersecurity defensive software and appliances are commercially available in the market, giving hackers relatively easy access to either procure or steal this technology and reverse-engineer it to determine how to advance their next offense. Cybersecurity software companies certainly can do the same to a black hat's creation, however, that typically entails someone falling victim to it in the wild—a much higher price for the white hat to pay to gain access to his opponent's technology.

5. *Black hats need only score once.* Black hats have the advantage of an asymmetric fight. While white hats must be vigilant in defending against all possible attacks (though admittedly at varying threat levels), black hats need only succeed once. They flood white hats with volumes of threats to attempt to simply land one if not provide a smokescreen for a more targeted attack in the making.

6. *Black hats leverage time to their advantage.* Time has been a major theme covered throughout this book. Depending on the adversary's motives, he will stealthily infiltrate his victim's "keep," lingering undetected for as long as possible to inflict harm. The latest spate of ransomware attacks has created a new threat category in cybersecurity—one in which the threat actor literally leverages time as the ultimate motivator to convince his victim to pay up. Of course, time can also be an advantage to white hats who are able to implement countermeasures quickly against the next attack. But, given adversaries are the ones who determine when the game starts, they naturally have the benefit of time on their side, at least initially.

7. *Black hats are clearly incentivized.* Whether for profit, principle, or province—just three possible motives covered in this book—threat actors have clear incentives motivating their next move. White hats are encumbered with office scorecards and political pressures that often motivate the wrong behavior. Many may feel pressure to simply show all cyberdefense metrics as being in the green so as to avoid uncomfortable discussions with executives and board members, assuming these conversations would be welcomed by these leaders at all, who are often overwhelmed and confused by the topic's inherent complexity. In fact, cybersecurity is not a domain measured in red or green—it lives in shades of gray as all organizations are under some form of threat (either from generic malware to highly targeted zero-day attacks) at any given time. The result? While black hats clearly know the score, white hats struggle to determine how it is even kept.

Each of these white hat disadvantages is exacerbated by an unenviable confluence within the game's macroeconomic dynamics. Simply put, there aren't enough white hats in the fight as the industry faces a labor shortage crisis. At the same time, the attack surface is exponentially increasing—with cloud, mobility and the Internet of Things creating new attack entry points for adversaries to encroach.

While white hats may largely agree that they face this unenviable set of constraints in a game rigged against them, half the market (according to McAfee research on the topic) is following the wrong strategy, ultimately giving their opponent an even greater upper hand. Specifically, thanks to the phenomenon of Grobman's Curve, where cybersecurity solutions provide diminishing returns with greater market adoption (because adversaries become increasingly motivated to develop countermeasures as more of their potential victims use a given technology), speed becomes of the essence when deploying the latest defense mechanism. Unfortunately, well-intentioned cybersecurity professionals struggling to prove their value are often compelled to adopt the latest point product in the market. And, with 1,400 cybersecurity vendors and counting, there is no shortage of wonder products promising to cure what ails them.

The problem with this strategy is that it creates one of two possible likely outcomes. The first entails a failure to implement the technology at all, known in the industry by the derisive term "shelfware," as covered in an earlier chapter. The second involves implementing the technology, only to be overwhelmed by a complex back-office operating environment comprised of fragmented tools oftentimes from multiple vendors. In either case, the white hat is not using the technology to his advantage as speed-to-implementation with workforce efficiencies are the elusive and often unattainable goals with such an approach.

We submit that Grobman's curve requires a different approach to the problem—one that focuses energy in implementing a platform capable of onboarding new security technologies quickly with simplified workflow management to optimize operations efficiencies. This isn't just a matter of our opinion. Those cybersecurity professionals with a more simplified back-office infrastructure, as provided by fewer vendors in their environment, report experiencing fewer threats, better detection times, and more confidence in their security posture than their counterparts with a more fragmented, multivendor approach.

But, you may rightfully realize that putting most of one's cybersecurity eggs in one vendor's basket is a risky game in and of itself. What happens if said vendor suddenly changes strategy or roadmap, is acquired, or simply ceases to innovate at the pace of the market? The CISO (chief information security officer) who recommended consolidating multiple workflows with that vendor will quickly be shown the exit door. Given this possibility, many cybersecurity professionals persist in broadening their vendor environment, in an attempt to also diversify their risks. Unfortunately, this is a losing strategy in a Red Queen Race where time makes or breaks a player.

We offer a different alternative: one that puts the focus on an integrated platform with unified workflow management but also leverages the power of a robust ecosystem of cybersecurity players. Finding the right partner capable of bringing to bear hundreds of providers across a fragmented industry over a common integrated framework offers cybersecurity professionals the best of all worlds.

- The ability to rapidly onboard and deploy new technologies with the lowest level of effort, allowing organizations to derive maximum utility from these defensive products before adversaries are incentivized to develop countermeasures

- The opportunity to simplify back-office management and processes, allowing existing limited resources to work smarter, not harder, in addressing more threats faster

- The benefit of tapping into the aggregate innovative capabilities of a vibrant ecosystem of hundreds of potential players, all connected over the same infrastructure and using the same management tools to simplify operations

This can no longer be a choice where cybersecurity professionals must decide between speed and effectiveness. Adversaries are setting the parameters of the game and it requires both. At the same time, white hats must demand more of their cybersecurity vendors. Threat intelligence sharing in the industry must occur at the vendor level and focus energies on specific campaigns of particular import. The good guys responsible for defending their organizations each day deserve more than superficial threat "intelligence" sharing that is often nothing more than vendors providing data on malware attacks. The Cyber Threat Alliance is a major step in the right direction but the industry can and must do more in this area. Each time an adversary's campaign is halted prematurely, it forces him to reinvest his efforts in developing his next menace vs. propagating one already created. This creates downward pressure on the adversary's return on investment (ROI), which forces him to re-evaluate his incentives—favorable outcomes for all white hats, both on the vendor and client side, in the battle.

Company executives must also do their part and a big role they play is in clarifying the cybersecurity incentives and reward structures within their own companies. Penetration testing should be ongoing, with rewards offered to red teams playing the adversarial role—who should be expected to *always* win if they are effective. Rather than require scorecards that simply measure how many security incidents the organization encountered the previous day, ask meaningful questions to assess the robustness of your cybersecurity posture. Identify your "keep" and what is most critical to protect in your organization. Find out how and where red teams managed to penetrate. Correlate threats with probabilistic indicators toward a specific campaign, particularly one that may be targeted at your organization directly. Inquire about the usefulness of installed security technologies and whether the organization is due for a refresh (for those on the declining slope of Grobman's Curve). Reward CISOs for candidly assessing where the organization may be vulnerable. Ensure your breach-readiness plan also includes communications policies for handling internal and external stakeholders when the critical moment of truth occurs.

Above all, critically assess your organization's own success in constantly evaluating the effectiveness of its cybersecurity posture by weighing the utility of any given product in your arsenal against the ongoing costs of maintaining it. Before attempting a forklift, determine if the organization has sufficiently milked the benefits of existing technologies, diligently pruning those that have outlived their usefulness, to avoid introducing unintended complexity, if not shelfware, into your environment. Many times, organizations are left holding the bag and unfortunate blame in the hindsight analysis of a cyberattack by simply failing to have maximized the yield of products, tools, and processes that were already available in their cybersecurity inventory.

In the game of cybersecurity, there are no easy answers, just easy problems. That said, there are practical strategies that cybersecurity professionals, their leaders, and vendors can take to alter the outcome of the contest in their favor. As in Connell's short story, the stakes for organizations in this game couldn't be higher. How an organization defends against an enemy and ultimately responds if breached have been the deciding factors in whether executives are required to relinquish their seats, if not force the company to close its doors. There is a happy ending to Connell's masterpiece: the protagonist wins. The reader is left to conclude he will forever be a changed man, and certainly a changed hunter, as a result of his experience— more cunning and more refined to meet his next match. White and black hats engage in a hunt each day in the virtual jungle in which we increasingly dwell. Our heroes can take a page from Connell's tale, but it will require that they first challenge their own playbook to change the outcome of this most dangerous game in *The Second Economy*.

Index

© 2016 by Intel Corp.
S. Grobman and A. Cerra, *The Second Economy*, DOI 10.1007/978-1-4842-2229-4

Get the eBook for only $5!

Why limit yourself?

Now you can take the weightless companion with you wherever you go and access your content on your PC, phone, tablet, or reader.

Since you've purchased this print book, we're happy to offer you the eBook in all 3 formats for just $5.

Convenient and fully searchable, the PDF version enables you to easily find and copy code—or perform examples by quickly toggling between instructions and applications. The MOBI format is ideal for your Kindle, while the ePUB can be utilized on a variety of mobile devices.

To learn more, go to www.apress.com/companion or contact support@apress.com.

Printed in the United States of America